Content

American Marriage

AMERICAN GOVERNANCE: POLITICS,
POLICY, AND PUBLIC LAW

Series Editors: Richard Valelly, Pamela Brandwein,
Marie Gottschalk, Christopher Howard

A complete list of books in the series
is available from the publisher.

American Marriage

A Political Institution

PRISCILLA YAMIN

PENN

UNIVERSITY OF PENNSYLVANIA PRESS

PHILADELPHIA

Published by
University of Pennsylvania Press
Philadelphia, Pennsylvania 19104-4112
www.upenn.edu/pennpress

Printed in the United States of America
on acid-free paper

10 9 8 7 6 5 4 3 2 1

Library of Congress Cataloging-in-Publication Data
Yamin, Priscilla.
   American marriage : a political institution / Priscilla Yamin.
— 1st ed.
      p. cm. — (American governance: politics, policy, and
public law)
   Includes bibliographical references and index.
   ISBN 978-0-8122-4424-3 (hardcover : alk. paper)
   1. Marriage—Political aspects—United States—History.
2. Marriage law—United States—History. 3. United
States—Social policy—History. I. Title. II. Series: American
governance.
HQ535.Y35 2012
306.810973—dc23   2012002589

For Joe, and for Ben and Adam

Abbreviations

ACF	Administration for Children and Families
AFDC	Aid to Families with Dependent Children
APD	American Political Development
CMFCE	Coalition for Marriage, Family and Couples Education
DLC	Democratic Leadership Council
DOMA	Defense of Marriage Act
ERA	Equal Rights Amendment
FMA	Federal Marriage Amendment or Marriage Protection Amendment
Freedmen's Bureau	Bureau of Refugees, Freedmen and Abandoned Lands
HHS	Health and Human Services
HMI	Healthy Marriage Initiative
LGBT	Lesbian, gay, bisexual, transgender
NAACP	National Association for the Advancement of Colored People
NOW	National Organization for Women
OFA	Office of Family Assistance
PRWORA	Personal Responsibility and Work Opportunity Reconciliation Act
TANF	Temporary Assistance for Needy Families
SNCC	Student Nonviolent Coordinating Committee

Introduction

Marriage as a Political Institution

For weeks during the summer of 2010, activists, pundits, and legal scholars paid close attention as the California Supreme Court heard testimony for and against the right to same-sex marriage in the case of *Perry v. Schwarzenegger*. When the decision to overturn the state's constitutional ban on same-sex marriage came down, one of the plaintiffs, Kristin M. Perry, said, "This decision says that we are Americans, too. We too should be treated equally. Our family is just as loving, just as real and just as valid as anyone else's." Theodore Olson, one of the lawyers for the plaintiffs, called the decision a "victory for the American people" and for those who had been denied rights "because they are unpopular, because they are a minority, because they are viewed differently."[1] Olson, who had worked in Ronald Reagan's Office of Legal Counsel, had represented George W. Bush in *Bush v. Gore*, and had served as Bush's solicitor general, surprised many observers who thought it incongruous that a veteran conservative would take up the cause of gay rights. While profoundly political, marriage does not so easily yield to ideological categorization. This is because marriage represents both the obligations and rights of citizens, which are elemental but disparate aspects of American politics. When we broaden our field of vision from the question of who should have the right to marry and look at marriage itself as a political institution, different questions come into view. Why and under what conditions does marriage come to matter politically? Why is it a site of such passionate political struggle? What kinds of political work do marriage do?

The institution of marriage is fundamental to American political development because it acts as a fulcrum between obligations and rights. Marriage represents communal duty, loyalty, moral education, inherited property relations, and social and civic status. Yet at the same time, marriage represents consent, contract, individual liberties, and independence from the state.

These opposing sets of characteristics in marriage generate tension between a politics of obligations on the one hand and a politics of rights on the other. As an obligation, marriage is seen to structure social, sexual, political, and economic relationships. As a right, marriage is meant to secure liberal freedoms and the privileges of full citizenship. Marriage defined as both an obligation and a right connects these disparate aspects of political life. To understand the politics of marriage we need to understand the interplay between questions of obligations and rights, whether the political issue concerns the status of ex-slaves at the close of the Civil War, immigrants at the turn of the twentieth century, civil rights and women's rights in the 1960s, or welfare recipients and gays and lesbians in the contemporary period. When extant political and social hierarchies become unstable, political actors turn to marriage to either stave off or promote political and social changes. Thus political struggles that have emerged historically in relation to race, gender, economic inequality, and sexuality have been articulated at key moments through the language of marital obligations and rights. Absent a political analysis of marriage, we cannot sufficiently understand these struggles.

The question of same-sex marriage is only the most recent public debate over marriage. In the 1990s, marriage played a significant role in conceptualizing the reform of welfare. The opening preamble in the 1996 welfare reform act stated that "marriage is the foundation of a successful society"[2]—a statement that both opponents and proponents of same-sex marriage might agree with. In the case of welfare reform, the associated marriage-promotion programs were designed to encourage and even require two-parent married families. In the case of same-sex marriage, the question is whether same-sex couples have the right to marry. On the one hand, the state strongly encourages poor single mothers on welfare to get married; on the other, gays and lesbians struggle for the right to marry and, in many though not all instances, they face resistance from the state. Here, the tension between marriage as an obligation and as a right comes into focus. When marital politics come prominently into play, certain marriages are pushed as obligatory and necessary for the good of society. Other marriages are contested or prevented. In the United States historically, there has been a consistent return to marriage when political questions of inclusion and equality surface. The politics of marriage embody central dynamics in American politics regarding matters of inclusion and exclusion, the status of citizenship, and the meaning of equality. For that reason, in shouldering the obligations of marriage or exercising the right to marry, we should question what we accept and what we authorize in terms of our relationship to each other, to society, and to the polity.[3]

The Politics of Marriage

The politics of marriage pivots between obligations and rights. As an obligation, marriage might be considered a form of what political scientist Karen Orren has, in another context, called "belated feudalism."[4] The obligations of marriage represent the survival of feudal relations in the United States. The hierarchies marriage defines and reinforces are vestiges of a pre-Enlightenment age, primarily maintained in our constructed differences. These racial, gendered, class, and sexual differences, as historian Nancy Cott has detailed, have been hierarchically reinforced through marriage as it draws the boundaries of national belonging.[5] Throughout U.S. history, marriage has been consistently defined by its upholders as the "foundation of society" or the "foundation of civilization," the integrity of which must not be compromised. This definition reflects the role of marriage in defining the norms, commitments, statuses, and practices of the American political regime, underpinning the organization of society economically, biologically, and socially. Finally, marriage defines and structures dependent relations. Thus, marriage not only supports hierarchical relationships, but also creates what political theorist Anna Marie Smith calls "disciplinary inclusion."[6]

As a right, marriage represents a liberal contract; a consensual agreement that orders property ownership in a liberal society. Marriage, as contractual, is also structurally central to liberalism. Indeed, in his *Second Treatise*, John Locke wrote that "the first society was between man and wife, which gave beginning to that between parents and children. . . . Conjugal society is made by a voluntary compact between man and woman."[7] Here, it is the freely chosen contract of marriage that takes us from the state of nature into that of society. This origin myth of marriage and society explains marriage's durability in a liberal society even as the myth obscures the feudal aspects of the institution. In fact, as both marriage scholar Stephanie Coontz and historian George Chauncey have demonstrated from different perspectives, marriage has moved steadily away from notions of economic and social necessity and toward a more liberal notion of choice governed by love and romance.[8] Marriage has come to represent freedom and personal expression as evidenced by an increasing emphasis on choosing one's partner and setting up one's private household. In this way, marriage shapes notions of privacy and conceptions of economic independence from the state. The 1967 Supreme Court decision in *Loving v. Virginia*, which rendered anti-interracial marriage laws unconstitutional, is an example of this particular development.

Marriage anchors two political logics: residual feudalism on the one hand and a modern legal-rational system of authority and legitimacy on the other. It is an institution that perpetuates both hierarchical status and individual rights, sometimes coexisting in tension and sometimes mutually reinforcing. Marriage embeds feudal norms in a legal system based on rights and democracy. Political theorist Carol Pateman explores this coexistence of the two ideological systems with her notion of a contractually based "modern patriarchy."[9] As Alexis de Tocqueville observed in the mid-nineteenth century, American women consent to marriage aware of the obligations that await them: "In America the independence of a woman is irrevocably lost in bonds of matrimony." Yet because she fully understands her obligations, he explains, "It may be said that she has learned by the use of her independence to surrender it without a struggle and without a murmur when the time comes for making the sacrifice."[10] These analytically similar (though politically divergent) observations capture the dual nature of marriage that is founded on both obligations and rights.

It is striking that while marriage is mobilized differently in distinct historical moments, marriage itself generates consistent thematic and political dynamics, especially after moments of political dislocation and change. In this book I explore five such moments. After the Civil War, amid a devastated society, state officials looked to marriage as they sought to establish national stability and transition ex-slaves into the polity. On the one hand ex-slaves were required to marry, but on the other hand their right to marry was limited by laws that prohibited interracial marriage. At the turn of the twentieth century, political and social norms were upended by the rapid rise in immigration. American values and norms were ushered in through new marital standardization laws that required state marriage licenses, while eugenic marriage laws preventing some marriages were enacted across the country. American women were obligated to marry American-born men or risk losing their citizenship, while at the same time foreign-born women were naturalized American when they married American-born men. In the 1960s, radical feminists protested against the obligation of women to marry, while policymakers promoted marriage as a solution to poverty and the Supreme Court legalized interracial marriages. The year 1996 saw the passage of two landmark statutes that dismantled the welfare state and defined marriage at the federal level as a union between a man and woman. Finally, at the beginning of the twenty-first century, a fledging Marriage Movement called on all American citizens to marry as a form of health policy, while simultaneously opposing the right of same-sex couples to marry. At each of these moments, social and political actors proclaimed a "marriage crisis." Yet fears about declining marriage rates or claims about rising threats to marriage were not reflected in actual marriage rates.[11] Rather, the striking pattern is that the development of "marriage crisis" language occurs at moments of broader political crisis. In all these examples we also see a pairing of struggles over marriage as an obligation and as a right, even as those conceptualizations of the obligation or right change and shift in each context.

While marriage does the work of the state, its imperatives not only emanate from the state toward the citizen. They also are generated by non-state political actors, some linked to institutional power, some not. At moments in U.S. political history when established social and political hierarchies—based on such statuses as gender, race, ethnicity, class, or sexuality—have been challenged, actors have turned to marriage to reestablish, revise, or reverse these categories. This tendency is evident in feminists who were criticizing marriage during the 1970s and in gays and lesbians who have expressly wanted to embrace it since the 1990s. In this way, marriage is a fulcrum on which political debates over inequality see-saw. Marriage is perpetually asserted as basic to American national identity, in both its pre-liberal and liberal expressions. Marriage shapes the grounds for inclusion by enforcing the heterosexual, monogamous expectations about family that apply to all; and marriage defines the hierarchy of citizenship by means of exclusion, in that only particular people may be allowed to marry. The dynamics that flow from the intersection of obligations and rights are politically vexing. Marriage is not merely oppressive and utilized to regulate behavior; nor is it simply progressively emancipatory and egalitarian. Marriage is a source of recognition, reward, and inclusion as much as it is a source of coercion, hierarchy, and exclusion. My aim is to reveal the enduring but evolving contradictory sets of characteristics in marriage and to explain how marriage is constitutive of politics. The pro-marriage of the Reconstruction-era Bureau of Refugees, Freedmen and Abandoned Lands (the Freedmen's Bureau)—the federal agency charged with aiding distressed refugees and freed slaves—is a case in point. This nuptial policy was based on the belief that if ex-slaves followed accepted bourgeois familial practices, they would become productive, worthy citizens. Indeed, some Freedmen's Bureau officials believed that the success and stability of the nation after the Civil War was premised on ex-slaves marrying.[12] One hundred years later, Daniel Patrick Moynihan echoed this view in his famous study of the black family, and the marriage initiatives put forth in contemporary welfare policy continue the tradition. Social Security, veterans' benefits, and mother's pensions are examples of social policies that use marital status as a reward. In addition, some activists argue for the right to same-sex marriage as a public obligation and others make a claim for it as an individual choice.

Marriage is a site of political contestation when the question of inclusion becomes a public issue and concern, whether that question is related to race, ethnicity, sex, or sexuality, whether it involves ex-slaves, immigrants, welfare recipients, women, or gays and lesbians, and whether it is put forward by lawmakers in the courts, laws, public policy, or social movement actors. Marriage concerns the public realm of citizenship, national identity, civic membership, and economic independence as much as it does the private realm of sex, parenting, relations of dependency, familial roles, inheritance laws, or weddings. These domains are not necessarily in conflict but they do clash when one highlights and examines competing discourses regarding the meaning and practice of equality, inclusion, and independence in the United States. In this way, marriage inhabits politics by shaping interests and either promoting or preventing change.

By criminalizing some marriages and encouraging others, marital regulations have drawn lines between citizens and created hierarchical statuses. Historically speaking, marriage has been a limited right, reserved for a few. It was not available to slaves prior to the Civil War, many immigrants during the Progressive Era, or same-sex couples today. Through marriage, policymakers have defined the society and polity by positioning the majority against marginalized others, be they African Americans, southern and eastern European immigrants, or gays and lesbians. At the same time, marriage has been a site for challenging those lines, whether by encouraging ex-slaves to marry, allowing some immigrant wives citizenship through marriage to American males, or even contesting unequal gender roles by denouncing marriage. During moments of social and political instability of the sort explored in this book, distinctions between legitimate and illegitimate marriages have sharpened dramatically.

Struggles over marriage as a right or an obligation, as legitimate or illegitimate, are in part debates over whether and how to incorporate groups on the margins of the national community.[13] Important here is that marital status is grounded in multiple sites of gender, racial, sexuality, and class differences. Antimiscegenation statutes, eugenic marriage laws, and the Defense of Marriage Act all constitute exclusion of difference embedded in marriage law. At the same time, *not* marrying has also been defined as a political and economic problem—as with ex-slaves, immigrant males at the turn of the twentieth century, and welfare recipients today. The state's push toward marriage for these groups did important political work, defining citizenship for ex-slaves, assisting in assimilation for immigrants, and shaping economic independence for welfare recipients. Seen this way, marriage is not outside the political realm but firmly embedded within it.

The Political Institution of Marriage

Historical moments in marriage politics show that marriage constructs multiple hierarchies by shaping the meaning and practices of the obligations and rights of citizens. This is why I define marriage as a political institution. By this I mean that marriage does the work that other political institutions do—it has a broad and discernible purpose; sets norms, rules and roles; clearly distinguishes between those inside the institution and out; and most significantly, attempts to control those inside and out.[14] This last aspect, according to political scientists Karen Orren and Stephen Skowronek, distinguishes political institutions from institutions more generally.

Like the political institutions of Congress, the presidency, voting, and even public education, marriage does not merely express, reflect, or deny political surroundings; rather, marriage participates actively in politics by shaping interests and motives, configuring social and economic relationships, and promoting as well as inhibiting political change.[15] In her book *Sexual Citizenship*, Barbara Cossman explains that "marriage is not simply a status line demarcating who is in and who is out. It is also an ongoing practice—a verb, something one does—and as such, must be done in a particular way."[16]

One important purpose of marriage is to institutionalize familial relations of dependency. It prevents women, illegitimate children, and others in need from becoming wards of the state. It clarifies who belongs to whom and who is responsible for whom.[17] It shapes familial norms and rules that define gender roles, sexual mores, racial categories, economic status, and the socialization of children. The boundary between those inside and outside is most evident in the everyday bureaucratic documents that we regularly fill out, marking ourselves as either "married" or "single." In these ways, the institution manages those within its walls. It also shapes those outside its confines, either by making it costly politically, socially, or economically for certain groups not to marry, or by denying certain people the right to marry entirely, thereby limiting their social and economic benefits.

Marriage not only orders sexual, reproductive, child-rearing, and economic practices within marriage; it also plays an important role in defining a range of political phenomena, from civil rights and notions of political membership, to immigration and citizenship, welfare policy and the state benefits conferred on citizens. Marriage is more than a right that is granted or denied a citizen. In different historical moments, political actors, political elites, policymakers, and opinion makers have interpreted marriage as a practice, using marriage to shape and reorder hierarchies, collective boundaries, and the meaning of social stability and nationhood.

I argue that marriage is one important way that Americans interpret notions of nationality, class, race, gender, and sexuality and have come, over time, to determine the practices of equality and hierarchy. Examining the political articulations of marriage in different historical moments illuminates how political differences are reflected and articulated through struggles to define the regulatory aspects, benefits, and conferred status of marriage. Marriage is not only political in the ways that it is a form of state governance or that it shapes identity categories of race, class, sexuality, and gender. Marriage itself has been a key site of contest within a wide range of institutional and social contexts. It has energized political actors over the political inclusion and equality of marginalized groups and the redefinition of the legal, economic, and cultural notions of nation. Indeed it helps define what political actors see as legitimate and proper interests.

For all of its political importance, marriage remains an underexamined topic in political science.[18] Analysis of marriage has generally occurred either in political theory or through behavioral approaches in useful ways, but not in ways that capture the plasticity of the institution. Political theorists from Aristotle to Rousseau, and from Tocqueville to contemporary feminists have analyzed marriage in terms of the split between public and private sphere. Modern theorists in particular have emphasized the importance of marriage both in liberal contract theory and for the founding of the liberal state.[19]

But often, work in political theory does not historicize the institution and neglects the multiple interpretations and uses of marriage at any one time. Behaviorists, by contrast, have used marriage as a variable in surveys (check the correct box: single or married), but they do not examine how the status designation itself changes across time.

I argue that analyzing marriage as a political institution with historical specificity allows us to distill its central political logic across time, to see how notions of obligations and rights get worked out in the terrain of marriage. This inquiry is built on the work of historians and marriage scholars, most recently Stephanie Coontz's *Marriage, a History* and Nancy Cott's *Public Vows*, and the scholarship of others, such as Hendrik Hartog and Michael Grossberg, who brought the political and contingent nature of marriage to light.[20] Cott in particular has demonstrated how the state has used marriage as a form of public policy. Drawing on these scholars, I study marriage as a political entity. In order to bring conceptual clarity and embrace the complexity of the role of marriage in U.S. politics, I analyze what exactly it does politically. I have sought to locate characteristics that are distinct and enduring, as well as to understand how and why it changes in relation to other political phenomena. To those ends, I explore how private citizens, political and cultural elites, and policymakers think about and interpret marriage politically.

As a political institution, marriage simultaneously organizes membership, rights, and obligations in civil society, and also socializes people into acceptance of certain social and political norms and patterns of beliefs and behavior. Debates over the definition of marriage do not simply concern people's sex lives, gender roles, and familial practices, but also political issues of inclusion, equality, and citizenship. In the United States, marriage is connected to the system of political liberalism, but it is also shaped by hierarchies of economic inequality, race, gender, and sexuality. Constituted as both an obligation and a right of citizens, marriage is contested in the democratic process over the status of ideas, and is also an object of struggle between different groups in society.

Though similar to other political institutions, marriage is also different. Enormous political work can be enacted through marriage, precisely because it *appears* as a nonpolitical or pre-political institution, and therefore beyond collective contest. Marriage is charged with great symbolic power that defines both individual endeavors and national ideals. In these two ways, marriage effectively pervades society. It is a powerful institution because of its cultural authority and its status as an agent of state control. It is a dominant institution because it is an everyday practice as well as a significant interpretative frame for political and social life.

In order to understand how marriage is a political institution, it is also necessary to see the way institutions are cultural formations that shape group identities and interests. Indeed, the governing authority and reach of marriage as a political institution is made possible precisely because of its discursive power to determine and define normal behavior, gender roles, racial classifications, and even class identity. The political questions that get contested through marriage have historically centered on identities based in race, gender, class, sexuality, and nationality, and thus I draw on theoretical work on identity, particularly intersectionality, social construction, and normalization; work that challenges the distinctions between public and private.[21]

As a political institution marriage limits and shapes how political actors define their interests, and how institutions shape identity categories.[22] The analysis of discourse, narrative, and identity are useful in understanding politics and how political actors use ideas, goals, and desires to define their interests and make judgments. Viewing marriage as a political institution shows how notions of normalization such as the construction of normal sexual practices have been crucial to the political development of the nation.[23] A focus on identity offers an opportunity to expand our notions of how institutions work, and how political problems are defined to include questions of culture, identity, language, and the political meaning of social practices. Sexual identity, race, and gender are key factors in both challenging and stabilizing a political order, particularly when questions of inclusion are at stake.

The emphasis on heritage, descent, and birthright citizenship in American culture and law makes marriage a crucial site for the political constitution of civic membership and notions of political order. Accordingly, discussions of nation-building and citizenship need to incorporate the role of social theorizing, culture, and the construction and deployment of ideals about marriage and family to obtain a more complete picture of how politics in the United States works. The study of marriage as a political institution concretely bridges the divide between the study of culture, discourse, and identity on the one hand and politics on the other.[24] For instance, marriage license laws passed at the start of the twentieth century were embedded in other pressing political questions around state-building and anti-immigration policies. I analyze the arguments, claims, and stories political actors at the time told about marriage to illustrate this link between culture and politics.

The institution of marriage organizes politics in distinct ways. It frames race, gender, class, nationality, and sexuality. It shapes notions of inclusion and civic belonging, and it is a language through which we discuss and debate national identity and economic equality. It does this by assigning the status and roles of wife and husband.[25] While these are gendered roles, they do not concern *all* men or women but only those legally able to become husbands and wives; in other words, these denominations are crucially undergirded by racial, ethnic, class, and heterosexual/homosexual categories. In other words, the political implications of determining who can marry, who is obliged to marry, and who cannot marry run deeper than a definition of rights. The roles of husband and wife clarify and circumscribe relations within the state and therefore their role is to stabilize society by defining the boundaries of the nation. This was the case, as I discuss further in the book, in 1907 with marital expatriation, where women lost their citizenship if they did not marry a man who was born in the United States. It is also evident today, in the political question over whether same-sex couples can inhabit the roles of husband and wife, or whether those roles change.

The American political system relies on marriage as a political tool and resource. Marriage is an obligation insofar as it is deemed necessary for society because of its role in creating statuses, and therefore its practice is one criterion for full civic inclusion. At different moments, the state and society have strongly encouraged matrimony, and even obliged citizens, or potential citizens, to marry as a way to carry on the cultural and political traditions of the nation. This was the case for ex-slaves during Reconstruction, African Americans in the 1960s, and welfare recipients today. At the same time, marriage is a right insofar as it has been granted to some and denied to others, such as people of different racial classifications, persons deemed unfit by eugenic criteria, or gays and lesbians today. By denying the right of marriage, the state—or non-state political actors—has sustained and reinforced hierarchical differences.

The construction of identity norms through marriage has been important in resolving broader political questions of citizenship, inclusion, and belonging in American politics. Thus, I primarily examine marriage from the vantage point of groups rather than individuals. My focus is on groups that have historically been placed outside the boundaries of membership and citizenship, and the way that marriage marks them by this exclusion and marginalization. Same-sex marriage debates concern individual freedoms, but at the heart of the issue is the question of inclusion of the group loosely defined as gays and lesbians. In other words, the issues do not just concern the individuals in that group, and whether they have the right to be married; they also tell us about the status of that group in the hierarchies in the nation. Marriage rights and obligations play a role in defining both the relationship of groups to each other and their relationship to the state.

For example, women have been and continue to be consistently targeted to fulfill their obligation to marry in ways that tend not to apply to men. In 1907, a woman lost her American citizenship if she married a foreign-born male. Liberal and radical feminist critics of marriage in the 1960s and 1970s opposed the obligation of women to marry, while in the contemporary era mothers on welfare are strongly encouraged to marry as a path out of poverty. Political scientists Gwendolyn Mink and Anna Marie Smith have pointed out that marriage promotion in welfare policy constitutes a challenge to the right of all women *not* to marry.[26] For some, marriage is a path to a certain kind of equality, one that is grounded in state identification. At the same time, women continue to be the primary objects of the institution; they are persistently faced with the obligation to marry, as articulated both informally within the political culture and formally through state legislation tied to receiving state benefits. And this, Mink explains, places severe limits on women's constitutional rights.[27]

People of color have also been the focus of the institution's imperatives, particularly as marriage has been conceptualized as an institution that fosters independence for citizens in both economic and patriarchal forms. Prior to emancipation the institution of marriage had been primarily white. Even though ex-slaves gained the right to marry, marriage remained racially and ethnically segregated, by virtue of antimiscegenation and eugenic marriage laws, for more than half of the twentieth century. Similarly, state actors have attempted to proscribe the biological boundaries of the nation, as seen in Progressive Era concerns about Anglo-Saxon "race suicide" in the face of growing immigration.

The issues that race raises in marriage are related to class and economic issues. A primary role of marriage has been to structure economic and dependent relations. And, though this function has decreased in the modern era, the promotion of marriage as an economic policy that addresses poverty and economic inequality has been central to its modern conceptualization. There are clear economic rewards to participating in the institution that start with tax benefits, yet more than that—and this is what I focus on in this book—marriage is justified in terms of fostering economic independence. As noted, this notion keeps surfacing in relation to race, poverty, and single motherhood.

Sexuality is yet another intersecting arena that has been crucial to understanding the institution of marriage, and state-building more generally, even beyond same-sex marriage concerns. At different moments, the state has acted, and even expanded, to prevent certain couples from coming together, and in this way prohibiting same-sex marriage is similar to prohibiting interracial marriage as well as international marriage. Indeed, Progressive Era eugenic concerns that specific marriages would produce "effeminate" or "feeble" offspring were also questions about sexual identity. Even as marriage has become over time a personal choice based in love, one's freedom to choose a partner has been limited by state concerns for children and procreation, reflecting the tension between obligations and rights. In other words, sexual orientation is more than a survey variable and homophobia is more than a set of irrational beliefs, but rather they are forms of political discourse.[28]

Marriage in American Political Development

Marriage rights and obligations have not progressed in a unilinear fashion in the United States.[29] Over time, marriage rights have expanded as the institution has undergone intensive regulatory transformations. The rules of marriage have become more regulated as their perceived connection to citizenship, state-building, and national identity have become more prominent. This was the case during the Progressive Era, when both the free love movement and the practice of polygamy were seen as social, even political, threats. Yet at the same time, as other political statuses loosen, the restrictions on marriage do as well. When *Loving v. Virginia* declared antimiscegenation laws unconstitutional in 1967, segregation policies and laws were waning, at least in their formal expression. At critical moments of political change in the United States, actors turn to marriage to resolve tensions and to justify new political arrangements or maintain hierarchical relationships with regard to the rights, obligations, and social status of specific groups. These political settlements, temporary by nature, include not only rights and inclusion but also restrictions, constraints, and exclusions. It is interesting, for example, that marriage represents civic incorporation that is justified as a right, yet marriage is at the same time a site of state disciplinarity and regulation. When interracial couples gained the right to marry as the basis of inclusion and citizenship, that right also was an expression of state governance and control; this will also be the case when gays and lesbians are granted the right to marry throughout the United States. As some examples in this book reveal, marriage rights have proven to be a way for the state to socially regiment minority groups seeking access, inclusion, and recognition.

The political dynamics surrounding marriage always involve marginalized groups who are attempting to transition into a stable location and status within the boundaries of the American nation; and thus as various groups fight to gain this status by means of marriage we see changes in the meaning of marriage. I explore the differences and similarities of this process in different historical contexts. Since the 1960s, the meaning of marriage has been deeply grounded in notions of social and economic equality, whether for interracial couples, black families, gays and lesbians, or welfare recipients. In earlier periods, particularly for newly arrived immigrants during the Progressive Era, marriage was used to determine access and national belonging. Before that, for ex-slaves during Reconstruction, marriage was critical in shaping the meaning of economic and political independence.

Institutionally, marriage has also been intertwined with the development of federalism in the United States. The tension between states rights and federal power has played a large role in marriage politics. Marriage law is neither uniform nor explicit in all instances, because it varies from state to state. It is the jurisdictional right of each state to create its own "marital regime."[30] The assertion by state legislatures of broad, plenary power over marital status is constitutional. The various religious denominations, in spite of their continuing interest in marital status and its obligations, are subordinate to the laws of each state.[31] In determining the capacity to marry as a civil act, states are permitted to establish their own statutory classifications to effectuate any legitimate legislative purpose. The state must show a legally valid purpose for each new law, such as promotion of public health, safety, or the welfare of the state. Accordingly, a marriage is generally considered voidable if either party is under consenting age, deemed mentally incompetent, or if the parties are related by blood. States can use marriage as a regulatory lever in the service of state interests.

Another noted characteristic of U.S. federalism is that the actions of certain states become templates for others. Through their separate marriage laws, states can distinguish themselves from each other; for instance, some states have more lenient divorce laws and have used their marriage and divorce laws to draw people to their states.[32] At the same time, states are influenced by each other, so that when one state passes a law, other states often follow suit. Witness how changes in state marriage laws occur in waves, such as the married women's property acts passed between 1848 and 1895, followed by the eugenic marriage laws that began in 1896 and were in existence until the mid-twentieth century, and the more recent proliferation of state constitutional and statutory bans on same-sex marriage.

Constitutionally, marriage is bound by the "full faith and credit clause," which addresses the duties that states have to respect the "public acts, records, and judicial rulings" of other states, as well as the responsibilities the federal government has toward the states.[33] In other words, the Constitution mandates that each state recognize marriages that are legal in other states. So states have an interest in "supporting" each other's marriage law choices. For most of U.S. history, the federal government had little constitutional control over marriage. While there have been calls for a national and uniform marriage law, primarily in the Progressive Era in response to polygamy and immigration, and today in response to same-sex marriage, in general the national government has played only a small role.

Just as marriage is determined constitutionally by federalism, so marriage as the basis of family is an expression of federalism. Legal scholar Jill Elaine Hasday writes that "family serves as the quintessential symbol of localism."[34] She explains that, in debates on federalism, family law is one area where state authority is privileged over federal involvement. While this has held true for some time, recently this view has shifted, notably with the reauthorization of the 1996 welfare reform policy in the 2005 Deficit Reduction Act. Since then, marriage has increasingly come under the policy purview of the federal government. Whereas conservatives such as political scientist and pundit Charles Murray have seen the institution of marriage as an alternative to reliance upon the institutions of the state, today many self-proclaimed conservatives support the idea of including marriage as an active policy realm of the federal government. The Defense of Marriage Act in 1996, and subsequent state-by-state legal struggles since then, potentially threaten the stability of this federalist arrangement.

The institution of marriage itself has changed, bringing with it shifts in the politics of obligations and the politics of rights. During Reconstruction, understandings of marriage were based in state common law, and marriage was viewed as an economic and sexual status defining reproduction. The Comstock Act of 1873 was passed in response to the distribution of free love, anti-marriage materials circulating in the late nineteenth century. By the turn of the twentieth century, in addition to being an economic and sexual relationship, marriage was also considered a personal choice based on romantic love. At this point, states took more control, bureaucratizing the process by which couples were married with the creation of formal state-based marriage licenses and official marriage officers. In the 1960s, the Supreme Court legally defined marriage as a fundamental right, overriding state laws that banned interracial marriage and institutionalizing the notion of marriage as a personal choice and private decision. By the 1990s, this view of marriage was tested and challenged by both welfare policymakers who supported federally funded marriage programs, and gay and lesbian activists and courts who continue to argue that marriage is a private right.

To argue that marriage is a political institution is to say that it functions via imperatives, norms, and practices that are produced by past institutional developments. The role of the institution is to create rules for the citizenry to live by. At the same time, the settled results of political, legal, and bureaucratic struggles over the definition of marriage in one era can have unintended consequences in another, or certain views of marriage can get reframed in another context.

The cases in this book demonstrate how the institution is lodged paradoxically (yet powerfully) between liberal notions of rights, contracts, and freedoms on the one hand; and obligations to the state and society on the other. During intense moments of cultural confusion and political strain, this tension between, as one Freedmen's Bureau official said, "the duties as well as privileges of freedom" is redefined.[35] Marriage is the language through which various political questions about inclusion, national belonging, and economic rights are interpreted and made comprehensible. In turn it is through questions of inclusion, socialization, integration, and independence that political actors, policymakers, and voters understand and make sense of what is at stake in marriage, family, and sexual practices.

Each chapter in this book examines a different time period where marriage is mobilized in two seemingly contradictory ways. In one place the obligation to marry was strongly promoted, even coerced, for certain groups; while in another marriage rights were either rewarded or denied to certain groups. These discourses were both simultaneous and in tension. In each example the privilege to marry was shaped, defined, or maintained through the obligations and rights of marriage.

This book is divided into two parts. Part I concerns the historical development of marriage, from Reconstruction through the Progressive Era. Part II is more contemporary, premised on the developments in the 1960s and their influence on subsequent decades, in particular the 1990s and the first decade of the twenty-first century. This structure enables me to track marriage politics in different eras of political change, with each chapter addressing how marriage specifically frames political debates over inclusion and citizenship.

I begin in Chapter 1 with Reconstruction, a founding moment for marriage politics in the United States. This chapter traces the tension in the institution of marriage between obligations and rights as reflected in the challenge of black political inclusion in the decade following the Civil War. Amid war, devastation, and the re-constitution of the nation, ex-slaves were granted the right to marry as part of the logic of emancipation and citizenship. While policies of the Freedmen's Bureau obligated ex-slaves to marry, racial and economic hierarchies remained intact because whites and blacks were prohibited from marrying each other. In the case of Reconstruction, then, I ask how marriage helped redefine relations of power between whites and blacks, and between the South and the North.

Chapter 2 continues the examination of the obligation/rights tension in marriage in relation to the restabilization of national identity at a time of major social and political change—in this case I look at nativist responses to the second great wave of immigration during the Progressive Era. With the rise of immigration, industrialization, and urbanization during the Progressive Era, eugenic laws prohibiting certain marriages were enacted across states, while the right to marry was institutionalized through the creation of marriage licenses. American women lost the right to marry foreign-born men and remain citizens, at the same time that marital naturalization allowed foreign women to gain citizenship through marriage to American men. In the Progressive Era, then, I examine how the institution of marriage was central to the shaping of the new progressive state and notions of national identity and civic membership.

Chapter 3 opens Part II by examining the politics of marriage during the 1960s, when significant shifts were taking place in the institution. Interracial couples gained the constitutional right to marry, while President Lyndon Johnson, via his labor secretary Daniel Patrick Moynihan, promoted marriage as a palliative for urban poverty. During this same period of time, feminists were railing against the obligation of women to marry. In the 1960s, then, I examine how the institution of marriage was central to both the opening up and the temporary settlement of political conflicts around race and gender.

Chapter 4 focuses on the position of marriage at the center of the culture wars in the 1990s. In 1996, President Bill Clinton signed first the Personal Responsibility and Work Opportunity Reconcilation Act—welfare reform that supported the use of welfare funds for marriage-promotion programs—and then four weeks later the Defense of Marriage Act, denying gays and lesbians the federal recognition of marriage. In the 1990s, the institution of marriage was crucial to Clinton's triangulation strategy. I argue that you cannot sufficiently understand this strategy without taking serious account of Clinton's utilization of the politics of marriage.

Finally, in Chapter 5, I examine how debates on marriage intensified in the first decade of the twenty-first century, as a result of both pressure from state officials to expand marriage promotion and the increasingly powerful movement to expand the right to same-sex marriage. I explore the rise of the Marriage Movement and their efforts to create a marriage culture. What is striking in this period is how it is non-state actors who struggle to limit marriage rights, as opposed to state elites who were the driving force in the past. In the first decade of the twenty-first century, then, I examine a return to marriage as an obligation of citizens and a mode of disciplinary inclusion. I show how marriage has shifted since the 1960s from an institution to be extended to an institution to be protected. In all these examples, we see a pairing of struggles over marriage as an obligation and as a right, even as the specific conceptualizations of obligations and rights change and shift in each context. In the conclusion of the book I discuss the implications of this study for American politics scholarship as well as for politics generally. And throughout the book, I argue that the role of marriage and family in shaping and reflecting politics, in each of the moments I cover, has been underexamined.

Each chapter in the book is an examination of how marriage frames political debates over inclusion and citizenship. The cases were chosen because they are the most prominent and illustrative examples of the tension between obligations and rights I am examining. African Americans in Reconstruction, new immigrants in the Progressive Era, and poor women, people of color, and gays and lesbians in the wake of the 1960s all elucidate the deep structure of marital politics in the United States. Of course, these are not the only examples.[36] That said, the cases I examine speak to the central struggles of these eras in U.S. political history. In this book, I ask how marriage shapes, defines and produces politics. Each example, from Reconstruction through debates over same-sex marriage today, shows the tensions, connections, and tradeoffs that marriage politics creates. Together, they reveal the centrality and persistence of marriage politics in American political questions, not just occurring at one isolated moment in time, not raised by just one political party or political group, but standing as an enduring feature of American politics. Like the planets circling the sun, notions of equality, inclusion, and citizenship are pulled into the orbit of the political institution of marriage.

PART I

Historical Development

Chapter 1

The "Duties as Well as Privileges of Freedom"

After the Civil War, agents of the federal Bureau of Refugees, Freedmen and Abandoned Lands (the Freedmen's Bureau), charged with inculcating former slaves with the precepts of freedom and American citizenship, imposed policies designed to teach African Americans the benefits and obligations of marriage. Also during this period, anti-interracial marriage laws were actively upheld in southern and northern courts as necessary to the protection and maintenance of "civilization." Thus, while ex-slaves were being pressed into one kind of marriage, they were legally prohibited from another, in both cases as the price of freedom and citizenship.

The period of Reconstruction (1863–77) was a time of intense political upheaval as the shape and scope of the American state were being reconfigured. The emancipation of almost four million slaves, the military and political defeat of the Confederacy, and a new phase of nation-building dramatically opened up and challenged prior definitions of freedom, citizenship, and political order. The ratification of the Thirteenth, Fourteenth, and Fifteenth Amendments and six major federal statutes restructured American citizenship laws in the United States.[1] Along with emancipation, citizenship, male suffrage, and civil rights, formerly enslaved African Americans were also granted the right to legal marriage. Thus, like voting and civil rights, marriage rights played a role in reshaping the political and social relationships between blacks and whites, in negotiating power relations between the North and South, and in defining the grounds of black citizenship.

Marriage rights helped distinguish between freed and slave status. Slave unions and families were neither legal nor protected. Families were broken up by the demands of their masters and the slave economy. Once ex-slaves gained the right to marry, however, they could establish legal households. At the same time, they also inherited the obligations of marriage, not only to family but to the state as well. As Freedmen's Bureau chief Oliver Otis

Howard explained, former slaves in their transition to citizenship must be "taught there are duties as well as privileges of freedom."[2] Delineating the obligations and rights of marriage for the newly established citizens was important in both promoting the civil status of former slaves and preventing change to the foundations of racial hierarchy.

During the nineteenth century, the scope of the marriage contract in the United States was dictated by the English common-law principle of coverture. Coverture placed married women's property and their own persons in the hands and under the legal "cover" of their husbands. English jurist and common-law scholar William Blackstone summarized the features of the doctrine in his 1765 book on English law in a chapter entitled, "Of Husband and Wife": "By marriage, the husband and wife are one person in law: that is, the very being or legal existence of the woman is suspended during the marriage, or at least incorporated and consolidated into that of the husband, under whose wing, protection and cover, she performs every thing."[3] Under coverture, a man's political and civic status stemmed from being the legal head—and legal representative—of a household, which included dependent women and children requiring economic and social protection. Marriage thus endowed men with the fullness of civic status, as independent individuals and as political decision makers. Women's political and civic status was also defined by their marital status, but it rendered them economically, civilly, and politically dependent.

In his commentaries on American beliefs and institutions during the 1830s, Alexis de Tocqueville found Americans' firm insistence on women's role to be "the chief cause" of the country's growing prosperity and power. His *Democracy in America* provided one of the most influential formulations of the nation's "separate sphere" ideology, relying on appeals to nature as well as political economy to suggest the appropriateness of purely domestic roles for women. Americans, Tocqueville wrote, "carefully divid[ed] the duties of man from those of woman [so that] the great work of society may be the better carried on." Women, he explained, received sufficient education to play their politically crucial role in shaping the mores of the nation's future citizens.[4] These embodied statuses were viewed as undergirding the progress and stability of the nation, and more specifically the white race.

As a common-law contract marriage was private and defined the private sphere. Yet, with the granting of marriage rights to ex-slaves, the interest of the state in the role of marriage as a relation and status expanded and evolved.

In the last third of the nineteenth century in particular, legislators, jurists, and social scientists assumed there was a close link between monogamous, patriarchal marriage and the state. Through marriage, the states were actively involved in creating social and civic statuses for both men and women, relying on these roles to order society. State power was seen as patterned on the male-headed family, its legitimacy dependent on the same source.[5] By protecting the family, then, the law also protected the state from disruption, instability, and discord. In this way, marriage was considered the foundation of the nation and society. It defined important statuses in the nation, which were unequal and based in privilege. Gender was crucial to the institutional framework of marriage.

After the Civil War, marriage became an important institutional site for the reestablishment of norms and the incorporation of ex-slaves into citizenship. Through marriage, political and social actors formulated and contested the rights and obligations of the newly defined citizens. As new citizens, many former slaves actively exercised the right to marry and create legal families. During this period of political instability and change, marriage was one way in which political inclusion and citizenship were reformulated; marriage was used to promote but also limit changes to status hierarchies based on race, class, gender, and sexuality. The obligations of citizenship were defined by the Freedmen's Bureau marriage policy that encouraged ex-slaves to marry each other; at the same time, southern courts curtailed and limited their right to marry through antimiscegenation laws. Thus, marriage was a political institution through which the economic, political, and social rights of the newly freed slaves were shaped.

Promarriage Policies and Defining Marital Obligations

Republican state legislators, in particular the federal Freedmen's Bureau, held that the practice of marriage, and its attendant gender roles, was a way to introduce ex-slaves into the moral and economic dimensions of American citizenship and belonging. After the war, states across the South passed laws that enforced marriage, attempting to substitute the patriarchal family unit for economic dependency on the state. Legal scholar Katherine Franke shows how the paternalistic marriage policies of both the Freedmen's Bureau and southern states were attempts to shape and direct black social, economic, and sexual behavior to ready the new citizens for the cultural and political norms of freedom and economic independence.[6] In essence, marriage helped define independent citizenship. The demands of the postbellum period resulted in the linking of marriage, citizenship, and economic independence, where each came to rely on the other. In addition to creating a new right that could be denied or granted, marriage for blacks also produced new obligations to the state and within families.

The right of former slaves to marry not only represented a new privilege but, more importantly, it delineated a new regulatory relationship to the state. Union officials and northern missionaries who came to the South during and after the war to "reconstruct" southern political society, and thus the lives of ex-slaves, taught ex-slaves in particular that freedom meant enacting the precepts of civilization through marriage. By insisting that marriage was a necessary foundation to citizenship and critical for grasping the value of independence—what was called "self-protection", "self-support," and "standing alone"—the relationship of former slaves to the polity was circumscribed by a notion of family obligation rather than citizenship rights.

This tension in marriage rights was not lost on ex-slaves, yet they also understood the right to marry as a crucial consequence of emancipation and as undergirding their new found rights. Franke describes how "after emancipation, formerly enslaved people travelled great distances and endured hardships in order to reunite families that had been separated under slavery."[7] Even though marriage rights also meant state power to compel former slaves to meet their new domestic obligations, African Americans saw that marriage was a way to protect not only their families but also a range of public rights. Historian Laura Edwards notes that at the same time ex-slaves appropriated certain tenets of legal marriage, they also maintained rules and practices that coalesced with those of many poor whites rather than bourgeois whites.[8]

Union officials and northern missionaries in the South came to understand the freedom to work and the freedom to marry as complementary and mutually supportive. As historian Amy Dru Stanley aptly explains, in order to create American citizens out of former slaves, they focused on teaching the freedmen and freedwomen both to work for wages and to honor the practice of marriage.[9] With the 1865 assassination of President Lincoln and the failure of Radical Reconstruction with its proposed program to grant ex-slaves plots of land, Republicans increasingly pushed ex-slaves toward marriage and working for wages as symbols of freedom, independence, and equality, as opposed to owning land.[10] Thus, after emancipation, marriage helped define one notion of equality as opposed to another. Political equality was not undergirded by economic access but marital obligations. This period also saw the beginning of a marriage policy that was government enforced. The link between membership in the polity and the practice of marriage limited the right of ex-slaves to demand and gain government aid.

Marriage Policies in the Contraband Camps

Not having the right to marry, and under the control of slave owners, slaves built families and relationships based on nonbinding traditions that defined a complex constellation of relationships, including "sweethearting," "taking up," and "living together." Sweethearting and taking up were considered open-ended and nonmonogamous relationships. Living together, however, was understood to be a more binding relationship that assumed a long-term commitment. Laura Edwards, among others, describes slave relationships as more fluid and open than the family structures of the then-dominant white society.[11] Once slaves became citizens, these familial practices were viewed by whites as incongruous with the principles and moral norms of American society that slaves were now entering. In fact they were considered an obstacle to the slaves' successful transition to living outside the bonds of slavery. Because monogamous unions and patriarchal gender roles served to define traditional marriage as the foundation of the nation, policies that encouraged ex-slaves to marry were widely encouraged by northern Republicans.

During the fall and winter of 1862–63, in a number of small towns across the Deep South and Southwest, General Ulysses S. Grant instructed his army to organize "contraband camps" where ex-slaves could be sheltered and supervised by Union officials, chaplains, and some civilians. Existing on the boundary of the North and South, between war and peace, slavery and emancipation, these camps also became liminal spaces where Union superintendents attempted to help former slaves adjust to, and understand, the meaning of living in freedom. Teaching the fundaments of formal, legal marriage was one of the first priorities. Camp officials were ordered to "lay the foundations of society" by not only setting up public schools, encouraging religious worship, regulating trade, but also by "enforcing laws of marriage."[12] These foundations of society and civilization defined what it meant to be living as free men and women. In other words, freedom and citizenship were characterized by certain acceptable behaviors.

The familial and sexual practices of the fugitive slaves who crossed over Union lines during the Civil War received intense scrutiny, and this was especially true for those who entered the camps. In trying to obtain information about former slaves and their habits, Chaplain John Eaton Jr., the general superintendent of the contrabands in Grant's charge, circulated a questionnaire in April 1863 to the director of each camp concerning the freedpeople's "marital notions & practices."[13] One of Eaton's questions concerned how ex-slaves understood marriage. A camp director from Corinth, Mississippi replied concisely that ex-slaves' understanding of marriage was "all wrong." Still another from Grand Junction, Tennessee responded that "most of them have no idea of the sacredness of the marriage tie, declaring that marriage, as it exists among the whites, has been impossible for them. In other cases, the marriage relation exists in all its sacredness without legal sanction." While officials reported that some slave unions could be characterized as committed unions, more often they noted that slaves "know what marriage is among the whites but have yielded to the sad necessity of their case." Chaplain Eaton charged that, "among the things to be done, to fit the freed people for a life of happiness and usefulness, it was obvious that the inculcation of right principles and practices in regard to the social relations ought to find a place."[14]

Linking the practice of marriage to freedom and a "life of happiness and usefulness," individual camp directors developed marriage rules. In 1863, the contraband camp in Corinth, Mississippi reported that "all entering our camps who have been living or desire to live together as husband and wife are required to be married in the proper manner, and a certificate of the same is given. This regulation has done much to promote the good order of the camp."[15] These rules were designed not only to maintain decorum as ex-slaves entered the camps, but also to emphasize that marriage, representing the "right principles and practices," was important because it promoted order grounded in moral, sexual, and gender norms that former slaves were to emulate.

By early 1864, the secretary of war had made marriage regulation official military policy and directed camp supervisors to "solemnize the rite of marriage among Freedmen."[16] By that spring the policy had expanded. A Union military edict had authorized army clergy to perform marriages among freedmen and women, instructing them to issue marriage certificates and record all marriages.[17] The policy was widely supported by superintendents of the contraband camps. Chaplain Warren from Vicksburg, Mississippi observed: "the introduction of the rite of christian marriage and requiring its strict observance, exerted a most wholesome influence upon the order of the camps and the conduct of the people."[18]

Early Union marriage policies were aimed at maintaining moral standards within the camps as well as fitting ex-slaves to be citizens. Camp directors argued for the necessity of learning social relations in transitioning to freedom. Their approach was based on the presumed organic relationship between morality and citizenship, and the importance of the principles of marriage and family to defining belonging. The obligations embedded in marriage, which included moral and gender norms, were crucial to this transition. Some of the testimonies from camp officials to the American Freedmen's Inquiry Commission illustrate this focus on social relations and morality as the basis for inclusion and freedom. The American Freedmen's Inquiry Commission was created by the War Department in 1863 to investigate the status of the emancipated slaves. The establishment of the Freedmen's Bureau was one of its recommendations. The commission was made up of three members, all of whom were abolitionists and reformers. They visited the South to hear testimony from former slaves and Union officers, and wrote two reports and many pages of individual observations.[19]

The testimony by Colonel William Pile, administrator of the Vicksburg contraband camp, illustrates the developing link between marriage, citizenship, and civic belonging. He explained to the commission that "one great defect in the management of the negroes down there was, as I judged, the ignoring of the family relationship. . . . My judgment is that one of the first things to be done with these people, to qualify them for citizenship, for self-protection and self-support, is to impress upon them the family obligations."[20] Pile explained that marriage was one of the "first things" necessary to qualify ex-slaves for citizenship.

An important part of this view of marriage was how it shaped understandings of economic independence. The commission urged that freedpeople should "stand alone" as soon as possible and that, while temporary government oversight was recommended to aid the transition to freedom, the dependencies of slavery should not be prolonged.[21] "Working for wages, they [ex-slaves] soon get an idea of accumulating," one commission report commented, continuing that former slaves should regard marriage "as a privilege appertaining to emancipation." Marriage was more than a right. It was also a privilege that slaves were obligated to enact. The institution would fit ex-slaves for citizenship by defining gender roles and economic independence. Marriage enabled "standing alone" because it encouraged self-protection and self-support, both economically and culturally—the commission urged that the wife must learn the "instinct of chastity" and the husband his "obligation to support his family."[22] In the commission's recommendations for emancipation, wage work and marriage emerged as important in defining freedom and civic belonging. These were mutually reinforcing notions that would lay the foundation of an economic and moral understanding of independence and self-support. Thus, a notion of family obligation, rather than one of rights, defined the foundation of citizenship, the value of self-protection and self-support, and ultimately the relationship of former slaves to the polity.

By focusing on the roles of marriage and family, camp directors understood marriage as a process of civilizing former slaves, inculcating them into the traditions and practices of the dominant society. The commission's final report to the secretary of war reflected the general view among whites that the rule of law and the kind guidance from whites together would civilize the uncivilized and unchristian ways of former slaves.[23] The commission concluded that "they [ex-slaves] will learn much and gain much from us. They will gain in force of character, in mental cultivation, in self-reliance, in enterprise, in breadth of views and habits of generalization. Our influence over them, if we treat them well, will be powerful for good."[24] As Katherine Franke explains, the commission urged and recommended an active, paternalistic role for the federal government in the moral cultivation of the black character.[25] In defining the rights and obligations of freed slaves through marriage, a racial hierarchy was reinforced under the banner of citizenship. Freedom and citizenship took form but were tempered by the social and economic obligations attached to the status of marriage. Here we see how marriage acted as a public and political institution that regulated and shaped obligations and rights of the newly defined citizens. Union officers in the Contraband camps used marriage to respond to political and social problems. Marriage became a legitimate venue for exercising state control and individual rights, structuring the economic and cultural notions of self-support and standing alone. This view of marriage as applied to ex-slaves affected how marriage would come to be seen more generally.

Postwar and the Freedmen's Bureau

After the end of the war, the Thirteenth Amendment did not clearly spell out the dimensions of freedom or the powers of Congress to enforce it. The devastation in the South called for immediate action, and federal aid was deemed necessary for providing relief, rebuilding, and reestablishing order. The South was unstable and destitute, with a desperate refugee population, widespread starvation, and no organized civil authority. In March 1865, Congress established the Freedmen's Bureau under the authority of the War Department, in an effort to begin the process of transition from war and slavery to order and freedom. The bureau was set up to coordinate a national program of relief, supervision, and management of "all abandoned lands and the control of all subjects relating to refugees and freedmen from rebel states . . . under such rules and regulations as may be prescribed by the head of the bureau and approved by the President."[26] The establishment of the Freedmen's Bureau represented an unprecedented federal effort as the government took responsibility for the relief and sustenance of the emancipated slaves.

The bureau, however, was unable to actually take full responsibility for the emancipated slaves because it lacked a clear mandate as to the scope of its authority and responsibilities. When Andrew Johnson was made president by Lincoln's assassination, he pardoned former Confederates and did not redistribute land.[27] Consequently, during the summer of 1865, it became clear that ex-slaves would not get the small farms many had expected; instead, they were reduced to working as hired laborers or sharecroppers on land owned by whites.[28] Following the Republican notion of free labor, the Freedmen's Bureau structured its approach to Reconstruction on the belief that economic mobility ensured social and republican order. The agency maintained that "personal habits of industry, frugality, integrity, and self-discipline would lead to independence and prosperity for both individuals and society."[29] These habits were essential not only for economic independence but for manliness. Freedmen, the bureau avowed, could become free men by working land rather than relying on government subsidy and protection.[30] Thus, with the failure of Radical Reconstruction, the Freedmen's Bureau evolved into assisting the transformation of ex-slaves into wage workers rather than landowners. In trying to help former slaves "stand alone," agents concentrated on familiariz-ing their charges with the idea of contracts, urging them to make contracts for work under white landowners as well as for marriage.[31]

As "wage laborer" took the place of "landowner" in defining freedom for ex-slaves, bureau agents impressed upon the former slaves that freedom was counter not just to bondage but also the habits of laziness and immo-rality.[32] In teaching freedpeople to be a "self-supporting class of free labor-ers" who understood the necessity of steady employment, the bureau also taught freedmen to be responsible husbands and fathers who provided for their families, and freedwomen to be devoted wives and mothers.[33] Marriage, which already defined patriarchal notions of independence prior to the Civil War, had become a useful framework through which to define freedom, eco-nomic independence, and self-support. Thus, reform of the sexual practices and family patterns of former slaves became crucial to the work of the Freed-men's Bureau.

The "Marriage Rules"

Freedmen's Bureau commissioner general Oliver Otis Howard considered the sanctity of contracts, self-support, and equal justice under the law as main-stays of Reconstruction and the new social order. In pledging to bar compul-sory, unpaid labor and to protect domestic rights, Howard declared it bureau protocol to write out wage agreements and officially register marriages to en-sure that both were enforceable by law. Former slaves were required to marry, and bureau agents were granted the authority to perform weddings, to create rules for certifying and dissolving slave unions, and to manage the complexi-ties that arose from the forced separation of slave couples.[34]

In 1866 the bureau issued a general order titled "Marriage Rules," in-tended to "correct, as far as possible, one of the most cruel wrongs inflicted by slavery, and also to aid the freedmen in properly appreciating and reli-giously observing the sacred obligations of the marriage state."[35] The rules stated clearly that "No Parties having agreed to enter the marriage relation will be allowed to live together as husband and wife until their marriage had been legally solemnized."[36] And teaching the precepts of marriage included more than just understanding the importance of living as man and wife. The rules also made clear that it was necessary to care for children: "if a man living without a wife find[s] two wives restored to him by freedom, the one having children by him and the other not, he shall take the mother of his children as his lawful wife."[37]

All across the South, Freedmen's Bureau agents proselytized marriage, attempting to counter what they considered informal, illegal, and illegitimate slave unions. An assistant commissioner in Kentucky asserted that "'taking up with each other' is an abominable practice, and must perish with the institution which gave it birth."[38] Wager Swayne, a Union general in charge of Alabama, insisted that those informally wed should engage in a "general re-marriage" or risk prosecution and punishment. Swayne focused on urging ex-slaves to form contracts, to "work energetically and patiently," and to establish lawful relationships, even while acknowledging that emancipated slaves faced "fiendish atrocity" form local whites.[39]

An assistant commissioner in Vicksburg was insistent on the value of marriage. He counseled freedpeople to be patient in their claims for jobs and schools, emphasizing that in order to revert the habits of slavery,

> regular lawful marriage is a most important thing. No people can ever be good and great, nor even respectable, if the men and women 'take up together' without being married, and change from one to another and quarrel and part whenever the fancy takes them. Sin and shame of this class always destroys a people if not repented of. . . . Let no woman consent to live with a man at all who will not at once marry her. Unfaithfulness to the marriage relation is such a sin and shame that it ought not to be heard of among free people.[40]

Thus marriage represented freedom whereas nonmonogamy was a savage practice that existed within the bonds of slavery.[41] Officials argued that regulation of the sexual practices of former slaves was crucial to freedpeople's understanding of American civic belonging. The practice of "taking up" disrupted the gender roles of patriarchal society and therefore the society they were premised upon. These marriage rules also suggest a belief that, without legal marriage, "taking up" threatened to create a new group of dependent African American women and children who, once under the care of plantation owners, would now look to the state for aid if no husbands were available. There were two views of marriage. On the one hand coverture and gender roles defined the foundation of the nation and the private sphere, and on the other marriage defined public freedom and manliness. Both sought to forestall public dependency.

The Freedman's Bureau instruction on marriage combined economic independence and patriarchal gender traits.[42] One bureau agent in Virginia reported that, at each meeting, the freedpeople in his charge learned "the duties and relations of the matrimonial state." The assistant commissioner in Tennessee impressed upon former slaves that a wife must be her husband's "help meet" and "the charm of the household." The wife must not be "a slovenly woman who goes about with her heels out of her stockings, her dress unpinned, her hair uncombed, with dirt under her finger-nails." In turn the husband must "Be a MAN. Earn money and save it." The assistant commissioner explained to the freedmen that, "Your wives will not love you if you do not provide bread and clothes for them."[43] The Freedmen's Bureau focused not only on enforcing marriage but also on reproducing the traits associated with gender roles in marriage.

Bureau agents were accustomed to understanding the social order based on male-headed households, and so they focused on policing and reforming the freedmen, and not freedwomen. In addition, they sought to halt the growing burden of orphans and an increase in relief funding. They assumed that freedmen should be the providers and protectors for their families. The effort to create monogamous husbands who were industrious and responsible providers for their dependents correlated with the aspiration to see them as citizens. Marriage and work reinforced the foundations of citizenship.[44]

Teaching the merits and practices of formal marriage was not the only way marriage defined freedom for ex-slaves and their relationship to the polity. As historian Eric Foner explains "with freedom came developments that strengthened patriarchy within the black family and institutionalized the notion that men and women should inhabit separate spheres." For instance, when the Freedmen's Bureau designated the husband as head of household, it insisted that men sign contracts for the labor of the entire family and established wage scales that paid women less for identical work.[45] In other words, labor contracts were structured to promote and enforce the patriarchal principles of marriage so that the wife's wages were not her own but belonged to her husband.

According to bureau agents, citizenship status was premised on a freedmen's control over family labor, acquired through marriage. Historian Nancy Cott explains "when a man had no property but only his own labor to indicate his independence and stake in society, he had greater interest in seeing his wife's labor as his own." This view was prevalent in the political context. Republican congressmen, in describing the rights of ex-slaves as citizens, contrasted the slave who had no rights and was economically dependent, with the free man with his rights and responsibilities as a husband and father.[46] Thus, freedom and citizenship came to be defined through the obligations of family life, particularly in the absence of other possibilities, such as owning land.

State Marriage Policies

Shortly after the end of the war, many southern state legislatures as well as the national Congress passed validation statutes or constitutional provisions rendering marriages begun under slavery legal. Some required registration of slave marriages; others just declared slave marriages legal if the couple was cohabiting as husband and wife when the law went into effect.[47] Mississippi's 1865 civil rights law was typical: "All freedmen, negros and mulattos, who do now and have heretofore lived and cohabited together as husband and wife shall be taken and held in law as legally married."[48] As another example, in North Carolina the legal status of slave unions was among the first issues on the agenda of the 1865 constitutional convention. The final act declared the unions of all ex-slaves who "now cohabit together in relation of husband and wife" to be lawful marriages from "the time of commencement of such cohabitation." As historian Laura Edwards argues, the date of commencement was important. "If the date had been set at either emancipation or the ratification of the act, then all children born in slavery would have been illegitimate and their maintenance could have fallen to the state."[49]

These state marriage laws tended to be coercive. In some states cohabitation without legal marriage was a misdemeanor punishable by a fine. Other states, in reestablishing their sovereignty, collected a fee for a marriage certificate. Once states reinstated their authority, the Freedmen's Bureau stopped granting marriages but assisted freedmen and women to comply with marriage regulations, in some cases arresting adulterers and bringing them before local state authorities.[50] Other states passed laws that gave former slaves time limits in which to remarry formally before a minister or civil officer. For instance, in Florida, "all colored inhabitants of this State claiming to be living together in the relation of husband and wife . . . and who shall mutually desire to continue in that relation" had nine months to file a marriage license with the county circuit court.[51] Former slaves who failed to comply and continued to cohabit would be criminally prosecuted for the crimes of adultery and fornication.[52] In North Carolina, ex-slaves had just less than six months to legalize their unions with the county clerk. "Each month after they failed to do so constituted a distinct and separately prosecutable criminal offense."[53]

These laws illustrate not only the strong regulation of ex-slaves' relationships but also how important it was to ensure that ex-slaves formed state-sanctioned marriages and families. State laws that enforced family and marriage stressed the obligations rather than the rights and privileges of citizenship. Through the rules surrounding marriage, then, a new relationship with the state was defined, one predicated on restrictions and obligations.[54] Freedmen's Bureau chief Oliver Otis Howard explained the logic behind enforcing both marriage and wage contracts, stating that if former slaves "can be induced to enter into contracts, they are taught that there are duties as well as privileges of freedom."[55]

Antimiscegenation Laws and Limiting Marriage Rights

In contrast to the federal marriage policy, white southern elites limited the reach of Reconstruction by using existing anti-interracial marriage laws to curtail the rights of black citizens, in order to maintain the racial hierarchy. By prohibiting interracial marriages, southern legislative and judicial bodies limited black entrance into the civic realm. After formal racial subjugation was abolished, southern courts held the line with antimiscegenation laws, fighting challenges to this form of legal segregation. The arguments the courts made on behalf of antimiscegenation policies focused on the relationship of marriage, gender, and family to the health of the state, and to civilization more generally. Through anti-interracial marriage laws, a concept of racial homogeneity was institutionalized as individual state policies and the ex-slave's relationship to the state were defined and curtailed. In particular, the courts argued that gender roles in marriage could not be maintained in the context of an interracial union, that a stable family was defined through its racial homogeneity. Thus, antimiscegenation laws were meant to reconstitute the political and social hierarchies that the Reconstruction Amendments were meant to abolish, and partially succeeded in doing so.

Southern judges in many antimiscegenation cases used the institution of marriage to re-impose a political and social race hierarchy. In the process they shifted the meaning of marriage itself, from a private nuptial obligation of men and women, as outlined by Blackstone, to a right that could be denied. Asserting that marriage provided a special status, in opposition to the view that Blackstone had articulated in contract philosophy in the eighteenth century, southern judges rendered state court intervention into the common-law marital union and the private sphere appropriate, even necessary. A distinction between social and political equality was further articulated, allowing the courts to push back the equalizing spirit of the Reconstruction Amendments.

While the Freedman's Bureau was promoting certain marital arrangements among African Americans, southern courts were prohibiting others. Laws against interracial marriage had been on the books since the 1660s, but after the Civil War, efforts to prevent interracial marriages in the South increased dramatically, not only through enforcing laws that already existed, but by passing new ones. By the end of the nineteenth century, interracial marriage was legally forbidden in at least twenty-six states, mainly in the South and West. Between 1865 and 1899, indictments of individuals who intermarried made up 72 percent of southern appellate cases.[56] During the latter half of the nineteenth century, antimiscegenation laws were consistently upheld as constitutional.[57] The examples below reveal that southern courts were combating the political changes wrought by Reconstruction, or were at least attempting to define and circumscribe black citizenship, through the very language of the legal rulings that knocked back challenges to these laws. Political scientist Julie Novkov explains that questions about "interracial intimacy" at this moment were more than concerns about sexual mores, but "many whites saw interracial marriage as a symbol of the most radical implications of freedom."[58] Thus the struggles over the constitutionality of interracial unions were matters of the state.

After the Civil War, the most challenging task facing the Union was reintegrating the nation, and doing so in a way that incorporated former slaves as citizens. For defeated Confederates, the postwar challenge was recovering some political power and, in particular, working out a new set of arrangements between the "races" to replace the political, social, and economic lines between whites and blacks once enforced by slavery. Between 1865 and 1866, the South looked to redraw the racial line, as legislatures across the region, in an attempt to reestablish white economic supremacy, enacted detailed codes of harsh labor laws that limited the economic rights of ex-slaves. The Black Codes, as they were called, varied by state, but generally authorized local officials to apprehend unemployed blacks and fine them for vagrancy. Some codes forbade blacks to own or lease farms. As a response to this attack on both ex-slaves and the power of the Union, Congress effectively struck down the Black Codes by passing the Civil Rights Act of 1866, which declared blacks to be citizens and empowered the federal government to intervene in state affairs when necessary.

After the installation of Reconstruction state legislatures in the former Confederacy, restricting interracial marriage was one attempt to revive the preexisting social and political order by sustaining white, masculine political sovereignty. But given the control exerted over the South by the Union during Reconstruction, how did southern courts exercise this power? After the adoption of the Fourteenth Amendment in 1868, the question arose as to whether state laws prohibiting interracial marriage denied people of color the equality guaranteed by the amendment. Challengers to antimiscegenation laws used federal initiatives, the Fourteenth Amendment (the privileges and immunities clause, the due process clause, and the equal protection clause),[59] the U.S. Constitution's right of contract clause in Article I, and the Civil Rights Act of 1866 to frame these kinds of marriage laws as an infringement of rights.[60] However, in constitutionality challenges, the laws were invariably determined to be valid.[61] The state courts' findings of constitutionality rested primarily upon three arguments: the statutes were not discriminatory because both races, black and white, were affected equally; the state had a rational, scientific basis for treating interracial marriages as threats to society; and, finally, marriage was under subnational jurisdiction. Southern courts mapped out legal and political territory for the institution of marriage, and in doing so attempted to reestablish white supremacy.

In response to the Reconstruction Amendments, southern courts differentiated social equality from political equality through marriage laws, and argued for limitations on the right to marry. In an 1869 Georgia case, *Scott v. State of Georgia*, a white man and black woman were convicted of intermarrying. The state supreme court proclaimed:

> Before the laws, the Code of Georgia makes all citizens equal, without regard to race or color. But it does not create, nor does any law of the State attempt to enforce, moral or social equality between the different races or citizens of the State. Such equality does not in fact exist and never can. The God of nature made it otherwise, and no hu-

man law can produce it, and no human tribunal can enforce it. There are gradations and classes throughout the universe. From the tallest archangel in Heaven, down to the meanest reptile on earth, moral and social inequalities exist and must continue to exist through all eternity.[62]

The law drew on then-current scientific definitions of race to establish Anglo-Saxons as the socially and biologically privileged race. The court argued that these natural inequalities maintained order in society and the polity, and it did so by asserting the distinction between political and social equality. While former slaves enjoyed political equality and protection from the federal government, social equality was not mandated or natural.

Thus, legal entitlement and notions of status and hierarchy derived from marriage were concerned not just with the statuses of men and women. Racial identity was also merged with stratified social and legal status. After the Civil War, whiteness was not just a privileged identity but also a vested political interest—an interest and right that could now be protected through marriage law.[63] In contrast to the Freedmen's Bureau Marriage Rules that asserted the obligation of ex-slaves to marry, here the right to marry was to be protected. Antimiscegenation laws served to protect racial identity and to keep property and financial inheritance entirely within white families, further limiting the access of black citizens. So, even though courts argued for the distinction between social and political equality, the construction of social inequalities undergirded political and economic interests and relationships.

Scientific racial and gender discourse of the time was also used as the legal argument against mixed unions. The court extolled the virtue of anti-miscegenation legislation, professing that "the amalgamation of the races is not only unnatural, but is always productive of deplorable results. Our daily observation shows us, that the offspring of these unnatural connections are generally *sickly and effeminate*, and that they are inferior in physical development and strength, to the full-blood of either race. . . . They are productive of evil, and evil only, without any corresponding good."[64] Calling the progeny of interracial unions "effeminate" suggests a cultural concern with masculinity and patriarchy, and thus shows a conflation of race and gender. Mixed unions would threaten not only whiteness but also patriarchy, and therefore also the core principles underlying political order and civic membership. The idea of interracial marriage threatened to contaminate the family, the foundation of the state authority. Such marriages also threatened to blur the line between whites and blacks and to "effeminize" politics. Thus, curtailing the right to marriage was considered both legitimate and necessary.

The threat of interracial marriage also had a more practical edge. In ways similar to poor blacks, poor whites lacked the means necessary to live up to elite white standards of marriage, manhood, and womanhood.[65] Thus included in the danger of interracial marriage was also the potential that poor whites would marry poor blacks, finding common cause against the bourbon elites. Because marriage formed a political relationship that defined the ideological basis of the state, this kind of union would not only upset the race and class dimensions of marriage, but threatened to unite poor whites and blacks in a class allegiance. In this sense, antimiscegenation laws reveal a distinctly politico-legal logic, a precursor to the language that led to the *Plessy v. Ferguson* "separate but equal" decision in 1896 and later the Jim Crow segregation laws. Southern judges substantiated a distinction between political and social equality, and between those inside and outside politics. They also institutionalized the notion of an "outside" within the confines of the polity. In doing so, they created the legal framework from which to codify "separate but equal." The forces animating this logic can be found in the links between the race and gender discourses of the time on a variety of issues that dealt with ideas of protecting the home, the family, civilization, society, and politics.

The role of marriage as a political institution regulated and defined those inside and outside the institution. After the Civil War, marriage as private contract was supplanted by marriage as conferring racialized hierarchical and privileged status. In 1871, the state court's decision in *Doc Lonas v. State of Tennessee* found a black man and white woman guilty of violating an 1870 act that made it a felony to intermarry. Judge Sneed, of the Supreme Court of Tennessee, argued that marriage was more than a contract. Rather, he ruled, "It is the civil status of a man and a woman, united in law for life . . . it is not a contract but one of the domestic relations . . . it is no more a contract than a fatherhood, or a sonship, or serfdom, or slavery, or apprenticeship, are contracts."[66] Because marriage, according to the court, was considered more than a contract, it constituted a relation of dependency and domination that could not be ended at will. It was not merely a right.

Against the political ambiguity of race relations during Reconstruction, the marital union was clarified as a domestic relation, bound as if by blood.

In arguing that the marriage relation was not something entered into freely like a contract, the court asserted its right to regulate the marriage relation. This view stands in tension with the attempts to link marriage with freedom and contracts, which was the work of the Freedmen's Bureau. In the context of establishing citizenship through marriage rights for ex-slaves, the more public the marriage status became, the more regulated it was.

After claiming that marriage was a status like "one of the domestic relations," the court went on to argue for the separation of the races, grounding the progress of civilization in a notion of racial homogeneity in the name of the public good: "The laws of civilization demand that the races be kept apart in this country. The progress of either does not depend upon the admixture of blood. A sound philanthropy, looking to the public peace and the happiness of both races, would regard any effort to intermarry the individuality of the races as a calamity full of the saddest and gloomiest portent to the generations that are to come after us." The decision here makes marriage a public concern, and what is good for the public is racial purity. In arguing for the separation of the races, the court legally defined order and peace through a notion of difference, that being racial difference, without which the progress and civilization of generations to come would be threatened.

The Tennessee court legitimated this claim to racial homogeneity by using the racist scientific doctrines of the time as evidence that racial inequalities were real and unassailable. Incorporating the precept of race as a physically defined reality allowed the law to assign social standing through the institution of marriage. Bowing to the rights acquired by former slaves, Judge Sneed explained, "They are among us. They were faithful slaves, and are becoming useful and valuable as laborers. . . . Their rights, social, civil, political and religious, will be jealously guarded; but [they] must not marry or be given in marriage with the sons and daughters of our people."

The court acknowledged the rights of ex-slaves, claiming to protect equal rights, but it also asserted that ex-slaves should not marry the children of "our people." Marriage, as the foundation of the state, would be ordered by racial homogeneity; the perceived purity of the black and white races had been and continued to be maintained as an institutional relationship, not merely a social one. Thus, institutionalized, marriage status determined a hierarchical relationship between men and women as well as between whites and blacks. Judge Sneed argued that it was necessary "to prevent the production of [a] hybrid race. To prevent violence and bloodshed which would arise from such cohabitation, distasteful to our people, and unfit to produce the human race in any of the types in which it was created. . . . The equality intended, is not equality in all things."

A decree on interracial marriage like this one was quite common in post–Civil War southern courts. Such rulings asserted the importance of keeping whites and blacks separate, and held that marriage was a realm where equality was neither required nor desirable.[67] The legal rhetorical logic went as follows: Interracial marriage was not just wrong, it was dangerous. The offspring of such unions were unfit for political life and violence would be inevitable, thus bringing the end of civilization. The courts conceded that ex-slaves had been granted political equality by the Reconstruction Amendments, but they did not allow that this guaranteed free blacks the right to marry white persons or that the laws were meant to legislate social equality.

Southern judges, allowing for some legal flourish and drama, expressed both real and imagined concerns over the scope and representation of the institution of marriage.[68] The courts considered marriage—the realm of the home and family—to be the legal and cultural foundation of the political and social order. By protecting the family, the law also protected the state from what southern courts characterized as the "disruption," "disorder," and "discord" of the mixing of the races. In other words, the courts argued that racial homogeneity, in stabilizing the family, was necessary to stabilize the state. Judge Sneed, and the southern courts generally, defined the home, marriage, and family as not just social categories but political ones as well.

In the South, the slave system had been the foundation of the patriarchal and white household. In turn, the white patriarchal family was the nursery of southern political order. In the 1877 case *Green v. the State of Alabama*, the state court reasserted this bedrock notion, claiming that state intervention and limits on marriage rights were necessary to maintain the integrity of the family against interracial unions. The family as the microcosm of the state had to be protected because as the family goes, so goes the state.

In this Alabama case, a black man and white woman were charged with "intermarrying."[69] The court argued for state intervention into the marriage contract because of the disruption that racial mixing brought to homes, the "nurseries of the state":

This institution [marriage] is indeed, the most interesting and important in its nature of any in society. It is through the marriage relation that the *homes* of a people are created—those homes in which, ordinarily, all the members of all the families of the land are, during a part of everyday, assembled together; where the elders of the household seek repose and cheer, and reparation of strength from the toils and cares of life; and where, in an affectionate intercourse and conversation with them, the young become imbued with the principles, and animated by the spirit and ideas, which in a great degree give shape to their characters and determine the manner of their future lives. These homes, in which the virtues are most cultivated and happiness most abounds, are the true *officince gentium*—the nurseries of the state.

If interracial marriage were tolerated, utter chaos would result. The decision continued, "Who can estimate the *evil* of introducing into their most intimate relations, elements so heterogeneous that they must naturally cause discord, shame, disruption of family circles and estrangement of kindred? While with their *interior* administration, the State should interfere but little, it is obviously of the highest public concern that it should, by general laws adapted to the state of things around them, guard them against disturbances from *without*."

In this logic, interracial marriages would disrupt the social and political order because such unions threatened to defile the "interior" of the household—the racial and gendered integrity of the nineteenth-century home. And it was the state's responsibility to protect the marital relation and the family. The state had to protect the family and home from the ensuing "discord" and "shame" of racial mixing. The heterogeneity of racial mixing would confound the order of things, causing "estrangement of kindred" and "disruption of family circles." The order to which the court referred was particular not only to a racial order but also to notions of domesticity, the role of women, and the sexual division of political labor. In the home, women, seen as the bearers of morality, created the conditions of "repose" in which children developed and cultivated "principles," "character," and "virtue." These were, in turn, the essential elements of public life that, the court asserted, were violated by blackness.

In its language of inside and outside, the *Green* decision attempted to redraw the political line between blacks and whites that the end of slavery challenged. According to the court, the state should guard against "disturbances from without." However, blacks were not "outside"; the Thirteenth, Fourteenth, and Fifteenth Amendments were already ratified. While legally

ex-slaves were equal citizens, the southern courts were redrawing that political line not only against blacks but also against federal intrusion. Here, then,
federalism is analogous to the protection of the home. In protecting the family from racial mixing, the courts were protecting the virtue and homogeneity of the southern states from the Union. Here again using the institution of
marriage to distinguish those inside from those outside is premised upon the
authority of the court to use antimiscegenation laws to define marriage as a
right that needs to be limited. Not only was interracial marriage beyond the
pale, but federal power over the south was as well. The institution of marriage, a subnational state jurisdiction, was one area in which states could exercise power outside the federal nation.

Marriage and the Racialization of Freedom

Reconstruction-era antimiscegenation court cases and the Freedmen's Bureau marriage policies were different attempts at addressing what had become the nation's greatest dilemma following the Civil War: on what grounds
would African Americans enter society and the polity? Freed slaves had been
granted citizenship, but the Fourteenth Amendment merely begged the question of how this group would become incorporated as participants in the
nation's future. In other words, formal citizenship rights did not guarantee
immediate black entrance into equal membership. The marriage laws of the
period reveal how notions of inclusion were marked by specific gender roles,
sexual practices, social norms, and economic behavior. The racialization of
freedom and paternalist policies toward assimilated former slaves defined
a racially homogeneous marital household as the foundation of respectable
citizenship. Furthermore, the interaction of race hierarchy and marriage during this time renders the political link between marriage and civic belonging
visible, revealing that marital status powerfully shaped ideas of inclusion and
responsible citizenship in the American nation.

In this era, the role of marriage as a fulcrum between the obligations and
the rights of citizens emerges. The Freedmen's Bureau vision of marriage as
an obligation conflicted with antimiscegenation laws that defined marriage
as a right subject to limitation. Freedmen's Bureau policies and state legislation introduced marriage as a way for the state to train and regulate ex-slaves:
marriage policies prohibited certain sexual and familial behaviors, structured
gender roles, prepared former slaves for wage work, prevented dependency,

and sought to make ex-slaves responsible for their own economic welfare. Instead of being a contractual right, marriage became a schoolhouse for citizenship—or, to use a more accurate if less appealing description, marriage became a disciplinary regime that penetrated the most private of relations to serve a public need for reordering society in the wake of war and emancipation. Family obligations were meant to motivate work, not only citizenship. Promarriage policies that enforced the obligation of marriage in order to enable economic independence, and promoted a notion of racial equality, reemerged a century later in the federal policies of welfare reform, discussed in detail in Chapters 4 and 5.

Though comprehended as an obligation for ex-slaves, at the same time, marriage was conceived of as a right that had to be limited through antimiscegenation laws in order to preserve the nation. In their rulings upholding these laws, southern judges sought to dictate how African Americans would enter the polity. The courts conceded that they had citizenship, granted by the Fourteenth Amendment. But for these southern justices the state (and civilization itself) was founded on—and would continue to be secured by— an understanding of marriage as a status under the protection and authority of the state. Marriage was not simply a right of ex-slaves, but the private realm of intimate relations and the rearing of children, and a homology of the nation itself.

Antimiscegenation laws and the rulings upholding them limited the rights of former slaves and maintained racial and gender hierarchies. Laws against interracial marriage, during the postbellum era, solidified the racial and gendered underpinnings and practices of civic inclusion and inequality. Marriage was a right that came with freedom but that also designated and represented a new obligatory relationship to the state. In other words, antimiscegenation laws served to sustain the white, masculine political order as well as to maintain a notion of citizenship and family based on racial homogeneity.

At the same time, within the context of the occupation of the former Confederacy by the Union, the granting of marriage rights to emancipated slaves made the institution available for the fashioning of new citizens in a reconfigured political order. In other words, the high priority that state policymakers placed upon marriage during Reconstruction suggests that they saw the racialized, economic and gendered roles in families and within civil society to be vital to political stability. An underlying political question was, if marriage defined the foundation of society and was the root of its progress, then what did it mean that legal black families were now part of the basis of the nation? In its role in negotiating and settling the terms of former slave inclusion, marriage itself and what marriage meant began to change as well, particularly as the racial restrictions on marriage became more pronounced in the law and through scientific racial discourse. While primarily shaped by common-law practices, the private marriage contract was now set against a view of marriage as a tool of public state interest. Thus, a direct consideration of marriage's transformation has much to offer the narratives of political development.

The prohibition of certain marriages for the good of the nation appears again at later moments—specifically in relation to immigrants in the Progressive Era and with respect to gays and lesbians at the turn of the twenty-first century. These linkages over time underscore that marriage is deeply, inexorably, and dynamically intertwined with notions of state order, citizenship, and belonging. The mandatory marriage policies of the Freedmen's Bureau were a form of inclusion, while anti-interracial cases tempered this notion of inclusion by limiting the right to marry. This tension between the obligations and rights of marriage with regard to racial hierarchy illuminates a central tension in American politics, one that emerges again at the end of the nineteenth century.

Chapter 2

"What Constitutes a Valid Marriage?"

In an 1881 essay that won a New York University Law School prize, lawyer Charles Noble lamented "the contradictory and indefinite rules which come to us from various parts of the United States, when we ask this most fundamental of questions, 'What constitutes a valid marriage?'"[1] Noble's anxiety reflected not merely growing concern over the inconsistency in American marriage rules. It also anticipated the more general impulse of many Progressive Era reformers who sought greater uniformity in American law, policy, and social practices. From 1880 to 1920, state marriage laws became part of a larger codification battle that was occurring in almost every institution in the United States as the substantive political changes that marked the Progressive Era proliferated nationally.

Marriage, however, was not simply one of many sites in which Progressive Era imperatives were articulated. Rather, marriage became a central institution through which to contest and resolve three perceived problems that defined the politics of the period. One of these problems was how to protect traditional norms in the midst of a rapid movement toward modernization, social complexity, and urbanization. A second problem was how to stabilize the nation's dominant racial identity at a moment when mass immigration from eastern and southern Europe threatened to overwhelm Anglo-Saxon hegemony. A third problem was how to produce a national uniformity of law and policy in the context of a solidifying nation-state. Progressives met these deeply intertwined challenges by attempting to define the boundaries of civic membership, a definition that concerned both the norms and practices of American citizenship, and also what they understood to be the genetic capacity for citizenship. To define the cultural and biological terms of immigrant assimilation, social reformers, immigration officials, judges, and legislators turned to marriage as the fundamental institution responsible for the reproduction (or dangerous decay) of both values and blood. Marriage in this era became a form of state obligation as its status as a locally practiced right correspondingly diminished. Examining marriage's role in the Progressive Era allows us to understand its centrality to the fundamental imperatives of that period.

Marriage underwent intensive regulatory transformation as its rules became more standardized and its connection to citizenship, naturalization, and national identity became more prominent. The institution was transformed by the imperatives of bureaucratization, democratization, centralization, the fostering of national uniformity, and the eradication of difference, either by exclusion or assimilation—what historian Robert Wiebe has called "the search for order."[2] Policies and decisions concerning the obligation and rights of marriage and family served to locate morality, sexuality, and the reproduction of civic values in the household as well as in the nation; to defend and reproduce biological purity and perfection as the new eugenic science demanded; and to secure and reflect ordered coherence in the modern nation-state over the individual's right to consent.

The expansion of marital law and policy in these years represented an attempt to preserve stable marriages and promote what were viewed as "fit" families in a society where the image of the ideal American household, and the environment in which that family was believed to flourish, seemed insecure.[3] But more than that, marriage was a regulatory instrument used to stabilize a national identity dislocated by the rapid rise of immigration. By the first decades of the twentieth century, a more forthright notion of a "public interest" in marriage had notably circumscribed nuptial privatism in marriage law, which had been eroding since Reconstruction.[4] Scholars of the Progressive Era have analyzed the political responses to immigration, industrialization, and urbanization, yet none have examined the key role marriage played in these struggles. Conversely, scholars of marriage have shown how the institution underwent regulatory transformations in the era, but have not linked those transformations to the establishment of a new civic order.

In the Progressive Era, marriage as an institution not only ordered sexual, reproductive, childrearing, and economic practices within marriage, but reproduction, cohabitation, migration, naturalization, and other practices outside of marriage as well. In this period, there was a critical relationship between the regulation of marriage as a form of obligation and the construction of a national political order. Three major changes in marriage law and policy reveal Progressive Era attempts to refashion national identity: first, solemnization statutes prescribed the obligatory and mandatory rites necessary for a legal union; second, eugenic marriage laws limited the right to marry and established standards of fitness for access to marriage, and thereby presumed to select for "fit" citizens; and third, for women marital naturalization and expatriation policies linked obligations and rights of marriage to nationality. In other words, how, what, and why one married became important questions in drawing the boundaries of U.S. civic belonging during this period.

Immigration, Progressivism, and Purity

During the Progressive Era, the American state went through a systemic transformation from a functionally limited "state of courts and parties," as political scientist Stephen Skowronek has described it, to a more centralized state with national governmental controls.[5] As such this period saw rapid movement from social and political simplicity to complexity, where once-isolated local communities were incorporated into an interdependent nation. Reformers and policymakers believed that the problems of the twentieth century would be addressed through the principles of continuity, regularity, functionality, rationality, administration, and management, all grounded in the perceived need for a strong and interventionist national government. Through the imposition of rules and regulations with uniform penalties, this new approach to social and political organization was an attempt to establish predictability in a changing world. Progressive Era reformers believed that, by granting greater power to government and encouraging the centralization of authority, they would be able to establish new norms of order, continuity, and community.[6]

At the same time, Progressive Era discourse embodied a political tension between democratic egalitarianism and hierarchical exclusion. Political scientist Rogers Smith explains that for centrist progressives such as Theodore Roosevelt and Herbert Croly, science, economic growth, equal rights, and democracy were part of a well-ordered society, but so were systems subordinating "inferior" races to "advanced" ones. Thus liberal principles of procedural and substantive justice coincided with and supported the trend toward restrictive, ascriptive Americanism.[7] At the same time, the period saw rising tensions over sexual morality. As James Morone explains in his book *Hell-fire Nation*, "By the turn of the century, the purity legions had turned the single sexual standard—self-control and continence—into the bourgeois norm. . . . This was one way they distinguished themselves from the dirty immigrants and the dangerous classes."[8]

The popular nativist response to the great wave of immigration in the 1880s reflected these themes. While economic elites had considered immigration essential to American material progress, the broader view was that immigration was an overwhelming problem that created conditions of social disintegration. Many Americans, fearing the effects of mass immigration, supported either total exclusion or absolute assimilation. An intensified nationalism, stressing the need for social homogeneity, expressed itself, on the one hand, in hatred of foreigners and, on the other, in a fervent desire to fully assimilate immigrants to "100 percent Americanism."[9]

The economic, social, and racial changes of the Progressive Era instigated a reworking of what constituted American national identity and notions of civic belonging. Political scientist Desmond King explains that, by establishing restrictions on immigrants' access to the United States, policymakers created and "privileged an Anglo-Saxon conception of U.S. identity, thereby rejecting the claims of other traditions in the nation."[10] As King makes clear, the restrictions were increasingly based on the presumed incompatibility or inassimilability of certain groups of immigrants.[11] Smith writes that "most policymakers believed that, in order for American civilization to be preserved and advanced, the highest stations of U.S. intellectual, economic, social and political life must, for the foreseeable future, be largely occupied by middle- and upper-class men of northern European descent. Most blacks, Native Americans, Latinos, Asian-Americans, immigrant working-class whites, and women were expected to be unfit for full and equal citizenship for generations to come."[12] This assumption lies behind the denial of access to education for certain groups. My concern here is how changes in marriage policy and attempts to control biological reproduction were part of the same drive to "preserve and advance" Western civilization, undergirded by the same ideological faith in the superiority of Anglo-Saxon men.

Many of the new marital regulations of the period were meant to check the growth of so-called genetically undesirable and sexually immoral populations. In the same way that political elites used increasingly restrictive immigration laws to filter out persons considered unfit for naturalization, restrictive marriage laws were intended to radically reduce the reproduction of new generations of Americans who fell outside the lines of the idealized image of the American citizen. Marriage reformers believed that regulating marriage and controlling reproduction would promote a homogeneous citizenry, in terms of both cultural values and biological capacities, and would serve as the foundation of a stable nation.

New Marriage Rites

The nuptial reform movement during the Progressive Era was made up of legislators, social scientists, journalists, and evangelical Protestants. These reformers believed, as legal scholar Matthew Lindsay explains, that marital legislation and regulation of the reproduction of citizens would reestablish the sense of security, morality, and community that was being lost to the rising rates of immigration and to industrialization and urbanization. Pervasive poverty, rising dependence on charity, the growing visibility of women in the labor market, and the increasing influx of immigrants were all factors indicated by reformers as having created a marriage crisis that threatened the material and ideological foundation of marriage, family, and the nation. In response to this perceived crisis, reformers worked for—and succeeded in—increasing state authority over nuptial celebrations and rites, as well as enhancing public supervision of marital fitness.[13] Their arguments for these new regulations were based on the idea that marriage and family were not only private cultural practices, but also institutions that should play a crucial role in establishing state stability. These arguments clarified that the right to marry was limited by state priorities.

During the Progressive Era, several states passed statutes formalizing the marriage process, involving a public wedding ceremony that was officiated by an officer of the state and attended by witnesses, as well as requiring a marriage license and registration.[14] This legislation was an attempt to rationalize and manage the marriage process against the dictates of common-law doctrine. States began to require public notification of new marriages, a regulation that was intended to guarantee publicity, acquire accurate information on the state of nuptials, and standardize family status for estate and property purposes. By 1907, twenty-seven states had instituted measures for the registration of new unions. Licenses served two purposes: to ensure the physical and mental fitness of the couple and to record marital information for statistical purposes.[15]

They also formalized the right to marry because, prior to this period, common law and what was called nuptial privatism had governed marriage. As discussed in Chapter 1, common-law marriage emphasized the private nature of contracts and relied on self-regulation, as opposed to state regulation, for nuptial supervision. Common-law marriage thus was based not on state sanction but rather on community acknowledgement, cohabitation, and the reputation of a couple.[16] When communities were smaller and more rural, where access to judges and magistrates was difficult, the majority of marriages were common-law. At the start of the Progressive Era, reformers criticized this informal marriage structure for failing to provide clear rules for legitimizing a marital union.[17]

Frank Gaylord Cook, a Massachusetts attorney and leader in the nuptial reform movement, exemplifies the position of the nuptial reformers. In an article in the *Atlantic Monthly*, he depicted a harmonious and tranquil past when settlers "of the same race and faith usually dwelt together"; when the population was "small," "scattered," "simple," and "conservative"; and when "respect for law and conformity to civil regulations were almost universal."[18] These local and rural communities, he argued, had "unanimity of sentiment in the protection of the common interest and the maintenance of social order" where "the statutory forms for the celebration of marriage had been generally observed." Cook described a notion of a stable community that was based on a link between shared social norms and "conformity to civil regulations." Thus, for Cook, the act of marriage was a basis of national unity, because it represented both shared norms and conformity to civil regulations.

Cook maintained that this unified community had changed because the "widest diversity of race, religion, and sentiments" now existed among the populace. He explained that cities grew, while laboring immigrants, "forsaking the fields," flocked to factories and tenements, and women's purity was at risk as they worked outside the home. The result, he bemoaned, was that "industrial struggle and discontent and social evils are rife in the community." Cook's contention was that conformity to civil regulations as a basis for shared social norms was less certain in this environment. With the rise in new immigrants, and the development of industrialization and urbanization, Cook argued, the foundations of social cohesion and national stability had been undermined by racial invasion and social breakdown. He turned to marriage to prevent changes in the racial and sexual hierarchies of the period.

Desiring conformity to civil regulations, Cook professed that the regulation of marriage, and ultimately the family, played a necessary part in recreating social cohesion in the community. Cook held that the family, the "source and mainstay of society," was harmed in industrializing America. The integrity of the institution, he asserted, was "dependent no less upon its legal inception than upon its legal termination." He called for state regulation of marital practices, which he argued should control and regulate not only how a marriage dissolved but also how it began. Linking marriage to the cohesion of the community, Cook reframed marriage from a private individual right, rooted in local community, to a public interest of the state and an obligation of citizens owed in exchange for the reward of civic inclusion.

Samuel Dike, secretary of the New England Divorce Reform League (later the National League for the Protection of the Family), another major supporter of nuptial reform, saw the changes of the period, and racial difference in particular, as destabilizing a shared notion of morality and social cohesion. He also looked to tightened nuptial governance as a way to redefine notions of national inclusiveness. Like Cook, Dike was concerned about the influx of immigrants into the United States. He argued for increased public and state attention to the foreign "source" of "our dangers." He wanted "careful supervision" over the domestic morals of the urban, poor, immigrant class through stronger, more selective marriage laws. Concerned about the "foreign element" in the country, he called for a "thorough study" of them by experts. He claimed that such a study would "show the need for more official and private watchfulness of the domestic morals of this class, and that a careful supervision of our immigrants would affect our domestic morals most favorably. The uncertain marital relations of some immigrants from countries where illicit unions take the place of lawful marriage . . . and where illegitimate births are . . . frequent, [and where] unchastity must exist among a very large population, . . . makes . . . legislation very desirable."[19]

Dike's rhetoric easily traversed public and private realms, calling for surveillance and control to mold immigrants into morally suitable Americans. Only state-sanctioned marriage and the practice of "domestic morals," overseen by the state officials, could act as a bulwark against the dangers to the

nation that immigrants posed. Thus, through marriage, Dike sought to define the terms of inclusion, manufacture shared values, and mandate uniformity of practice by requiring couples to obtain a marriage license and have a
public wedding performed by a state official.

At the same time, these regulations were not just meant to constrain and
direct sexual practices; they were also aimed at what these sexual practices
represented. For reformers, uncontrolled sexual practices undermined the
ability to be a wage-earning, contributing citizen in a democratic society, and
in this way stable marriages were linked to a stable society. Reflecting the
tension within the Progressive Era generally, these new marriage rites were
about the obligations and rights not only of marriage but also, and just as
importantly, of citizenship.

In the 1892 case *In re McLaughlin's Estate*, the judges in Washington
State's high court clarified the link between marriage rites, on the one hand,
and the public order and boundaries of national inclusion, on the other.[20]
Concerning a dispute over the rights to the financial holdings of Hiram
McLaughlin, who was survived by a common-law wife and daughter, the
court decided against the validity of common-law marriage, delegitimizing
unions that did not comply with statutory requirements. Judge Scott argued,
"By adhering to the statutory provisions, parties are led to regard the contract as a sacred one, as one not lightly entered into, and are forcibly impressed with the idea that they are forming a relation in which society has
an interest, and to which the state is a party."[21] In other words, he contended
that laws circumscribing the legitimacy of marriage would force couples to
view the marriage contract not only as sacred and personal but also as public and as forming an important relation to society and the state. The court
suggested that by publicly exchanging vows, citizens both produced and
subjected themselves to state governance. The very act of marrying, then,
connected citizens to the state. The goal of reformers, in replacing common-
law practices with new marital solemnization statutes, was both to regulate
the institution itself and to establish a way of fostering shared values and
civic responsibility. While the move to solemnize statutes did not go uncontested, as the turn of the century approached, state courts increasingly
adopted the *McLaughlin* approach.[22]

Solemnization laws were an attempt to codify the increasing belief that
legally sanctioned marriages and families—by fostering unanimity of sentiment, conformity to civil regulations, and the protection of common inter-

ests—provided a stronger foundation on which to define the boundaries of citizenship. In these ways, marriage became a regulatory lever to help fashion and direct an emergent national identity and sense of social and political cohesion. The regulation of marriage meant greater state intervention into nuptials and an emphasis on the public act of marriage in supporting the nation. Through the streamlining of marriage law and careful record-keeping of marital unions, the state transformed marriage. Finally, policymakers and reformers invoked the sovereign right of states to protect society and nation by defining a notion of unanimity of sentiment on one level, and by preventing undesirable marriages on another.

Eugenic Marriage Laws

In bringing sexual and reproductive practices under greater state control, *In re McLaughlin's Estate* demonstrates how the new state interest in institutional inclusion, through curtailing the right to marriage, was at the same time an interest in exclusion. Among the arguments that paved the way for state-regulated eugenic marriage laws, the court held that

> there is a growing belief that the welfare of society demands . . . that an institution like marriage, which is so closely and thoroughly related to the state, should be the most *carefully guarded*, and that *improvident and improper marriages* should be prevented. All wise and *healthful* regulations in this direction prohibiting such marriages as far as practicable would tend to the prevention of pauperism and crime, and the transmission of hereditary diseases and defects, and it may not be regarded as too chimerical to say that in the future laws may be passed looking to this end.[23]

Stepping beyond Samuel Dike's concerns about "illicit unions" and "illegitimate children," the Washington judge set out to define an "improper marriage." Solemnization laws were not only about legitimizing marital unions in the eyes of the state but about defining proper marriages. Marriage licenses and public ceremonies served to "carefully guard" the institution from marriages and families that did not fit within the emerging notions of civic identity. Here the court argued to guard the institution because it was "so closely and thoroughly related to the state." "Improvident" or "improper" marriages were not only illegal unions but marriages that would, under the logic of eugenic science, produce unfit children. Thus, solemnization laws concerned not only the regulation of marriage but control over the reproduction of future citizens. Eugenic marriage laws could serve to protect society's interests and prevent the passing down of hereditary defects, believed to be the source of society's most tenacious problems, such as poverty and crime. These laws could limit the potential for unborn citizens who would not meet reformers' basic standards of American-ness. In all, according to the judges who decided *McLaughlin*, the "welfare of society demanded" that the institution of marriage be limited as a right, in order to create, maintain, and protect cultural and biological notions of national cohesion and order.

At the end of the nineteenth century, the reigning racial ideology held that racial differences were fixed and immutable. This belief was reflected in and augmented by the rise of eugenic science, which stressed the biological significance of hereditary traits.[24] Reformers rallied for new regulations that would prohibit certain kinds of marriages believed to be genetically unsound. Consequently, state legislatures across the country passed a series of eugenic marriage laws that dramatically limited who could marry and who could not. In 1895, Connecticut adopted the first such law, which barred "feebleminded, imbecilic, and epileptic men and women under 45 years of age" from marrying.[25] This legislation targeted both men and women, and violators were sentenced to a minimum of three years in prison. Some laws mandated proof of marriage applicants' eugenic fitness by requiring sworn written statements in addition to extensive blood tests. By the 1930s, forty-one states had passed statutes that required tests of mental capacity, using such terms as "lunatic," "feeble-minded," "idiot," and "imbecile."[26]

In the public arena, fears about "improvident and improper" marriages abounded. Penal reformer Charles Reeve expressed his fears of the hereditary transmission of defects through marriage in his 1888 address to the powerful reform organization, the National Prison Association. He argued that the weakness and deformities of the "dependent classes" stemmed from "erroneous and perverted" marriages through which many a "viciously diseased man or woman was being permitted to procreate."[27] In other words, marriage was an institution that might produce physically and mentally unfit future citizens if the obligations and rights of marriage were not clear. Reformers used such terms as "erroneous," "improvident," and "perverted" to describe marriages they believed would produce such undesirable outcomes for the nation. In 1901, a highly regarded study by Frances A. Walker, president of the Massachusetts Institute of Technology, attributed the decline in the birth rate of the native white population to competition with the population of immigrants.[28] More specifically, upper-class nativists feared that working-class immigrants were reproducing faster than the native white population, seeing the latter as committing "race suicide."[29] Economist William Ripley suggested in 1908 that racial intermixture would weaken the dominant Anglo stock.[30] In the *Independent*, one writer opined that the nation's "best blood fails to perpetuate itself" while "the poor and worthless marry and have many children."[31] The notion of race suicide articulated the elite's fears about the declining birth rate of native white Americans and, with this decline, the lost dominance of an inherently superior Western civilization.

Within an intellectual context of nearly hegemonic scientific racism, public policy expressed in practice the widespread fear of racial mixing. From 1880 to 1920, twenty states and territories strengthened or added antimiscegenation laws.[32] In the name of the "purity of the races," local governments added these statutes to many state codes and constitutions in an attempt to control the reproduction of interracial citizens, who posed a threat to the nation.[33]

For Reeve, Walker, and others, fears of race suicide led directly to marriage policy. Reformers were clearly anxious about the inevitable results of allowing unfit married couples to reproduce, because the resulting children would, by constitutional dictate, be U.S. citizens by birth. In 1906, Elsie Clews Parsons, anthropologist and social critic, wrote at length about the obligation of some people *not to marry* in order to protect society. She stated that science demonstrates "the disastrous results of the mating of those handicapped by . . . taints or lacks, [thus] the social obligation in marriage will be held more and more considerable."[34] Society, she contended, required a population endowed with "progressive traits, physical, moral, and mental as well as lack of disease on the part of child bearers and begetters." She professed that the "costs to the state" to manage the "reproduction by its diseased and vicious subjects" were too great and that those deemed unfit but who married would be "morally guilty" and socially condemned. She added that a greater obligation fell "upon the individual" to protect society and the nation.[35]

These sentiments were codified into eugenic marriage laws. The 1909 Washington State nuptial regulation and prohibition stated that "*no woman under forty-five years, or man of any age*, either of whom is a common drunk-ard, habitual criminal, epileptic, imbecile, feeble-minded person, idiot or in-sane person, or person who has theretofore been afflicted with hereditary insanity, or who is afflicted with pulmonary tuberculosis in its advanced stages, or any contagious venereal disease, shall hereafter intermarry or marry any other person within this state."[36] Marriages in which one or both of the spouses exhibited any of these characteristics were deemed "perverted" and "erroneous" because they would produce ill and parasitic citizens. The age limit of forty-five illustrates the emphasis on reproduction; past the age of forty-five, the state was no longer interested in controlling a woman's marriage choices because no offspring would result. Categories of exclusion showed up in marriage laws because reformers argued that the family was the site of both the biological and cultural reproduction of society. In this way, marriage and family were crucial to the reshaping of notions of civic inclu-sion and national political identity in the ideal image of white, Anglo-Saxon citizens.

Often, scientific arguments were mapped onto notions of cultural degen-eracy. In 1905, Indiana passed a law that prohibited a marriage license from being issued to "any male person who is or has been within five years an inmate of any county asylum or home for indigent persons, unless it satis-factorily appears that the cause of such a condition has been removed and that such male applicant is able to support a family and likely to continue to do so."[37] This law restricted a male's access to a marriage license if he had been in a jail, insane asylum, or halfway house. Preventing access to mar-riage on these grounds illustrates how behavior was thought to be passed on biologically; marriage regulations were not just about preventing the passing of physical and mental incapacities, but certain degenerate behaviors as well.

However, like the solemnization statutes, laws prohibiting marriages based on physical and mental incapacity and/or cultural degeneracy did not go uncontested and were subjected to judicial review in many states. These legal challenges illustrate another important thread in how marriage and family produced and reflected the Progressive Era impulses toward marital obligation, because they highlight the tension between an individual's right to consent in marriage and a state's power to deny marriage in the name of the public interest.

In the 1905 case *Gould v. Gould*, Marion Gould sued her husband for di-vorce because he had neglected to alert her of his epilepsy not only prior to their wedding but during the four years of their marriage.[38] The case concerned the 1895 Connecticut statute and was one of the first eugenic marriage laws to be contested in the courts. The court found the statute to be constitutional because it was "in the interest of public health" to prohibit certain marriages. Judge Baldwin supported the law's eugenic foundations when he wrote that epilepsy was a "disease of particularly serious and revolting character, tending to weaken mental force, and often descending from parent to child, or entailing upon the offspring of the sufferers some other grave form of nervous malady." This, he asserted, was a "matter of common knowledge." The decision further explained that it was necessary to "forbid sexual intercourse with those afflicted by it, and to preclude such opportunities for sexual intercourse as marriage furnishes."[39]

The way to "preclude" the transmission of this disease was to impose "a restriction of the right to contract marriage." Judge Baldwin made clear that it was important to guard against the "perpetuation" of such ill-founded marriages. In this case, eugenic marriage laws overrode claims to the right to contract in marriage, because such laws protected wives and future children from this disease of "revolting character." Baldwin reasoned that "to impose such a restriction upon the right to contract marriage . . . is no invasion of the equality of all men. . . . A law of this kind is necessary for the preservation of public health."[40] Once marriage law cast the institution in a more public role, an individual's ability to assert his/her consent in certain marital circumstances was diminished. The decision in *Gould* highlights the reproduction of citizens and the role of marriage as a regulatory force in compelling marital obligation.

Determining the terms of consent in marriage—that is, who was capable of consenting and under what circumstances—fell increasingly to the discretion of state lawmakers. The 1915 Wisconsin Supreme Court case *Peterson v. Widule* affirmed the range of state authority.[41] In this case, the question was whether a 1913 statute requiring a groom to test negative for venereal disease before being granted a marriage license was constitutional. The court held that it was within the power of the state legislature to aggressively regulate entry into marriage by preventing those with physical disease from marrying. Judge Winslow declared, "The power of the state to control and regulate the marriage relation and to prevent the contracting of marriage by persons afflicted with loathsome or hereditary diseases, which are liable either to be transmitted to the spouse or inherited by the offspring, or both, must on principle be regarded as undeniable."[42] He went on to assert that "society has a right to protect itself from extinction." Echoing fears of race suicide, Judge Winslow's judgments served not only to limit certain people's ability to choose a marital partner, but in some cases to totally deny it. *Peterson* reflected the emerging view that strict control over access to marriage was a rightful exercise of states' police power to protect public health, safety, and morality.

In 1923, in *Schoolcraft v. O'Neil*, the supreme court of New Hampshire voided a marriage because the wife, Mary Josephine O'Neil, was found to be insane.[43] The couple was married in May 1920. In the January before the marriage, O'Neil had been hospitalized and diagnosed with dementia praecox (today known as schizophrenia). She was released after four days, although her condition did not improve. The future groom, Schoolcraft, met her two months before their marriage. He met her family too, and he claimed no one informed him that she had been committed to the state hospital or that she had been "mentally deranged." The court ruled that her history of mental disease was "fraudulently concealed" and that "the marriage contract [was] thus tainted with fraud." The court ordered that the marriage be annulled.[44] Not only was her disease fraudulently concealed, but her mental illness called into question her ability to consent to marriage in the first place. Thus in extending the doctrine of concealment and fraud to marriage the court privileged the authority of the state to control marriage, in this case to prevent the transference of hereditary disease, over an individual's right to consent in marriage.

The struggle over eugenic marriage laws and defining notions of national belonging turned in part on this issue of individual consent versus the responsibility of the state to protect society from eugenically unsound marital unions and future unfit citizens. This tension mirrors the larger Progressive Era trends of faith in democratic ideals, support for a stronger federal state, and the rise of civic ascriptive hierarchies. Nuptial reformers and proponents of eugenic marriage laws believed that the statutes determined whether a mentally and/or physically deficient person was able to perform the duties of matrimony and, as a consequence, of citizenship itself. Those duties included maintaining moral standing, economic independence, and the ability to rationally consent. Reformers minimized the importance of consent as a key premise of liberal democracy in favor of the majority's desire to define and reproduce order in the American polity through racial purity and cultural homogeneity.

Marital Naturalization and Expatriation

The policies of marital naturalization and expatriation enacted in 1907 created notions of marital obligation and also played a role in reconstituting notions of national identity and uniformity.[45] Based on the doctrine of "family unity," these laws endorsed the principle that all members of the household—the wife and children—should have the same nationality as the male head of the household. Immigration law tended to support family unity and encouraged the admission of immigrant wives. Wives, for example, were exempted from the literacy test that was mandated in 1917. As political scientist Virginia Sapiro points out, in a time of growing international migrations, family unity provided an expedient means to clarify loyalties among shifting populations. Granting naturalization based on family unity also addressed concerns about existing and future households in which husband and wife were of different nationalities.[46] Policies based on the principle of family unity, then, ensured national homogeneity within the family, a policy also thought to encourage the prosperity and stability of the nation.

At the same time, through marital naturalization and expatriation, marriage directly affected a woman's nationality in ways it had not prior to the Progressive Era. Common-law marriage did not explicitly include nationality; a married woman could maintain her premarital citizenship regardless of her marital status. By 1907, the right of a woman to consent to her marriage was curtailed by her obligation to marry an American-born male. With marital naturalization and expatriation, the law further presumed that if a woman married a foreign national, she had consented to renounce her U.S. citizenship.

Originally passed in 1855, the Naturalization Act allowed that "any woman who is now or may hereafter be married to a citizen of the United States, and who might herself be lawfully naturalized shall be deemed a citizen."[47] Thus, all foreign-born women married to American-born men were granted citizenship. Politicians and policymakers viewed this automatic naturalization of citizens' foreign-born wives as a gift to the worthy wife of a valued American. Following the dictates of the doctrine of family unity, the policy invested in the national culture by maintaining one nationality within the family.

However, in 1907, during the height of the immigration wave as nationalist sentiments grew, the principles of family unity seemed to conflict with the growing trend toward restrictive immigration policies. The debate

positioned the virtues of restriction and national homogeneity against the
virtues of family unity. A range of institutional actors articulated different
views on the ideals of marriage and family, and on what role the state and
society should have in producing and reproducing those ideals. Between
1910 and 1920, while Congress made it more difficult for immigrants to attain permanent residency and citizenship in the United States, the practice
of marital naturalization was essentially a path of open admission for mi-
grating wives. In many of their decisions on the constitutionality of marital
naturalization, U.S. judges and the courts sought to protect the doctrine
of family unity through adherence to legal precedent. But marital naturalization came under strong criticism from the Bureau of Immigration and
Naturalization, and legislators and immigration officials thought that the
borders needed to be resecured by severely limiting the practice. Driving
this need, more specifically, was the anxiety that foreign-born women were
not "true" wives but rather were using the marriage license to gain access
to the United States.

In particular, some legislators and immigration officials thought immigrant prostitutes were taking advantage of the law by fraudulently marrying American male citizens to avoid deportation. Officials worried that any
male procurer or pimp with American citizenship could protect a foreign-
born prostitute from deportation by marrying her. They also believed that
prostitutes married citizens hastily and on purpose, as soon as deportation
proceedings against them were initiated, in order to avoid the web of immigration officials.[48] The commissioner general of the immigration bureau
envisioned prostitutes and the men who protected or exploited them as cal-
lously employing both marriage and citizenship for their own immoral and
illegal ends.[49] Access to American citizenship through marriage functioned
as an opening to national membership in support of immigrant families, but
at the same time officials believed the boundaries of that membership needed
to be carefully safeguarded against immoral women who threatened the integrity of the nation.

Bureau officials, anxious about the proliferation of potentially fraudulent marriages, struggled to narrow the application of marital naturalization, giving immigration officials the power to deport suspect wives. Not
surprisingly, these efforts focused on Chinese women. Since the 1875 Page
Law, immigration officials had generally assumed that all incoming Chinese women applying for naturalization as wives of citizens were part of the

international prostitution trade. Once again, sexuality and morality played a role in shaping both the possibility of inclusion and, in equal measure, the grounds of exclusion. However, unlike most other foreign-born wives of citizens, if a Chinese woman married an American citizen, she was still racially ineligible for naturalization.[50] Yet, if these Chinese women gained access to the United States, any of their children born on U.S. soil would be American citizens.[51]

In a 1907 report from the Bureau of Immigration and Naturalization titled *Facts Concerning the Enforcement of the Chinese-Exclusion Laws*, the secretary of commerce and labor alluded to concerns that American men of Chinese ancestry routinely abused their right to bring wives and children into the country. He wrote that the number of fraudulent wives had reached "alarming proportions."[52] Convinced that the vast majority of Chinese women who came to the United States as wives of Americans had married for illicit purposes, he even went so far as to put the word "wives" in quotation marks to emphasize their counterfeit marital status: "There are, doubtless, cases of a bona fide character—that is, cases in which a real Chinese American citizen brings a real wife to this country, but it is not believed that the files of the Bureau of Immigration contain a record case of the importation of a 'wife' of a native that is free from at least a strong suspicion that such 'wife,' if married to the American Chinaman at all, was made a party to such marriage solely for the purpose of evading the exclusion laws and entering this country."[53] As part of the larger trend toward restrictive immigration policy, cracking down on fraudulent marital naturalization cases became an important part of marking the limits of inclusion.

In 1907, Congress formed the Dillingham Commission—or the U.S. Immigration Commission—to investigate the effects of immigration, and in 1911 the commission issued a forty-one-volume report based on four years of research. One of those volumes was titled *Importing Women for Immoral Purposes* and also included anxieties about the fraudulent wife. The commission's evidence of fraudulent marriages between American men and immigrant women was primarily anecdotal. In one instance, foreign-born "Mary Doe" was arrested in Manhattan in 1908 for prostitution. Though she was convicted, her expulsion was delayed by immigration officials so that she could serve as witness in another prostitution case. During this time "Richard Roe," an American, applied successfully to the Department of Commerce and Labor for permission to marry Doe. Once married, Doe was discharged to Roe. Several days after the marriage, the arresting officer met Doe on the street and, according to his account, she offered a full confession.

> Don't you know what he wanted from me, that fellow Roe? Don't you
> know that he had another girl in his house at ——— street, and when
> we got there he introduced me to her (an old prostitute named Laura)
> and told me she was his wife, but that I would stay with them and
> that we both would make good money but both hustling from his
> house? . . . I now make $5 or $6 a day, which I keep for myself and
> Roe stays with his affinity, Laura. Of course, you know, John, that if I
> married that fellow Roe, it was only to beat deportation and be safe
> forever, as I am now an American citizen.[54]

The report gave three other stories of this kind, which Congress accepted as sufficient corroboration of the immigration bureau's contention that fraudulent marriages were increasing. The report also raised concerns about how easily these "Jane Does" could speak about the shady circumstances of their marriages because the marriage certificate safeguarded them from further entanglements with immigration officials.

The act of challenging or even just questioning the legitimacy of a foreign-born wife was a way to exclude immigrant women from the dominant definitions of "wife." Historically in the United States, racial classification has been intertwined with representations of gender and sexuality.[55] One of the most common reasons to detain immigrant women was the charge of being part of the "sexually immoral" class—or a prostitute.[56] There was a general societal interrogation and suspicion of immigrant women's morality and sexuality, and a corresponding willingness to deny their right to privacy and the right and power of their husbands to protect them. By categorizing foreign-born wives as potentially fraudulent, immigration officials rendered immigrants and naturalized citizens powerless against the intrusion of the state into their private lives. Detainment by an immigration official was frequently the first contact point for the intrusive role of the state in legislating and enforcing racialized immigration policies, policies that in turn served to reproduce hierarchical and racialized notions of American citizenship, national identity, and belonging.

Immigration officials tried to stop the practice of marital naturalization from undermining the country's increasingly restrictive immigration policy.

At the same time, the courts routinely decided in favor of family unity, citing the force or power of marriage. The struggle that ensued among different state actors over the proper role and scope of marriage and its effects on immigrants lasted through the 1920s. A significant and even defining question was whether the roles of husband and wife transformed immigrants into ideal Americans, or whether immigrant men and women were outside the borders of the American state and therefore could not be seen as husbands and wives.

The contrasting positions can be seen vividly in the debate between Secretary of Commerce and Labor Charles Nagel and Attorney General George Wickersham. The argument between them concerned an "alien prostitute," a native of Belgium, who had entered the United States in 1907 and was unmarried at the time. After working less than a year as a domestic, she "began to live the life of a prostitute."[57] She was eventually arrested and, during the course of her deportation proceedings, she lawfully married a native-born citizen, a private in the U.S. Army. In challenging the government's authority to deport her, she explained that it was her "professed intention" to "abandon her previous mode of life." Secretary Nagel argued against marital naturalization and asserted that an alien woman could not break free of the deportation net simply because she married an American.

Attorney General Wickersham disagreed. He explained that her marriage to an American citizen was "indicative of her good character, whatever she may have been previous to her marriage." He further clarified that "character is not immutable, and while acts of prostitution are indicative of bad character, the entering of a prostitute into the lawful state of matrimony indicates reformation and present good character, which it is the duty of society to encourage."[58] Even though Nagel submitted more evidence of fraud—that the husband had been paid to enter into the marriage and allowed his wife to return to prostitution—the Attorney General's Office remained firm. In response to Nagel's claims, Acting Attorney General Wade H. Ellis said fraud in marriage must be prevented. However, he stated that "the mere intention" to prevent the woman's deportation "would not in itself be sufficient to invalidate what would otherwise be a lawful marriage."[59] Eventually, automatic naturalization through marriage was abolished in 1922 with the Cable Act.[60]

While marital naturalization was the site of a gendered struggle over citizenship, the inverse scenario played out in the form of political battles over the policies of marital expatriation. Marital expatriation legislation, enacted in

1907, asserted that "any American woman who marries a foreigner shall take the nationality of her husband," thereby forfeiting her American citizenship.[61] From 1907 until it was overturned in 1922 with the Cable Act, this law stripped thousands of women of U.S. citizenship. This statute was part of a group of expatriation laws enacted in the early decades of the twentieth century that were designed to denaturalize individuals who, according to the federal government, had voluntarily forsaken their allegiance to the United States. One objective of the marital expatriation law was to ensure the unity of nationality within the family under the male head of household, even if it meant expatriating American women citizens. Prior to this time, the majority of executive and judicial decisions did not consider an American woman's marriage to an alien to be an act of expatriation. However, by 1907, marriage became, by law if not by explicit declaration, an expression and test of political loyalties for women.[62]

Amid the gains in women's rights and women's public activism at the time, marital expatriation strikingly reiterated that a wife owed her primary political allegiance to her husband. However, as historian Candice Bredbenner explains, marital expatriation was not an attempt to revive coverture; rather it involved issues of immigration control, dual nationality, and naturalization, of which patriotism and prejudice were a part.[63] At the same time, domestic and international policy objectives of national stability and uniformity meant that a woman's consent to marry was simultaneously constructed in relation to husband and nation. In the 1915 case *Mackenzie v. Hare*, the U.S. Supreme Court supported the constitutionality of marital expatriation when it declared:

> The identity of husband and wife is an ancient principle of our jurisprudence. It was neither accidental nor arbitrary and worked in many instances for her protection. There has been, it is true, much relaxation of it but in its retention as in its origin it is determined by their intimate relation and unity of interests, and this relation and unity may make it of public concern in many instances to merge their identity, and give dominance to the husband. It has purpose, if not necessity, in purely domestic policy; it has greater purpose and, it may be, necessity, in international policy.[64]

Here again we see the emphasis on marriage as a public concern. Once public, marriage became a regulatory lever through which to ground "unity of interest," not only within the marital union but in the national union. In particular, the role of marriage in domestic policy was necessarily shaped and given greater weight by its "necessity" as a component of U.S. international policy, according to this judicial opinion.

In supporting marital expatriation, the Supreme Court reframed the "ancient principle of jurisprudence," namely coverture, from control of the economic and social resources of women/wives to control of national and political identity. With marital expatriation, a woman lost all her rights to her own nationality. A woman's marriage vows now represented a voluntary oath of naturalization or declaration of expatriation.[65] In this way, the doctrine of family unity, expressed both through marital naturalization and marital expatriation, institutionalized patriarchal forms of authority in order to stabilize and unify American civic belonging, citizenship, and national identity.

Marital expatriation law sought to rid the country of Americans who compromised their citizenship status by maintaining or establishing foreign ties of some type, particularly the tie of marriage. In this political culture, defined by the rhetoric of "100 percent Americanism," a female citizen's marriage to a foreigner was an un-American act, punishable by expatriation. In this context, marital expatriation colluded with exclusionary immigration policy. It represented desires to keep foreigners out, and supplemented efforts to preclude future international marriages and the progeny of those marriages.[66] The 1907 marital expatriation law discouraged American women from marrying immigrants and foreign nationals, and it punished American women who introduced foreign elements into the body politic. The logic at work was implicitly, and sometimes explicitly, concerned with the production and reproduction of U.S. citizenship and national identity, an important component of which was one's choice in matrimony. This logic thereby conveyed the idea that it was the social obligation of citizens to link their commitment to the nation to their commitments to each other, even in the seemingly most private of settings and practices.

The Rationalization of Marriage
and the Marital Control of the Citizenry

Through contrasting languages of rights and consent, and obligation and public interest, the institution of marriage both promoted and prevented changes in the social, gendered, and racial hierarchies of the time. In the Progressive Era, policymakers justified the unprecedented level of state regulation of private relationships on the grounds that the preservation of the nation's social order, moral character, and political stability demanded extraordinary forms of intervention. The confluence of middle-class anxieties about social dislocation caused by urbanization and industrialization, nativist fears of Anglo-Saxon race suicide, and the belief among Progressives that greater rationalization, administration, and scientific management could solve social problems all shaped a political environment in which policymakers were more inclined to see the native-born white American's contribution to the civic realm as distinctly expressive of American national ideals. Marital regulation simultaneously concerned the fashioning of sexual and familial norms, bureaucratic and legal rationalization of marital practices, and control over the genetic suitability of current and future members of the polity. Marriage also underwent change as it shifted from a primarily economic arrangement to an institution representative of national and political identity. Marriage came be seen as central to the shaping and creation of national identity and social cohesion. Political actors from Congress, state legislatures, the courts, state institutions, and social reform organizations all turned to marriage to direct the massive changes of the era.

Marriage was an influential political institution during the Progressive era, shaping politics of both incorporation and exclusion. Few accounts of the Progressive era examine the subtle but significant role marriage played in the politics of the time. The regulation of marital relations helped usher in a concept of social and political order, and the institution itself changed radically from a private to public relationship, regulated by the state and limited by immigration status. As a political institution, marriage defined and controlled those both inside and outside its boundaries; while at the same time, it shaped norms and practices that tipped back and forth between obligations and rights. Institutionally marriage thus allowed state actors a way to regulate the flow of immigrants and a way to restrict that flow.

The legacy of both Reconstruction, discussed in Chapter 1, and the Progressive Era's marital battles and reforms has reverberated across a century, and we see echoes of the themes surrounding the obligations and rights of marriage in the 1960s, 1990s, and the beginning of the twenty-first century. In the Reconstruction and Progressive eras, not only did public power operate in the realms of intimate and familial relationships, but these relationships also were politicized by judges and policymakers in relation to the imperatives of the state. In the 1960s, these trends continued but also shifted.

The Supreme Court declared marriage a fundamental right of individuals, overshadowing past state calls to marital obligations in the name of national stability. This decision also meant that the state courts could no longer mandate racially homogeneous families. At the same time, the understanding of marriage as an obligation did not disappear, but resurfaced both as a revised policy aimed at addressing economic inequality among African Americans, and as a focal point for feminists. These turns in the politics of marriage again reveal the central role that marriage plays as a fulcrum in American politics in the articulation of diverse visions of community and nation by various political actors.

PART II

The Long Culture Wars

Chapter 3

"Marriage Is One of the Basic Civil Rights of Man"

Chief Justice Earl Warren, writing for the majority in *Loving v. Virginia* in 1967, asserted that "marriage is one of the 'basic civil rights of man,' fundamental to our very existence and survival."[1] The court claimed that antimiscegenation statutes deprived Mildred and Richard Loving of liberty without due process of law. The state of Virginia could not deny "this fundamental freedom" on the unsupportable basis of race: marriage as a civil right could not be restricted by race. This ruling was seen as a major step forward in race politics. It reflected one aspect of the development of the country towards inclusion and racial integration. Yet as civil rights proponents hailed the right to interracial marriage as a victory, marriage politics played out differently in other arenas. Women's movement activists challenged the obligation to marry as oppressive to women, and political elites claimed that the absence of marital family structure was a principal cause of black poverty. Marriage became a central site though which activists, policymakers, and state officials addressed pressing issues of the day, namely questions of social and economic inequality and the disempowered status of women, African Americans, and poor people.

The period we know as the sixties (which stretched into the mid-1970s) was a time of intense political, social, and cultural upheaval as societal norms and practices were upended with the rise of multiple social movements. In particular, social and political conflicts over issues of race and gender were central tensions of the time. In 1964, President Johnson announced his Great Society program to fight poverty and promote racial equality; and the courts by this time had begun the process of legal desegregation in schools, restaurants, and workplaces. Political activists were seeking to dislodge existing unequal power hierarchies and practices, while policymakers and politicians were trying to resettle them.

Various political and social actors invoked the legitimacy of obligations and the necessity of rights of marriage to frame struggles for inclusion, equality, and self-determination. Differing factions turned to the institution of marriage to promote, prevent, or settle the deep changes wrought during the period. Marriage, in other words, became a site of heated debate over social equality and liberation. Three major interventions in the laws and practices surrounding marriage reveal sixties-era attempts to define equality, to challenge the status quo, and to refashion a sense of normalcy and stability in this period of discord: first, the public policy framing of marriage as an institution to promote black equality; second, the feminist challenge to marriage as patriarchal; and third, the Supreme Court's declaration of marriage rights over and against race-based restrictions. In other words, the why, if, and who of marriage became important questions in addressing pressing issues concerning social and economic independence and equality.

According to marriage scholar Stephanie Coontz, the period from 1947 through the early 1960s was the time marriage had shifted fully into a love-based model, where couples married for love, independent of extended family. As Coontz writes, "Never before had so many people agreed that only one kind of family was 'normal.'"[2] While the relationship between men and women had shifted dramatically, with women gaining more legal and social rights, a commitment to monogamous, male-headed family based in love and personal fulfillment prevailed as the norm. As legal scholar Milton C. Regan, Jr. explains, marriage in the 1960s had come to be understood as a relationship "constituted by personal choice, the natural character of which is rooted in the desire of individuals to seek happiness through intimate association with another."[3] With such a view came the expectation that marriage should be the focus of people's emotional and moral strivings; the nuclear family came to be seen as the central repository of loyalty, obligation, and personal satisfaction. At the same time, the more that people hoped to achieve personal happiness within marriage, the more critical they became of "empty" or unsatisfying relationships (setting the stage for the "divorce revolution" of the 1970s).[4]

This privatized and personalized approach to marriage converged with the politics of the time and figured significantly in shaping the political terrain in terms of the definition of individual rights and the practices of self-determination. The civil rights climate also encouraged people to think of marriage as a basic human right. Both state and non-state actors used marriage when conceptualizing individual rights, civil rights, black liberation, poverty, and women's movement politics. Prior political conceptions of marriage as a right to be limited and protected were opened up as its constitutive relationship to the goals of desegregation, equality, and citizenship became more prominent. On the one hand, the right to marry became a vital sign of rights and freedom. On the other, feminist and black power activists questioned the importance of the right to marry in creating a politics of equality and self-determination. In fact, many activists viewed marriage as a source of institutionalized gender and racial inequality. Thus, for many activists marriage was a critical site to deeply question the prevailing social and political order in the name of individual rights.

At the same time, the declaration of the right to marry did not eliminate the role and view of marriage as an obligation. Some women's movement activists saw marriage only as an obligation and not a right. Policymakers in the Johnson administration, drawing on the Freedmen's Bureau "Marriage Rules" framework, offered marriage and family structure as crucial to building paths out of poverty for poor, single-mother-headed households. Policymakers and judges pushed marriage to address questions of inequality and to create order and stability. Marriage, in other words, fostered a policy of obligation to encourage economic independence. Finally, in the context of civil rights, the acceptance of interracial marriages represented a "domestication of rights," or in other words, rights and inclusions grounded in acceptable familial structures.

This period from the mid-1960s to the 1970s marks a turning point in marriage politics, when policymakers advocated for marriage in one arena, it was challenged by activists in another, and in still another realm, marriage was declared a fundamental right by the Supreme Court. By the late 1960s, legislation and court rulings had lifted racial limits on marriage, opening up the right to all heterosexual couples, a positive assertion of marriage rights not seen before. Progressive era concerns about national identity and civic belonging were replaced by questions of social equality. Rather than asking: Who belongs? On what grounds? People were asking: What do women want? How could equality among the races be created? Who is responsible for poverty? Social movement actors and policymakers turned to marriage to answer those questions, and in turn marriage shaped the meaning of equality in this period. The focus on marriage politics shifted to asserting marriage rights rather than limiting them. Thus, the politics of marriage during this period reveals marriage as central both to the reestablishment of order and to cultivating the seeds of change and challenge to that same order.

The Great Society

Extraordinary and destabilizing changes marked the 1960s. The assassination of President John F. Kennedy in 1963, the assassination of Martin Luther King, Jr. in 1968, the Vietnam War, the explosion of social movements, and unprecedented urban unrest helped produce a society steeped in discord. Accepted hierarchies between whites and people of color, and between men and women, came under assault. Civil rights protesters had already placed the issue of racial inequality on the national agenda, and Johnson placed the Democratic Party firmly on the side of equal rights for blacks. Introducing and successfully signing the Civil Rights Act of 1964, the Voting Rights Act of 1965, and the Fair Housing Act of 1968, among other pieces of legislation in the context of the Great Society, Johnson made the federal government an engine of civil rights promotion.[5]

As the federal focus on supporting civil rights developed, changes in the civil rights movement also occurred. The onset of urban rioting in Watts in 1965 and in several other northern cities over the next few years, the increasing visibility and authority of the "black power" movement, the rejection of the integrationist ideal, and the extension of the civil rights struggle to the North all served to nationalize the politics of race and merge it with other developing social movements. The new left and counterculture, based on campuses across the country, engaged in civil disobedience, protesting the Vietnam War and challenging conventional norms of behavior, particularly around sex and drug use. The rise of the women's movement and sexual liberation also was aligned with these developments, and the Supreme Court issued a series of decisions that seemed to support this questioning of tradition.

In response, and attempting to preempt further tumult, Johnson introduced the Great Society and the War on Poverty in 1964, a multitude of policy initiatives aimed at wholesale reconstruction of the social, political, and economic arenas. As part of this effort, the Johnson administration succeeded in passing not only the Civil Rights and Voting Rights Acts, but also a host of social welfare initiatives, with federal money allocated to education, antipoverty projects, Medicare for the elderly, Medicaid for the poor, and hundreds of other programs.

The Great Society offered a vision of social equality that aimed to eradicate the ills of poverty and urbanization. As Johnson described in his 1964 State of the Union address, the approach was "cooperative" and community-based. "The war against poverty will not be won here in Washington," he proclaimed. "It must be won in the field, in every private home, in every public office, from the courthouse to the White House."[6] Johnson also emphasized the importance of ensuring formal racial equality, employment opportunities, and access to healthcare and education. And he stressed the importance of both the home and family in pursuing and fulfilling the central aims of the Great Society.

The Economic Opportunity Act of 1964 (EOA) reflected Johnson's community approach. Designed to help poor Americans rise out of poverty, the EOA directed funds for the creation of youth programs, work training programs, work study programs, and Community Action Programs (CAPs). The results are familiar to this day, among them Head Start, VISTA (Volunteers in Service to America), and Job Corps. The Civil Rights Act of 1964 was even more fundamental, prohibiting employment discrimination on the basis of race, color, religion, national origin, and sex.

However, the combination of the expanded welfare state and the escalation of U.S. involvement in Vietnam created some tensions.[7] Funding for the War on Poverty and the war in Vietnam was difficult to maintain and led to increased inflation and higher taxes. Political scientist Michael Brown explains that beyond a financial tug of war between domestic and foreign policy, the Great Society's welfare state program was destined to fail because it was "predicated on a strategy of fiscal conservatism, which necessitated targeting social programs on the ghetto," and tension arose over taxes and spending.[8] The aid, especially in the form of the EOA programs, was the object of severe attacks. The funding of these expanded entitlements was expensive, and they came to be viewed as the government giving "something for nothing."[9] A growing body of working and middle-class whites—a demographic Richard Nixon would later describe and claim as the Silent Majority—believed that the Johnson administration was making them pay for ever-increasing services to the primarily black poor. Middle-class whites increasingly lost sympathy for low-income urban minorities, especially as the economy declined during the 1970s, and this led to diminished support for welfare programs. Dissatisfaction with governmental intervention in social and economic problems began to mount.[10] Amid this rising instability, within the government and in the streets, political and social actors turned to marriage to promote, prevent, and direct emerging tensions about the politics of race, class, and gender. In this political and social context, marriage played a central role in negotiating the tense terrain.

The Moynihan Report and the Obligation to Marry

On June 4, 1965, President Johnson gave the commencement speech at Howard University, in which he said that the next stage in securing freedom and equality for African Americans was to translate newly reinforced legal rights into "equality as a fact and equality as a result."[11] The reorganization of the poor black family figured prominently in that process. Johnson declared in the speech that "family was the cornerstone of society," suggesting an important shift in the civil rights stance of the federal government. The "next and more profound stage" of the civil rights struggle would not have to do with legal protection of rights, but with the provision of resources that would enable African Americans to turn freedom into economic and social equality. Real freedom would not be found in law and court-ordered guaranteed justice, nor simply in job creation, but in shoring up family life. Johnson turned to marriage as an institution through which to revise and rework federal policy on racial equality. While the policy was not ultimately developed by Johnson, he used the language of marital obligation as one approach to conceptualizing civil and economic rights, and sparked a debate on the role of marriage in racial equality.

As the Freedmen's Bureau officials had thought during Reconstruction, so Johnson suggested that without the proper structure of a two-headed marital family, black Americans could not be proper citizens. At the heart of Johnson's appeal in this Howard University speech was the metaphor that likened racial inequality to different "nations" inhabited by black and white Americans, made so by their different family structures. "In far too many ways," he told the Howard audience, "American Negroes have been another nation, deprived of freedom, crippled by hatred, the doors of opportunity closed to hope." The "breakdown of the Negro family structure," in Johnson's view, was perhaps the most important obstacle to black equality, and thus the family was crucial to articulating racial equality. But Johnson's promised equality was premised on reorganizing the female-headed black family into one with a male head of household. Patriarchal marital family structure would create a bridge between the black and white nations.

The Howard speech was received favorably by both the press and main-stream civil rights organizations. According to a *New York Times* article at the time, the speech's content had been "under study for about two months. Much consultation with civil rights leaders and experts in the social sciences went into its preparation."[12] Among the leaders named were Martin Luther King, Jr. and Roy Wilkins, executive director of the NAACP. Some newspaper columns after the speech focused on how the president had "begun to examine the full sordid fabric of racial inequality rather than simply its tattered fragments."[13] One journalist noted that "it was one of the few such speeches not aimed directly at the South"; instead, it focused on the whole nation and "the total social and economic plight of its Negro citizens."[14] In a *New York Times* piece, Wilkins wrote that the speech marked "the first time in the history of our country that a President had spread the whole difficult, intimate and extremely complex racial picture before all the people."[15] Wilkins further stated that Johnson was correct to describe the complexities of racial inequality in the United States as part of a "seamless web." Wilkins commended Johnson for recognizing that it was not enough to raise one corner of the "blanket of circumstance that buries the Negro community," but that it was necessary "to raise the entire cover if we are to liberate our fellow citizens." The family was posited as one important component in the web of racial inequality.

The Howard speech was written by Daniel Patrick Moynihan, the author of the then-private report, *The Negro Family: The Case for National Action*, from the Department of Labor's Office of Policy Planning and Research. The Moynihan Report, as it came to be called, had been completed in March 1965, when Moynihan was the assistant secretary of labor, in collaboration with two members of his staff, Paul Barton and Ellen Broderick. The report emphasized social science as the basis for policy recommendations.[16] Similar to the structure and spirit of the "Marriage Rules" put in place by the Freedmen's Bureau after the Civil War, the Moynihan Report saw family and marriage as the basis of economic and social independence, equality, and full citizenship, and on that basis advocated for federal policies that would encourage African Americans to marry. The Howard commencement speech reflected this same view, and it also echoed Freedmen's Bureau policies in its assertion of the African American obligation to marry. Marriage, then, for Moynihan and by extension for the Johnson administration, was defined as an obligation that came with the effort to achieve equality.

A key and controversial passage in the report explained that "at the heart of the deterioration of the fabric of Negro society is the deterioration of the

Negro family."[17] The "fundamental problem" with the black community, Moynihan claimed, was "that of the family structure."[18] He wrote that "at the center of the tangle of pathology is the weakness of the family structure. Once or twice removed, it will be found to be the principal source of most of the aberrant and inadequate or antisocial behavior that did not establish, but now serves to perpetuate the cycle of poverty and deprivation."[19]

Moynihan's framing of racial poverty as an issue of family structure was in part an attempt to help the Johnson administration lead and direct the civil rights movement. Civil rights struggles were becoming increasingly militant as Johnson looked for a way to manage the growing crisis. Moynihan explained later that the speech at Howard University was intended "to deliberately leapfrog the civil rights movement—to get out in front so far that you would avoid chasing it."[20] To do so, Moynihan put forth the patriarchal family structure as a solution to the problem of racial difference and inequality, and suggested a central role for the federal government in developing black patriarchy within a marital structure.[21] This role required, according to Moynihan, "a national effort" to define "programs of the Federal government" that will work towards "enhancing the stability and resources of the Negro American family."[22] Thus the basis of civic inclusion, equality, and success begins with the marital family structure.

Moynihan supported marriage and family policies as an answer not only to poverty but also to social inequality. Because of this, *not* marrying was defined as a political and economic problem. By postulating two societies within one nation, Moynihan raised the question of what constitutes citizenship, and what comprises the obligations of U.S. citizenship. He suggests that if a poor nonwhite single mother married, the act would represent a desire for civic membership and therefore legitimize government help.

Undergirding Moynihan's ideas was a larger sociological scholarship that argued that slavery had "broken the backbone of the slave family" and had created black families in which mothers rather than fathers were heads of households.[23] The link between family and poverty was the basis of the "culture of poverty" arguments that explained urban poverty and ghetto life by cyclical pathological behavior that was passed on through the generations.[24] According to a *New York Times* description of the report, "essentially what has happened . . . is that white Americans by means of slavery, humiliation and unemployment have so degraded the Negro male that most lower class Negro families are headed by females."[25]

President Johnson, through the influence of Daniel Patrick Moynihan, argued that the relative absence of marriage in black communities hindered black collective freedom and equality. The argument resonated with the logic of the Reconstruction-era Freedman's Bureau, claiming that full realization of citizenship for blacks required a structure of familial dependence based on marriage and paternal authority. Johnson and Moynihan's diagnosis and remedy for black poverty and disempowerment were echoed by supporters, but were challenged by the increasing militancy of black protests as well as urban unrest.

The initial favorable responses to the ideas in Johnson's Howard University speech soured once the Moynihan Report became public on August 9, 1965 in a *Newsweek* article.[26] A frequent complaint leveled at the administration's policy approach was that the generalized idea of a "Negro family" did an injustice to those whose lives could not be characterized as unstable and pathological. In addition, the Watts Riot in Los Angeles, beginning on August 16, 1965, proved a turning point in the civil rights movement and the conversation over civil rights legislation. The riot lasted for five days before it was put down by National Guard troops. Thirty-four people died, a thousand were injured, and more than six hundred buildings were burned or looted, causing upward of $200 million in damages. At the time, it was the worst urban violence in U.S. history. Many saw it as an assertion that legal protections were not enough; black Americans demanded jobs. It also transformed the national debate about civil rights legislation into a conversation focused on racial confrontations and blame. The Moynihan Report and the issues it raised over the role of marriage and family were a focal point of the debate. This was evident in *Los Angeles Times* reporting on Johnson administration policy that came after the riots. "The administration," said the *Times* staff writer Thomas J. Foley, "is redirecting its main focus on racial problems from the South to large urban areas as the result of an unpublished report that blames Negro unrest on the breakdown of Negro family structure."[27] A shift in the framing of racial politics had taken place: the Moynihan Report was said to "blame Negro unrest" instead of to *explain* Negro inequality. That shift was accompanied by another shift that placed the "blame" of poverty and violence in the hands of African Americans rather than in the social, political, and economic systems. This change in focus would not take firm hold until the 1980s, when it began to structure discourse around welfare policy, but its roots are in these responses to the racialized violence of the mid-1960s.

Two critiques of the report emerged. Some were critical because the report ignored economic needs, while others rejected the assimilationist approach that assumed aspiration to the norms of white America. Some African American leaders were enraged by Johnson's focus on the family and argued that it was more important to provide jobs than to worry about a strong male image.[28] Civil rights leaders vehemently attacked the Moynihan Report because "they feared it would fuel racism and detract from economic remedies."[29] They were irritated by the Moynihan Report's implicit suggestions that blacks ought to take more responsibility for self-improvement and they ought to mimic white society. Floyd McKissick of the Congress of Racial Equality (CORE) admonished the report's focus on the family when he said that, "it's the damn system that needs changing."[30] Critics of the report saw it as bolstering the culture of poverty arguments—that is, the idea that links black poverty to the deterioration of the black family—that directed resources and attention away from economic concerns. The negative response to the report halted federal policy efforts aimed at African American families. No longer was a focus on family structure an assault on the "seamless web" of racism; it was instead an attack on black males.

Critics knew that marriage policy did not translate into economic support—as indeed it had not during Reconstruction. Rather, the turn to marriage took the responsibility for economic well-being out of the hands of legislators and the state and placed it into the hands of African Americans. Finally, the turn to marriage constituted a policy of assimilation, attempting to address problems of inequality by a policy of disciplinary inclusion.

With the emergence of a new generation of black leaders dedicated to "black power" and a militant politics based in civil disobedience, as well as the politics of feminist and women's rights activists, a strong group of vocal activists came to reject the focus on marriage and family as a solution to equality questions. (After *Loving*, it would not be until the same-sex marriage debates in the 1990s that the institution would again be used to advance equality, and then the effort would come from rights-seeking activists, not the state.) In fact, the Moynihan approach, according to its critics, served to maintain status quo racial hierarchies, not challenge them. The civil rights movement increasingly focused on the ghettoes of northern cities, as the black power movement spoke to the rage of young urban blacks. Political scientist Sidney M. Milkis examines the tension between the growing black power movement and the Johnson administration. He explains that Stokely Carmichael, head of the Student Nonviolent Coordinating Committee (SNCC), and Floyd McKissick of CORE, among others, were frustrated with the achievements of the Johnson administration's civil rights program as well as the racial integration program. In the manifesto entitled *Black Power*, Carmichael and political scientist Charles V. Hamilton wrote, "the goal of the black people must *not* be to assimilate into middle class America, for that class—as a whole—is without a viable conscience as regards humanity."[31] The focus on the obligation to marry reflected middle-class white America and thus was antithetical to social and political transformation. As Carmichael later wrote in his autobiography, "the underlying and fundamental notion" of *Black Power* "was that black folks . . . had the right and duty to define ourselves, *in our own terms*, our real circumstances, possibilities, and interests relative to white America."[32]

In many ways, the debate that ensued was precisely over whether marriage was a right or an obligation, a personal choice or a public status. Patricia Harris, co-chair of the National Women's Committee for Civil Rights in the Kennedy administration and Johnson's ambassador to Luxembourg, explained that, for Moynihan, family issues "became *the* explanation rather than *an* explanation of the problems with Negros."[33] She objected to the implied claim that marriage was an obligation and central to notions of equality rather than existing outside of politics, and therefore she asserted that Moynihan's formulation was an insult to the pressing questions of economic inequality. Likewise, James Farmer, leader of CORE, saw marriage not as a central structural factor that created inequalities but as a private individual right, writing in the *Amsterdam News* that the Moynihan Report would be "fuel for a new racism." He condemned it as "another one of those academic efforts to get our eyes off the prize. . . . Nowhere does Moynihan suggest that the proper answer to a shattered family is an open job market . . . or that high illegitimacy rates . . . may be partly explained by the fact that birth control information and covert abortions are . . . the exclusive property of the white man."[34] Some critics argued that income levels were key forces behind variations in family structure and that many impoverished white families were threatened too.[35] In the context of the time, where marriage was considered a love-based institution, the notion of marriage as an obligation was not politically viable.

The disagreement over the Moynihan Report was in part a struggle over the status of marriage and family in defining racial difference and equality. Civil rights leaders such as Whitney Young and Martin Luther King, Jr. were sensitive to the report's claims because they feared it stigmatized a whole group, suggesting innate black weaknesses.[36] The claims that Moynihan was misguided were based in part on the report's view that marriage was private and therefore a choice, suggesting that poor blacks were actively not choosing to marry. The sociologist Christopher Jencks wrote a critique of the report in October for the *New York Review of Books*, saying that "the guiding assumption [of the report] is that social pathology is caused less by basic defects in the social system than by defects in particular individuals and groups which prevent their adjusting to the system. The prescription is therefore to change the deviance, not the system."[37] Critics argued that it was not about whether blacks choose to marry or not. Moynihan argued that it was necessary to create the obligation to marry, because marital structure was at the center of defining inclusion and economic justice.

Like Johnson's Howard University address, the Moynihan Report was welcomed by some elements of the civil rights community and the Left, illustrating widespread ambivalence around this issue of marriage and racial equality. Michael Harrington, author of *The Other America*, as well as Charles Silberman, author of *Crisis in Black and White*, defended the report. In October 1965, Martin Luther King, Jr. saw the relative strength of focusing on marriage and family as political sites, but also the risk of laying the problem at the feet of African Americans rather than society as a whole. In public addresses, he spoke movingly about "the shattering blows" of slavery that had made the Negro family "fragile, deprived, and often psychopathic."[38] At the same time, he articulated the "dangers and opportunities" of focusing on the family, explaining that "the opportunity will be to deal fully rather than haphazardly with the problem as a whole . . . and meet it as other disasters are met with an adequacy of resources. The danger will be that the problems will be attributed to innate Negro weaknesses and used to justify neglect and rationalize oppression."[39]

Both the Moynihan Report and the Howard University speech demonstrate how marriage and family figured in negotiating the political problem of racial stratification laid bare first by the civil rights movement and then by growing urban unrest. In the view of Moynihan, marriage and family were structural factors and the bridge between formal equality and real equality; marriage and family created a common practice in which all citizens could exercise their rights of freedom, and unify the nation; the institutions of marriage and family thereby remedied economic inequality and social delinquency. Here we see the way in which, during this tumultuous political era in U.S. history, marriage was presented as a solution to multiple political and social problems.

Questions about the role of marriage and family were significant in the unfolding debates concerning race during this era. For Moynihan's critics, marriage was not central to addressing the larger economic and systemic issues of racial inequality. The political response to Moynihan can be explained in part as the tension between a view of marriage as a right and personal choice, and a view of marriage as a component of the societal structure and thus an obligation. Opponents of the Moynihan Report read the report's formulations as a political dodge that ignored other structural issues such as unemployment. The debates surrounding the Moynihan Report questioned the separation between social and political equality, which was also a central issue of the women's movement at the time, to which we now turn.

Feminists Challenge the Obligation to Marry

The political movements for black civil rights and against the war in Vietnam in the 1960s were followed by an attack on the 1950s belief system about what constituted American values, and in particular on beliefs about women's roles in regard to courtship and marriage.[40] The shift in marriage to a love-based model, easier access to legal divorce, and the introduction of birth control[41] coincided with and informed the development of the women's movement and the heated critiques of both marriage and the role of women as wives.

New trends in divorce, women working outside the home, and reproductive laws were changes that in many ways represented a rejection of prior understandings of what constituted a traditional marriage in favor of women's empowerment. At the same time, most of the changes supported women's roles in the public sphere, while their obligation and expectation to care for dependents and to maintain a household remained relatively unchanged. This role for women, as caring for dependents, matched or coincided with the culture of poverty arguments that also supported women staying in the home. Meanwhile, arguing the "personal is political," radical feminist groups launched a thoroughgoing critique of the bonds of marriage and women's role in the home.

Echoing President Johnson's claims about racial equality, women's movement activists came to argue that legal rights to voting, education, and nondiscrimination were not enough to create equality. Rather, by the 1960s women began challenging and interrogating the institution of marriage and, in particular, the obligation of women to marry. Some activists, such as SNCC veteran Casey Hayden, described gender inequality as a caste system, while others, such as the radical feminist group in New York who called themselves simply The Feminists, launched a full attack on marriage, likening wives to slaves.[42]

Radical feminists pushed against what they characterized as women's slave-like submission to husbands within the institution of marriage. Under the love-based model, husband and wife were supposed to be equal partners contracting in marriage because both retained an independent legal existence, yet women were still limited by "bonds of matrimony." Radical feminists claimed that women were not really equal as long as their work in the home had no value or recognition. So while President Johnson looked to the institution of marriage to fulfill the rights created by legal equality for African Americans, feminists saw the institution of marriage as limiting the fulfillment of their freedom and equality.

These feminists also focused on the obligation of marriage but, in contrast to Johnson and Moynihan, found an opposite logic: the duty did not lead to emancipation from poverty and inequality, but rather toward oppression within a patriarchal social order. For many in the white women's movement, freedom and equality required a reworking or abandonment of the responsibility of women to marry. Their critique was that while women had gained political and economic rights, their role in the home was still unequal. And though liberal and radical feminists saw the role of marriage and family in women's lives differently, in general feminists believed that the institution of marriage was at the heart of women's inequality, preventing them from becoming free, equal, and self-determined individuals.

The marital struggles of the 1960s drew from postbellum Freedmen's Bureau reasoning about the relationship between black citizenship and marital duties, but they also posed new challenges to the legitimacy of marriage itself when understood in relation to questions of gender equality. Two main political approaches to marriage came out of the primarily white women's movement. One was liberal and the other radical, the difference being that liberals wanted to reform marriage while radicals wanted to abolish it. For all, however, critiques of marriage were tied to exploring, challenging, and reforming gender norms.

The National Organization for Women (NOW) in its founding statement, written in 1966, asserted:

> We believe that a true partnership between the sexes demands a different concept of marriage, an equitable sharing of the responsibilities of home and children and of the economic burdens of their support.

We believe that proper recognition should be given to the economic and social value of homemaking and child-care. To these ends, we will seek to open a reexamination of laws and mores governing marriage and divorce, for we believe that the current state of "half-equity" between the sexes discriminates against both men and women, and is the cause of much unnecessary hostility between the sexes.[43]

The statement drew out the relative burdens that men and women endure in marriage and called for a reevaluation of those roles. NOW's position on marriage rejected "the current assumptions that a man must carry the sole burden of supporting himself, his wife, and family, and that a woman is automatically entitled to lifelong support by a man upon her marriage, or that marriage, home and family are primarily woman's world and responsibility—hers, to dominate—his to support."[44] The group did not reject wholesale the concept of marriage but rather believed it could be reformed to meet the needs of men and women. This view was possible in part because of the legal rights married women had gained since the nineteenth century, including rights to own property, earn wages, and own a credit card.

The question of whether marriage could be reformed, however, was open. Liberal feminist writer and activist Gloria Steinem wrote in *New York Magazine* in 1967, "Once upon a time—say, ten or even five years ago—a Liberated Woman was somebody who had sex before marriage and a job afterward. Once upon the same time, a Liberated Zone was any foreign place lucky enough to have an American army in it. Both ideas seem antiquated now, and for pretty much the same reason: Liberation isn't exposure to the American values of Mom-and-apple-pie any more (not even if Mom is allowed to work in an office and vote once in a while); it's escape from them."[45] For Steinem, questioning marriage went hand in hand with questioning other powerful institutions like the military, suggesting that these two pillars of the American nation —the military and marriage—cannot foster equality or liberation, but in fact stand in the way of their achievement. Moreover, what this quote shows is a shift in how marriage is viewed.

Feminists who questioned marriage were also questioning the grounds of women's inclusion, their status in relation to marriage, and their obligation to marry. Liberal feminist Betty Friedan characterized women's angst as "a problem with no name," as she wrote about her deep feelings of being trapped by marriage and family. In *The Feminine Mystique*, published in 1963, Friedan described traditional homes, in which wives were solely home-

makers without outside employment, as "comfortable concentration camps."
Women's identity, she said, was stilted by the feminine mystique: "by choosing femininity over the painful growth to full identity, by never achieving the
hard core of self that comes not from fantasy but from mastering reality," girls
are "doomed to suffer" feelings of boredom, purposelessness and even non-
identity. Friedan asserts "the housewife's problem that has no name" can be
seen "in a more pathological form" in the children of these mothers in a pas-
sivity and softness that has been passed on to American children.[46] So tightly
bound to the institution of marriage and to the roles of mother and wife,
women were compelled to retreat to marriage and remain passive. Friedan's
work shows how the institution of marriage was crucial to shaping women's
experience.

In part, what Friedan and later the radical feminists articulated was how
the obligation of marriage defined the social group of women. Friedan's aim
was to empower women rather than to dismantle the institution of marriage
itself, and this came to define a central difference between liberal and radical
feminism. She turned to the liberal promises of individuality, education, and
work outside the home to help women break out of the feminine mystique. She
suggested that women must shed their focus on the home and on their roles
as wives and mothers through nondomestic work. By moving into the public
sphere, women could fulfill their potential as free humans and attain equal status. Friedan, a founding member of NOW, went on to struggle to reform political and economic rights for women along liberal individualist lines.[47]

By the late 1960s and early 1970s, an emergent radical feminism had
pushed beyond the positions represented by NOW feminists like Freidan.
Younger women comprised the majority of this new women's liberation
movement, and they began to organize in 1968 and 1969 as a distinct branch
of contemporary feminism.[48] While not a cohesive collection of groups, radical feminists exhibited certain common themes, one being overt hostility to
the institution of marriage. Women's liberation movement activists saw patriarchy as integral to the functioning of society and as enforcing an obligation
for women to marry; they attacked the notion that women had to marry to
maintain societal stability. For many radical feminists, the institution of marriage was so embedded within society that it could not be reformed, but had
to be dismantled in order for women to achieve liberation. They were critical
not only of the institution of marriage but also of the ideologies of whiteness,
heterosexuality and patriarchy that went with it.

Kate Millet in her 1969 best-selling and influential book *Sexual Politics*, for example, took a different tack from liberal feminists such as Friedan. Millet forthrightly defined the "problem with no name" as patriarchy. Whereas Friedan discussed the feminist mystique as a "damaging problem of socialization, Millet understood patriarchy as a profound organizational principle that affected all of culture and society."[49] Millet argued that, "in spite of modifications of law in women's rights, under patriarchy marriage and kinship remain in the *feudal* position as kind of property right of man." Millet wrote that "patriarchy's chief institution is the family."[50] Quoting eighteenth-century jurist William Blackstone, Millet argued that marriage made women chattel.[51] Millet was one of the first to define the relationship between men and women as one of political domination. Millet explained that "so long as every female, simply by virtue of her anatomy, *is obliged,* even forced, to be the sole primary caretaker of childhood, she is prevented from being a free human being."[52] The family, she argued, "must go." Radical feminists like Millet challenged the distinction between the public and private. In so doing, they questioned the natural place of marriage in society and the nation as well as the supposedly natural unequal roles of men and women.

Shulamith Firestone, author of the 1970 best-selling *Dialectic of Sex,* also took marriage on directly. She wrote that the institution of marriage "consistently proves itself unsatisfactory—even rotten. . . . The family is . . . directly connected to—is even the cause of—the ills of the larger society."[53] Firestone's and Millet's critique of marriage and family was embedded in their view that sex, not class or race, was the root of oppression. Interestingly, Firestone's analysis of how patriarchal gender roles worked in marriage was like Daniel Patrick Moynihan's. While she opposed this framework as oppressive to women, Moynihan promoted it as the path out of black poverty. Both Firestone and Moynihan, though from very different perspectives, saw the institution of marriage similarly as an obligation and status.

The crux of the radical feminist critiques was the comparison of marriage to a system of slavery. In 1969 the Redstockings issued a manifesto declaring that marriage turned women into "breeders" and "domestic servants."[54] Shelia Cronan, a Redstockings member, wrote in her 1970 essay, "Marriage," that the institution "is a form of slavery. . . . Freedom for women cannot be won without the abolition of marriage."[55] One group, The Feminists, staged a demonstration at the Marriage License Bureau in New York City in 1969 and passed out a pamphlet titled, *Women: Do You Know the Facts about Marriage?* "Do you know that you are your husband's prisoner?" the pamphlet asked. "All the discriminatory practices against women are patterned and

rationalized by this slavery-like practice. We can't destroy the inequities between men and women until we destroy marriage. *We must free ourselves.
And marriage is the place to begin.*"[56]

A crucial concept that came out of the radical feminist movement was the
idea that "the personal is political." The phrase was originally coined by Carol
Hanisch, a member of the New York Radical Women in 1968. The phrase captured what the critiques of marriage were based on: that there were political
and hierarchical dimensions to private life that needed to be viewed through
a lens of inequality. As historian Ruth Rosen explains it, the phrase conveyed
the idea that "power relations shaped life in marriage, in the kitchen, the bed-
room, the nursery and at work. . . . politics existed beyond Congress."[57]

The attempted revolution in marriage peaked in the late 1960s and early
1970s, as feminists and other activists challenged the economic, social, and
political limits imposed upon women by marriage. The radical feminist
movement, which launched the most thoroughgoing critique of marriage,
was short-lived. By the end of the 1960s, most women were apprehensive
about supporting even the more moderate ideas of women's liberation. Moreover, by the 1970s, right-wing activists aggressively challenged changes in
gender roles and sexual norms. Conservative activists such as Phyllis Schlafly
mounted an effective battle against liberal feminist's long sought ratification
of the proposed Equal Rights Amendment, in part because of the threat it
posed to marriage.[58] New groups advocating "traditional" marriage arose,
and any article by a reformed or repentant feminist was virtually guaranteed
publication.[59]

The story of the women's movement reveals the importance of marriage
to notions of equality and self-determination, though how marriage figured
in women's equality and what the implications of the institution were for
women was contested. Constant, however, was that the institution of marriage was crucial to the development and articulation of women's politics.
While some women were challenging the confines of the institution of marriage, sociologists and policymakers like Moynihan looked to marriage as a
path out of poverty. The critiques of marriage laid out by the different types
of feminists both confirmed and challenged explicit racial marital discourses,
revealing how policies like Moynihan's defined racial equality based on unequal gender norms. While this was happening, in 1967 the Supreme Court
ruled against antimiscegenation statutes in *Loving v. Virginia*. The Supreme
Court officially granted interracial couples the right to marry, calling this
right fundamental. The decision made marriage a crucial site of equality and

rights, which indirectly helped to override and delegitimize the feminist critique. In interesting ways, these approaches played off one another.

Loving v. Virginia and Domesticating Civil Rights

In 1967, as civil rights leaders debated the aftermath of the Moynihan Report and federal policies on race, and as feminists were beginning to challenge the very structure of marriage and family, the Supreme Court decided *Loving v. Virginia*, which made anti-interracial marriage laws unconstitutional and defined marriage as a fundamental right. For Moynihan, marriage was an obligation to be upheld, and for feminists it was an obligation from which to escape. But in *Loving* it was a fundamental right to be extended, a civil right crucial to the pursuance of life, liberty, and the pursuit of happiness. "Under our Constitution, the freedom to marry, or not marry, a person of another race resides with the individual and cannot be infringed by the State," wrote Chief Justice Earl Warren for the majority.[60] The courts were also overturning most other segregation laws, and for the liberal establishment *Loving* was the keystone to establishing racial equality. But for the burgeoning Black Power movement, interracial marriage undermined racial solidarity. Thus, in the context of changing racial politics, the meaning of marriage persisted as a site of intense political debate.

During the 1950s, interracial marriage rights were not at the top of black leaders' list of political priorities. By the 1960s, however, black leaders began to see interracial marriage as a civil rights issue.[61] Even though the white South was still overwhelmingly against it, public opinion had shifted measurably toward acceptance. By 1967, the outcome of *Loving v. Virginia* was almost expected.[62] Antimiscegenation statutes were the last holdout among segregation laws. Since its *Brown v. Board of Education of Topeka* decision in 1954, the Supreme Court had made the notion of "separate but equal" unconstitutional and untenable. As civil rights activists challenged Jim Crow laws, the federal courts invalidated laws that mandated segregation on buses, in parks, and in public accommodations, and discredited the larger system of racial regulation of which antimiscegenation laws were a part. In the years after *Brown*, states reconsidered their antimiscegenation laws so that by 1967 only sixteen states, mostly in the South and Midwest, still barred interracial marriage, down from twenty-nine states in 1959.[63]

In 1958, Richard Loving, a white man, and Mildred Jeter, a black woman, left their Virginia home to wed in Washington, D.C., where interracial marriage was legal. They returned home and were eventually arrested and convicted of violating their home state's antimiscegenation statute. Under Virginia's law, the one- to five-year prison sentence for marrying across racial lines applied even if the couple was married in a state that allowed interracial marriage. In lieu of a one-year jail sentence, the Lovings were banished from the state for twenty-five years. For nine years after their arrest, they waged a legal battle through the courts. The American Civil Liberties Union filed a motion on their behalf in the state of Virginia on the grounds that the violated statutes ran counter to the Fourteenth Amendment. This set in motion a series of lawsuits that ultimately reached the Supreme Court. In 1967, the Supreme Court reversed the Lovings' convictions, effectively invalidating all existing antimiscegenation legislation. In *Loving*, the court moved beyond race discrimination and asserted that the right to marry was itself protected by the Constitution. As a civil right, it could not be restricted by race, nor could the state infringe upon a person's choice of whom to marry. Racial classifications were deemed subversive to the principle of equality.

The *Loving* decision constitutes an important moment in marriage politics and in the development of marriage in the United States. While *Loving* was not the first court ruling to claim that marriage was a civil right, it was the first Supreme Court case to explicitly decide so.[64] With emancipation in 1865, ex-slaves had gained the right to marry along with freedom from bondage—except that intermarriage with whites was illegal in most states. The decision to render antimiscegenation laws unconstitutional marked the final step in formal civic inclusion for African Americans, and redefined marriage as a right of individuals, protected from state interference. *Loving* thus also reasserted the importance of the institution of marriage as a public political issue, as central to constituting citizenship, and at the same time as a private, personal prerogative.

The case for marriage in *Loving* is both similar to and different from the views put forth by Daniel Patrick Moynihan. It is similar in that it posits marriage as central to collective life, or as President Johnson put it, as the cornerstone of the nation. It is different in that marriage in *Loving* is a right of personal fulfillment rather than an obligation necessary to secure social cohesion. With the racial restrictions on marriage lifted, marriage became a fundamental right more than an obligation. The case recast the meaning of equality to encompass the freedom to choose marital partners without state intervention on the basis of race. Here we have two different approaches to

civil rights. Whereas Moynihan had suggested that marriage was an obligation, *Loving* defined marriage as a right.

In the amicus brief submitted by the Legal Defense Fund of the NAACP,
Robert Carter took up the personal fulfillment side of this see-saw, explaining that marriage was an individual choice that had nothing to do with race:
"the choice of a spouse is a subjective act, the act of an individual and not
that of a race or group."[65] He went on to explain that "Negroes cannot be considered to have obtained equal rights or to have gained full freedom as full-
fledged citizens of the U.S. until they are free to make the individual decision
as to whom they will marry without legislative interference or proscriptions
based solely on the accident of their color. It is to assert this individual right
to freedom and full-fledged citizenship that the NAACP is filing this brief."[66]
Carter argued that differences in marriage and family, along with education
and health, were not racially based. The differences, he suggested, would
change when economic discrimination ended. Like the critics of Moynihan,
Carter viewed marriage as a personal choice, unrelated to larger societal and
political questions.

During the hundreds of years in which antimiscegenation laws were in
place, they channeled property, morality, legitimate procreation, and notions
of belonging into a specific form of monogamous marriage: one man and one
woman, whose sameness of race was required by law and "whose difference
of sex was taken entirely for granted."[67] *Loving* legally voided racial restrictions on marriage, asserting on the surface that marriage was "colorblind"
and suggesting that there are no racial differences within marital discourse.[68]
Yet *Loving* did not challenge the definition of marriage itself. Consequently,
it reinscribed the centrality of the institution and the primacy of the white
family as the ideal structure.[69] The *Loving* decision legitimated theories of
the family based on a white, middle-class model, as well as the discourses of
racialized family breakdown and the culture of poverty ideology. Notions of
marriage and family formation turned out not to be colorblind, and the line
between rights and obligations was not so clear. While *Loving* established
a rationale for rejecting racialized limits on marriage, regulatory and legal
mandates on family formation and marital structure still had strong racial
distinctions. *Loving* reaffirmed the role of marriage and family in shaping
equality, inclusion, and the obligations and rights of citizens. It asserted marriage as personal right but not a fully open one. The right to marry, in other
words, was not entirely free of the politics of obligation. When interracial
couples gained the right to marry as the basis of inclusion and citizenship,

the court's decision also represented a politics of disciplinary inclusion and a domestication of civil rights, setting the terms of inclusion.

The court explained that "the freedom to marry has long been recognized as one of the vital personal rights essential to the *orderly pursuit* of happiness by free men."[70] I highlight "orderly pursuit" here because, in declaring that marriage was a fundamental right, the court, as state proxy, still maintained an interest in defining the *way* in which individuals pursued happiness. The phrase first appeared in the 1923 case of *Meyer v. Nebraska*, which challenged a state law prohibiting the teaching of foreign languages to elementary and middle school children. Speaking for the Supreme Court in *Meyer*, Justice James Clark McReynolds stated that the liberty guaranteed by the Fourteenth Amendment included not only freedom from restraint, but also the right to work, to marry, to raise a family, and "generally to enjoy those privileges long recognized as essential to the *orderly pursuit of happiness by free men*."[71] The *orderly* pursuit of happiness suggests that one can pursue happiness as long as it conforms to the rules and norms of law and society, which impress upon citizens the need to engage in "normal" and stabilizing behaviors. That the court invoked the "orderly pursuit of happiness" both in a case that concerned public education (*Meyer*) and a case that concerned marriage (*Loving*) underscores the political role of marriage in determining the rights and obligations of citizens: like public education, marriage is a political institution because it manages and shapes the rights of citizens in relation to the state.

In the case of *Loving*, coming as it did in the midst of societal upheavals in the 1960s, the phrase "orderly pursuit" was meaningful. In other words, judges turned to marriage to make a powerful yet subtle statement about stability, which offset the radical shifts in racial power relations that were under way. In the context of the civil rights movement and the discussion of the "failing" black family, *Loving* recentered the institution of marriage as an important issue in civil rights.

In addition, it also indirectly supported policies that focused on the black family, and on the actions of black people in general, rendering the black family a legitimate site of state intervention over individual privacy. The right to marry could not be denied, but at the same time this right raised anew the Johnson administration's concern for the "breakdown of the African American family" and the alleged political problems entailed when people do not marry.

In the aftermath of *Loving*, with antimiscegenation laws rendered mute, and with the last formal element of racial segregation thereby overturned, the leaders of the integration movement began to retire from the scene. The generation of civil rights leaders who replaced them had to walk a fine line between the old liberal commitment to individual rights and racial integration, and the burgeoning radicalism and racial solidarity expressed by the black power and black nationalist movements. At the same moment that whites began to revoke their opposition to interracial marriage, black communities began to openly critique it.[72]

Malcolm X, a leader who inspired the subsequent generation of black nationalists, said in 1964, "We are as much against intermarriage as we are against all of the other injustices that our people have encountered."[73] Black nationalists, committed to the project of black pride and an all-black nation, ridiculed many black leaders and activists with white spouses and criticized them for betraying racial solidarity.[74] The rising black power movement rejected interracial marriage because it represented something deeper. Black nationalists increasingly understood intermarriage as an engine for assimilation that would allow successful blacks, especially black men, to leave the community behind as they focused on their own economic and social advancement. As historian Renee Romano describes it, "debates about interracial marriage reflected a growing concern about how the black community could continue to produce strong families and inculcate a sense of racial responsibility at a time of expanding individual opportunities."[75]

The role of interracial marriage in furthering racial equality was up for debate, however. Author Joseph Washington argued in *Marriage in Black and White*, written in 1970, that until whites began to liberate themselves from their "fear" of interracial marriage, there could be no real racial progress, even though most blacks considered interracial marriage peripheral to black liberation. "To the degree we come clean on marriage in black and white," he wrote, "everything else can be worked out, and to the degree we are dishonest about marriage in black and white, nothing else will work."[76] Marriage itself could not resolve U.S. racial tensions. But he argued that complete resolution of racial conflicts had to involve the removal of stigma from interracial unions.[77]

The *Loving* decision was a historic step in this direction. But it was only a temporary settlement to the civil rights tensions of the time. It bolstered marriage norms as much as it changed them. *Loving* served to reaffirm marriage as a central organizing institution in society and the nation. This is not to erase its significance for racial equality, but we should not ignore an important contradiction within the ruling. On the one hand, *Loving* reveals the liberatory potential of marriage as a right to civic inclusion. On the other hand, the terms of that inclusion are hemmed in by preexisting ideals of marriage, which is an under-examined implication of this decision in the context of the vibrant and multivalent nature of marriage politics.

The Reaffirmation of Marriage in a Time of Upheaval

Across the sixties era, the definitions and politics of marriage pivoted between obligations and rights. On the one hand, there was a consistency between the understanding of marriage as fundamental right, and the role of the federal government as a supporter of civil rights and equality. On the other hand, there was an antagonistic relationship between marriage as a form of obligation and the critiques of marriage articulated by radical feminist and black power movements. We have seen three areas of controversy that show the centrality of marriage in defining and shaping politics, interests, and political identity during this era: first, Moynihan's focus on family as a solution to racial inequality; second, feminists' challenges to women's obligation to marry and to the patriarchal order established in marriage; and finally, the Supreme Court's assertion of marriage as a fundamental right. Once again, as in other periods, the how, what, and when of marriage became important political questions.

The institution of marriage underwent significant changes during the 1960s and early 1970s. Though challenged to its core, marriage was sustained and even strengthened during this tumultuous period. This happened in part because it straddled competing political, economic, and social frameworks that looked to marriage to address deep inequalities in society. The debates over marriage enacted the competing discourses of obligations and rights as state actors, civil rights activists, and feminists questioned what marriage and family should look like and what it should mean to the state.

Policymakers, in the tradition of the Reconstruction-era Freedmen's Bureau, made family structure and status a focal point in developing federal policy on racial equality by advocating marriage as the obligatory path to full civic inclusion for poor blacks. Feminists also saw marriage as an obligation, but an oppressive one. They argued against the obligation to marry and the pressure to maintain gender roles. On the rights side, the Supreme Court's decision voiding antimiscegenation laws, and the support of that decision by civil rights groups such as the NAACP and American Civil Liberties Union, positioned marriage as a right integral to individual civil rights, self-determination, and freedoms.

The ideological confluences between the legal right to marry as defined by the court and federal policies that focused on family structure were not part of a grand scheme; rather they show that in moments of crisis and change, when notions of equality and inclusion are shifting, political and institutional actors turn to marriage in both complementary and contradictory ways. Moynihan and President Johnson turned to marriage to address racial inequality, as did the Supreme Court in *Loving v. Virginia*. But *Loving* also constituted a move toward challenging accepted notions of race categories by asserting marriage as liberatory, while the Moynihan and Johnson policies reinscribed those categories by proposing to "fix" black marriage and family structure to cure poverty. Marriage remained a central institution because, though it was threatened by feminists and the sexual revolution, it was invoked to manage and domesticate the emergent crisis of civil rights.

The obligation and rights forces within marriage were in a tug-of-war, shaping marriage as an institution and revealing it to be changeable over time. In the Reconstruction era, marriage shaped the contours of the obligations and rights of ex-slaves transitioning out of slavery and into citizenship. In the Progressive era, marital obligations and rights were crucial to conceptions of belonging and national identity, set against rising immigration rates. In the 1960s, the different political uses of marriage were part of the decade-long call to address the pressing issues of social inequality. In the same way that political elites looked to family structure to deal with racial and economic hierarchies, the Supreme Court decision in *Loving* dealt with marriage as the last step in overturning Jim Crow laws. Feminists believed that the institution of marriage was at the heart of their inequality, preventing women from becoming free, equal, and self-determined individuals. These three views represent very different ways to address social inequality. At the same time, the common focus on marriage reveals and raises the obstacles to achieving full social equality.

The rights and obligations of marriage were central to defining left, liberal, and progressive politics, as well as the conservative agenda that would take off in the 1980s and become entrenched by the 1990s. Marriage was not just one of many areas of political formation, but in fact it was central to debates that challenged, changed, and restructured the social and political order of the nation. The privatization of marriage that resulted from the *Loving* decision opened the door for challenges decades later around the right to same-sex marriage. And marriage's obligatory cast that began with the Moynihan Report would become a key battleground in the culture wars of the 1990s and in the 1996 Welfare Reform Act, which I discuss in Chapter 4. The politics of marriage during this period reveals marriage as central both to the reestablishment of order and to the seeds of change for re-casting that order.

Chapter 4

"Marriage Is the Foundation
of a Successful Society"

The political and cultural challenges sparked in the 1960s and early 1970s by the civil rights movement, feminism, gay liberation, and the counterculture congealed by the 1990s into what came to be known as the "culture wars." The term, as employed by conservatives, was meant to evoke a historic conflict pitting those Americans who believed in a nation of traditional heterosexual two-parent families, religious morality, law and order, and economic independence against feminists, gays and lesbians, criminals, rioters, welfare cheats, and those who mocked the Christian values upon which the nation rested. Marriage became a major front in these wars. It was there that the battles over race, poverty, gender, and sexuality were waged across the decade.

The role of marriage was central to the political developments of this period, as various actors turned to the institution to affirm, contest, or amend the Great Society policy orientation towards promoting civil rights and alleviating poverty. Through debates over marriage, conservative policymakers successfully redefined and reframed rights issues, the claims to self-determination and equality of the 1960s, to "lifestyle" issues that selfishly threatened the stability of the nation. The decade of the 1990s saw rapid rejection of the progressive policies and ideals of the 1960s, the effects of which continued into the twenty-first century. Thus marriage was not simply one of many sites in which the country moved politically rightward, but *the* institution through which to contest three major political legacies of the 1960s. The first was the attempt to roll back changes in race and gender equality. The second was the effort to reaffirm heteronormativity at a moment when gays and lesbians increasingly challenged their own cultural stigmatization and marginalization. The third was the assault on New Deal and Great Society social programs. The simultaneous promotion of marriage for welfare recipients and the prohibition of marriage for gays and lesbians meant that marriage in this decade became a form of state obligation for some, and a denied right for others. State actors and others employed marriage in the dismantling of welfare, the curtailment of gay rights, and the promotion of a particular vision of family. Whereas during the Progressive Era marriage policies and obligations helped create a national uniformity in the context of a solidifying nation-state, in the 1990s, marriage policies and obligations helped to end an "era of big government" under a Democratic president.

For the Republican Party and conservative activists, marriage associatively linked the black poor, feminists, and gays and lesbians in a narrative of national decline. For Bill Clinton, a centrist Democratic president who faced strong challenges from an antagonistic Congress after 1994, marriage provided a way to underscore his political differences from the progressive liberals in his party by focusing on issues of race, poverty, feminism, and gay rights. Two major pieces of federal legislation that received bipartisan support during the first Clinton administration placed marriage at the center of political questions of equality, inclusion, and the role of government: the Personal Responsibility and Work Opportunity Reconciliation Act (PRWORA) passed on August 22, 1996, and the Defense of Marriage Act (DOMA) passed a month later on September 21, 1996. Each law responded to political and cultural rifts originating in the 1960s, and each addressed perceived threats to marriage. PRWORA proclaimed that "marriage is the foundation of a successful society,"[1] while DOMA asserted itself as an act to "define and protect the institution of marriage."[2] PRWORA made marriage a key remedy for problems of poverty, while DOMA shielded the institution of marriage from participation by lesbian, gay, bisexual, and transgender (LGBT) citizens. On the one hand, with PRWORA, the state promoted marriage as an obligation and means to full civic inclusion and citizenship benefits; on the other, with DOMA, the state denied marriage as a right and thus circumscribed equality and citizenship for some groups. Together they placed the institution of marriage at the center of political debates on national identity, economic entitlements, gay rights, and the rise of conservative anti-statism.

Cultural and fiscal conservatism shaped the political climate in which Congress enacted PRWORA and DOMA. Both conservative Republicans and centrist Democrats argued for a return to two-parent, heterosexual, and monogamous families as the basis of American political culture and against the increasing cultural visibility of homosexuality, reproductive rights, no-fault divorce policies, and the welfare state. Marriage promotion, as seen in PRWORA, became a popular antidote to perceived excesses of government spending, and the denial of marriage rights through DOMA aimed at restraining sexual freedom and choice as a way to protect the institution of marriage itself.

This period is marked by a return to Progressive Era definitions of marriage as a regulatory lever, enforcing the obligation to marry and limiting the right to marry in the name of the public interest, and a turning away from the view that marriage is a fundamental right. Over time and through the competing and shifting definitions of marriage, as an obligation that would shore up societal norms or as a right of personal fulfillment, marriage became a central vehicle through which the legacy of the 1960s and the political tensions over race, gender, and sexuality were debated. In this context, PRWORA and DOMA defined a political, though temporary, settlement between a Democratic president and Republican Congress, and a middle ground between accepting the social and cultural changes represented by the 1960s and a turn to more traditional values. Marriage became a crucial nexus for the allocation and limitation of public and private rights and benefits—whether through promotion of marriage in welfare policies or denial of marriage to gays and lesbians—imposing significant cultural, economic, and legal consequences for those vulnerable to this political reframing of the meaning of, and access to, the institution of marriage.

Changing Trends and Views of Marriage since the 1960s

Marriage underwent a number of interrelated changes in the wake of the 1960s, with far-reaching effects. Sexual and familial behavior shifted dramatically. As counterculture upheavals challenged the norms underlying sexual identity and traditional notions of marriage and family, American society witnessed a gradual shift toward more open definitions of gender identity, sexual relations and family.[3] In Reconstruction marriage was linked to citizenship rights. This development was halted in the Progressive era, and revisited in a different form in the 1960s, when the popular imagination increasingly defined marriage as an individual choice and its goal as personal fulfillment. At the same time, the loosening of gendered division of labor and changing norms about sexuality opened up possibilities for marriage between two people of the same sex.

As historian John D'Emilio has argued, the family and living arrangements of heterosexual Americans had become "bewilderingly" variable.[4] Divorce became commonplace. There was greater access to abortion, and there was an increase in the number of women having children outside of marriage. The number of single-parent households grew exponentially. Women were participating more and more in the paid labor force, and birth rates sank.[5] In the wake of the cultural changes in regard to sexuality in the 1960s, and with the rise of public gay activism, the 1970s saw increasing social acceptance of gays and lesbians.[6]

Since the 1970s, cohabitation among heterosexuals had become so commonplace that the Census Bureau struggled with how to categorize and count these new familial arrangements.[7] Based on such changes in families throughout the 1990s, in 2002 the American Law Institute published *Principles of the Law of Family Dissolution: Analysis and Recommendations*. According to the institute's press release, the recommendations offered a "coherent legal framework, sensitive to both the traditional value systems within which most families are formed and the nontraditional realities and expectations of other families, a framework the earlier drafts of which have already begun to influence both courts and legislatures."[8]

Deeply related to these social, personal, economic, and institutional changes was the idea that marriage was a fundamental civil right and not a mandatory practice. Over the latter half of the twentieth century, marriage was understood primarily through a liberal, rights-oriented framework. Institutionally, after the *Loving v. Virginia* decision in 1967, the political definition of marriage shifted toward being a right and a matter of individual choice. The Supreme Court continued the *Loving* precedent into the 1970s and 1980s by rendering marriage a fundamental right. In *Turner v. Safley*, a 1987 case that concerned the right of prisoners to marry, the court declared that "the decision to marry is a fundamental right."[9] In the 1978 case *Zablocki v Redhail*, the court maintained that marriage was "of fundamental importance to all individuals," "one of the 'basic civil rights of man,'" and "the most important relation in life."[10] The court also noted that "the right to marry is part of the fundamental 'right to privacy'" in the U.S. Constitution.[11] With these rulings, the freedom to marry and the freedom to choose one's partner in marriage had been established as fundamental rights. Yet, as the 1990s began, the marriage pendulum would begin to swing back toward the view that marriage was an obligation in service of the stability of the nation.

Culture Wars and the Marriage Crisis:
From Personal Fulfillment to Selfishness

The assertion of marriage as an individual choice and a right were met with growing opposition from an ascendant movement of cultural conservatism dating from the Reagan era. In 1983 conservative activist Phyllis Schlafly organized the STOP ERA campaign, which argued that "equal rights" had negative effects for women because they would take away privileges and protections that women require.[12] And in the mid- to late 1980s, the Christian Right began to articulate a politics of "family values." According to many voices on the Right, white middle-class professional women, abortion advocates, welfare mothers, gays and lesbians, and liberalized divorce laws all threatened both basic gender norms of society and the institution of marriage that grounded these norms.[13]

The rifts of the 1960s over questions of race, gender, sexuality, and class defined the main terms of conflict in U.S. politics for the following four decades, as the Republican and Democratic parties realigned along consistent ideological lines of conservatism and liberalism.[14] The term "culture wars" gained currency after the 1991 publication of sociologist James Davison Hunter's *Culture Wars: The Struggle to Define America*, which argued that a deep cleavage existed within American culture over issues of gender, family, sexuality, religion, and race, among others.[15] The term became more salient after what became known as Pat Buchanan's "culture wars" speech at the 1992 Republican National Convention, where he spoke of feminism, gay rights, and the Los Angeles riots in the wake of the Rodney King verdict as sites of skirmishes in that so-called war.[16] Over the course of the 1990s, a full-fledged "marriage crisis" became the focus of media and political attention, specifically concerned with who should and should not marry—that is, with the obligations and rights of marriage. Well-funded

secular and religiously based conservative institutes, think tanks, and programs focused on marriage began to proliferate, among them the National
Marriage Project, Focus on the Family, Smart Marriages, Marriage Savers,
the Center for Marriage and Family at the Institute for American Values,
and the Institute for Marriage and Public Policy. Pundits such as Margaret
Gallagher and Robert Rector significantly raised their public profile by promoting marriage.

For conservatives, the different strands of culture war rhetoric were woven together after the April 1992 Los Angeles riots, in which South Central
Los Angeles erupted in five days of violent reaction to the acquittal of four
white officers accused of beating a black motorist, Rodney King. This trau-
matic episode, the most severe social unrest since the New York City Draft
Riots of 1863, left 53 dead, over two thousand wounded, and between $800
million and $2 billion in property damage. The riots brutally exposed the
conflicts over race, class, and culture still unresolved since the 1960s, but the
meaning of the riots themselves was open to interpretation.

Vice President Dan Quayle delivered a polemical speech on the riots to
the Commonwealth Club of California in May 1992, saying, "In a nutshell:
I believe the lawless social anarchy which we saw is directly related to the
breakdown of family structure." This diagnosis echoed Daniel Patrick Moynihan's culture of poverty argument from 1965, linking black poverty to marriage and family. Quayle also connected black lawlessness to the excesses of
feminism in popular culture: "It doesn't help matters when prime time TV
has Murphy Brown—a character who supposedly epitomizes today's intel-
ligent, highly paid, professional woman—mocking the importance of fathers,
by bearing a child alone, and calling it just another 'lifestyle choice.'"[17] Fears
of black criminality and opposition to women's rights had been staples of
conservative backlash politics since the 1960s, but in this calculus they were
each part of a causal loop that threatened traditional values: black communities were the leading edge of family breakdown, while white feminists
mocked the importance of fatherhood and instead legitimated single-parent-
ing. As *Time* magazine observed, "critics suspected that the Vice President's
remarks fit into a calculated strategy to suggest that L.A.'s rioters, who were
mostly black and Hispanic, have in common with feminists and other Democrats a shoddier moral standard than nice people (who therefore should vote
Republican)."[18] Although Quayle's framing of black poverty and feminism
together through the lens of traditional marriage would become hegemonic

within a few short years, at the time his comments were controversial enough that he backpedaled within a couple of days, saying that he had "the greatest respect" for single mothers.[19]

For all the criticism the speech generated, Quayle's remarks garnered considerable support. Among the supporters was scholar and journalist Barbara Dafoe Whitehead, who wrote an influential 1993 article in the *Atlantic Monthly* titled "Dan Quayle Was Right." In it she described a debate in American culture over deeply held and often conflicting values of women's equality and the welfare of the nation's children. She asserted that "all domestic problems" of crime, poor school performance, and unemployment were "closely connected to family breakup."[20] Thus, for Whitehead, the alternative was either supporting women's rights or stabilizing the family and the community. She lamented that Murphy Brown, an unwed mother, was portrayed as honest and courageous, as asserting her rights and demonstrating "true moral heroism." Whitehead argued that disruption of the traditional marital family had far-reaching impact, and that "new families," such as same-sex unions or single mothers, harmed society. "It is not an exaggeration," she wrote, "to characterize [these new families] as a central cause of many of our most vexing social problems. . . . These new families are not an improvement on the nuclear family, nor are they even just as good, whether you look at outcomes for children or outcomes for society as a whole. In short, far from representing social progress, family change represents a stunning example of social regress." The implication was that a woman's right to work outside the home undermined broader social goals and was a form of shameful self-gratification. Women therefore had an obligation to marry, not a right to choose to marry or not.

As cultural conservative discourse and politics continued to develop, controlling out-of-wedlock births and preventing same-sex marriage were twinned as fundamental political problems. Political scientist James Q. Wilson, in a 1996 *Commentary* article, questioned "why an alternative to marriage should be invented and praised when we are having enough trouble maintaining the institution at all." He claimed that same-sex marriage would "call even more seriously into question the role of marriage at a time when the threats to it, ranging from single-parent families to common divorces, have hit record highs."[21] Modern society did not resist same-sex marriages entirely out "irrational prejudice," said Wilson. Rather, he claimed that "marriage is a union, sacred to most, that unites a man and woman together for life." In other words, most societies choose heterosexual unions over homosexual unions because "these distinctions involve the nature of marriage and thus the very meaning—even more, the very possibility—of society."[22]

William Bennett, President George H. W. Bush's drug czar and a cultural conservative critic, made what became the core argument of social conservatives: gay marriage was a countercultural legacy of the 1960s. Writing in the *Washington Post* in 1996, he said, "The institution of marriage is already reeling because of the effects of the sexual revolution, no-fault divorce and out-of-wedlock birth. We have reaped the consequences of its devaluation. It is exceedingly imprudent to conduct a radical, untested and inherently flawed social experiment on an institution that is the keystone on the arch of civilization."[23] Bennett linked changing sexual mores to conceptions of marriage as a private right (which is what socially authorizes no-fault divorce), to illegitimacy, and to same-sex marriage. In doing so, he articulated the connection for social conservatives between welfare and gay rights in the "keystone" issue of marriage. The absence of marriage among welfare recipients and the possibility of marriage for gays and lesbians threatened to bring civilization crashing down. The laws that eventually emerged out of these debates and arguments were PRWORA and DOMA, which both defined marriage as something other than a love relationship or a site of emotional fulfillment, as it had been articulated in *Loving v. Virginia* in 1967. As political figures like Bennett used debates over marriage to give expression to broader political claims, marriage itself moved from an institution grounded in individual rights to an institution grounded in national obligations.

The Personal Responsibility and Work Opportunity Act of 1996

Before passage of the Personal Responsibility and Work Opportunity Act in 1996, there was considerable public debate on the shortcomings of the welfare system and Congress's proposed solutions. Notions of personal responsibility and citizenship framed the reform debate. Conservative critics of welfare policy questioned whether poor single mothers deserved to receive government financial aid, and the "problem of dependency" emerged as a common theme.[24] Illegitimacy allegedly forced the care of children and mothers onto the state, so that the decline of the two-parent heterosexual family ensured by marriage increased in tandem with the expansion of the welfare state. Such criticisms, however, arose not only because poor single mothers were economically dependent; they were also *unmarried*. In this logic, the system encouraged welfare recipients to renege on their obligation to marry and to rely instead on what critics described as handouts. It encouraged them to be irresponsible. In response to this perceived crisis, policymakers succeeded in dismantling welfare entitlements by encouraging work and marriage. The notion that marriage ought to be an obligation of poor women went hand in hand with the shrinking of big government.

Both conservative and liberal social and political scientists in the 1980s and 1990s continued to look at marriage and family as a central factor in explaining black poverty, a holdover from Daniel Patrick Moynihan's attempt to advance this perspective in the 1960s. Yet, Moynihan was a liberal democrat arguing for government policy, whereas these views were picked by conservatives arguing to limit government. Political scientist Charles Murray, a fellow at the conservative American Enterprise Institute, author of *Losing Ground* (1984), coauthor of *The Bell Curve* (1994), and an early advocate of welfare reform policy, believed that marriage was the only economically and socially viable domestic relationship. Murray argued that the then-current welfare program, called Aid to Families with Dependent Children (AFDC), which granted aid on the basis of single motherhood, actually encouraged women to have more children out of wedlock. Linking this directly to the 1960s, Murray blamed "the revolution in social policy" that started with Johnson. For Murray, the idea of an underclass, or culture of poverty, defined the behavior of the racialized poor as both different and deviant.[25]

Throughout the 1990s, Murray framed the absence of marriage as not just a political problem but *the* political problem of the day. "My proposition," he wrote in a 1993 *Wall Street Journal* opinion piece, "is that illegitimacy is the single most important social problem of our time—more important that crime, drugs, poverty, illiteracy, welfare or homelessness because it drives everything else."[26] Marriage in this view does more than socialize citizens; it is an institution that organizes both social and economic relations of dependency. Murray posited marriage as an institution that stabilizes society by controlling sexual behavior. Order comes, as Murray described, from "thick walls of rewards and penalties" generated and maintained through marriage. It is, in other words, an obligation of poor citizens. For Murray, marriage sets norms and rules of sexual conduct; assigns the roles of husband and wife, father and mother; sets the boundaries of who can and should be married and who cannot; and, in the context of both welfare and same-sex marriage debates, controls those inside and outside the institution. It also importantly limits the relationship between individuals and the state.

Conservatives were not the only ones to tie welfare and race to marriage. In his influential 1987 book, *The Truly Disadvantaged*, the social democratic sociologist William Julius Wilson presented an economic argument, making the case that the truly disadvantaged (the new category of permanent, generationally immobile poor made up primarily of black unmarried mothers and the jobless fathers of their children) came into being largely as the result of the deindustrialization of the inner city. This situation, Wilson asserted, caused "social isolation" and the creation of an underclass "whose behavior contrasted sharply with the behavior of the general population."[27] Declines in marriage rates did not cause poverty but rather were a symptom of poverty.

Wilson's explanation for the decline in marriage rates received a great deal of attention. He asserted that the decrease in marriage rates among blacks—particularly among poor, inner-city black—was due primarily to declining black male employment levels, resulting in a shrinking pool of acceptable marriage partners for black women. To support his claim, Wilson constructed a "male marriageable pool index," or MMPI, which represented the number of employed men per women of the same age and race. The MMPI for young blacks trended downward from the late 1960s through the early 1980s, a period of rapid decline in marriage. Wilson claimed that, "clearly, what our 'male marriageable pool index' reveals is a long-term decline in the proportion of black men, and particularly young black men, who are in a position to support a family."[28] Wilson concluded from these coinciding trends that declining black male employment was a major source of the declining rates of marriage among blacks. While he took pains to argue that the problem was fundamentally economic rather than cultural, he still asserted that the dissolution of the black community and of black families created a destructive culture in the inner cities.[29] Although Wilson strongly opposed PRWORA, he served as an informal advisor on poverty issues to Clinton in the early 1990s. Clinton, in seeking to take the "family values" ground from Republicans, drew on Wilson's ideas about marriage and poverty while ignoring his equal emphasis on employment and economic opportunity.[30]

In a speech titled "The New Covenant: Responsibility and Rebuilding of American Community," then-governor Clinton, having just declared his run for the presidency, announced his ambition to "end welfare as we have known it." He couched welfare reform within a larger framework of mutual responsibility, calling for a "new covenant" between the government and citizens. Clinton's notion of individual or "personal responsibility" was both "prowork" and "profamily."[31] This linking of responsibility to employment and family was a key principle of the Democratic Leadership Council (DLC), the organization of centrist Democrats founded after the 1988 presidential election to steer the party rightward, away from a liberalism they saw as no longer viable after the Reagan Revolution in the 1980s. Asserting that "new approaches should emphasize individual and parental responsibility, strong families and the moral and cultural values that most Americans share," the DLC placed the heterosexual, married, two-parent family at the center of its social policies. Clinton, longtime member and former chair of the DLC, carried these principles forward into his 1992 presidential campaign and into his administration.[32]

The DLC also advanced a conservative antistatist politics, articulated most succinctly in Clinton's campaign promise that "the era of big government is over."[33] This small-government principle dovetailed with the argument that fathers, not the state, had to be held responsible for children born out of wedlock.[34] The DLC's position was that families were in crisis due in part to "sharply rising rates of divorce, births to unwed mothers, runaway fathers, and irresponsible parents." The organization argued that "forty percent of our welfare dollars are spent on children with fathers who could contribute to their support, and too many women are forced to bear the financial burden of raising a child alone," saying that "a growing body of evidence supports the conclusion that the intact, two-parent family is usually best suited to the task of providing for the economic and moral well-being of children."[35] The DLC also supported the paid employment of women as a path toward independence. Thus, the solution of work and marriage, meant to appeal to both Republicans and moderate Democrats, shifted the need to fix the broken system of welfare to a campaign to right a problem of dependency through fostering responsibility, characterized by some legislators as "tough love."[36]

These welfare debates descended both from the Moynihan Report of thirty years prior and, even more directly, from the Freedmen's Bureau link between work and marriage in the Reconstruction era. In all cases, the link between work and marriage was designed as an alternative to government entitlements or state benefits. Unlike these earlier periods, however, by the 1990s, the assertion was that government handouts *caused and encouraged* dependency. An early attempt to reform welfare in Wisconsin also drew on work and marriage as opposed to the state. Republican Wisconsin governor Tommy Thompson began reforming his state's welfare program as early as 1987. In 1993 he proposed replacing the state's AFDC program with an employment program called "Wisconsin Works," which went into effect in 1997. However, prior to proposing his work program, Thompson was already focused on marriage. In 1992 he introduced his Bridefare program, which encouraged poor, single teenage mothers to get married. At a conference in 1995, he explained, "The welfare system is a perfect example of what I refer to as government sense. When you pay people not to work, not to get married, and to have children out of wedlock, guess what happens? People do not work, they do not get married, and they have more children out of wedlock."[37] Thus for Thompson, getting people married and getting people working were ways to knock that "government sense" right out of them.

On the national level, House Republicans led with their 1994 Contract with America manifesto and set welfare reform as a priority for the 104th Congress. House hearings starting in 1995 featured testimony that built the case for replacing welfare entitlements with marriage and work. Peter J. Ferrara, a senior fellow at the National Center for Policy Analysis, testified that "the current system [was] not just a failure" but was "counterproductive" because it promoted behavior "such as nonwork, nonmarriage, illegitimacy and family break up."[38] In welfare communities, said Ferrara, "the whole idea of marriage has been obliterated."[39] This recalls the postbellum Freedmen's Bureau accounts of the freed slave's view of marriage. Yet, Ferrara blamed the government, whereas the Freedmen Bureau officials blamed slavery. Foreshadowing later policy initiatives under President George W. Bush, Penny Young, representing the conservative women's organization called Concerned Women for America, argued, "As the cornerstone to a healthy future, government should work to encourage marriage, not undermine it."[40]

Woven into the debates over welfare, and particularly apparent in the 1995–96 congressional hearings on welfare reform, were claims that marriage was an obligation of citizens. Advocates of welfare reform regularly invoked racist and gender-biased images of "welfare queens" out to cheat taxpayers, refusing to marry and having children out of wedlock. As Florida representative E. Clay Shaw, Jr. (R) testified at the March 1996 "Causes of Poverty, with a Focus on Out-of-Wedlock Births" hearing, "a primary cause of the trend towards birth outside marriage is the dramatic increase in sexual activity outside marriage that has afflicted culture since the sixties." He argued that poverty could only be fought by "changing values." What was characterized as freedom from sexual controls and marriage by feminists in the 1960s was reframed in the 1990s as irresponsible behavior that caused poverty. He said, "The fastest ticket to poverty is to have a child without being married."[41] This refusal to marry in particular harmed children. Representative James M. Talent of Missouri (R) testified at the same hearing in March 1996 that "the growth in illegitimacy is the single most important change in our country in the last generation. It is a fact so powerful that it annihilates all other facts. Nothing the government does in school, day care, job training, family planning or any other programs can overcome the damage done to our children."[42]

Clinton vetoed two early versions of the PRWORA bill, for two reasons, according to Ron Haskins, senior fellow at the Brookings Institution and welfare policy expert: (1) he thought the bills were too punitive; and (2) he was trying to force Republicans to make the final legislation more amenable to Democratic support.[43] Democrats were concerned about putting young mothers and their children at risk by cutting off too much aid. At the same time, according to political scientist Gwendolyn Mink, Democrats supported the bill's focus on marriage promotion. The revisions that Clinton agreed to included paternity establishment, which had negative effects on women in the program.[44] After some back and forth, half the Democrats in Congress voted in favor of the bill and Clinton signed PRWORA on August 22, 1996.

The legislation changed the basic structure of the American welfare system.[45] It eliminated the statutory entitlement to poverty assistance: the need for benefits alone was no longer a sufficient requirement to demonstrate eligibility.[46] Instead, an applicant had to fulfill other requirements in order to obtain aid, and states were required to observe the limitations established by the welfare law. Any state that did not adhere to the federal regulations risked losing block grant funds. The major program in the welfare system prior to 1996 was Aid to Families with Dependent Children (AFDC), which was now replaced by Temporary Assistance to Needy Families (TANF). Under PRWORA, every state was required to compel each TANF recipient to work in order to receive benefits, and a lifetime limit of five years of aid was imposed.[47] In some cases, the establishment of paternity also became a precondition for establishing eligibility for benefits.[48]

The first passage in PRWORA's purpose clause incorporates the promotion of both work and marriage: "The purpose of this part is to increase the flexibility of States in operating a program designed to 1) provide assistance to needy families so that children may be cared for in their own homes or in the homes of relatives; 2) end the dependence of needy parents on government benefits by promoting job preparation, work and marriage; 3) prevent and reduce the incidence of out-of-wedlock pregnancies and establish annual numerical goals for preventing the incidence of these pregnancies; 4) and encourage the formation and maintenance of two-parent families."[49] Two of these four program goals did not specify need, but instead established marriage and two-parent families as of central importance. Work and marriage were posited as alternatives to government benefits and were seen as encouraging the responsibility of individuals.

While jobs and workfare framed the law primarily at this point, the act did provide bonus grants to states that implemented abstinence and marriage education initiatives. A total of $100 million was set aside for bonuses to the five states that had the greatest success in reducing out of wedlock birth rates while also reducing abortion rates. TANF money was appropriated to marriage promotion programs, allowing states to administer and provide welfare funds through nongovernmental entities. Arizona and Oklahoma were the first states to use TANF money to fund marriage initiatives, followed by Utah and West Virginia. Beginning in 1996, West Virginia provided a $100 monthly welfare bonus to recipients who married, though the program would eventually be suspended.[50]

In early versions of the welfare reform legislation, Clinton was criticized process for putting more emphasis on the role of work rather than marriage as the solution for dependency. Robert Rector of the Heritage Foundation in particular said that Clinton's bill did not go far enough in promoting marriage, as it only proposed employment as a means of exiting welfare—and Rector believed this would not reduce the welfare rolls. Rector continued to push marriage promotion, claiming in a House hearing prior to passage that "marriage still remains the most effective mechanism for reducing dependency."[51] The only real solution to the problem of poverty was promoting "marriage and reducing out-of-wedlock births," not training and putting a "lot of people in the labor force."[52] Replaying debates about poverty from the

1960s, Rector argued for a marriage solution to dependency over economic remedies, a formulation that offered marriage as a structural solution to poverty. By the time welfare reform was reauthorized under George W. Bush in 2005, marriage became the central language through which to discuss and address economic issues and inequalities.

The development of marriage promotion in welfare programs and the focus on marriage as an obligation constituted a contingent political settlement between anti–Great Society conservatives, social traditionalists, and liberal culture-of-poverty proponents seeking to come to terms with the social crises laid bare by the 1992 Los Angeles riots and the growing cultural wars dividing the nation ideologically. It allowed Democrats to signal that they too could support small government programs. And it served to reassert traditional gender norms in marriage.

Initially, the object of this settlement was poor mothers, especially poor single black mothers. However, preventing same-sex marriage was just as important in reconciling these various political stances. By comparing the debates surrounding PRWORA and DOMA, we can see the continued interplay between assertions of marriage as a right and marriage as an obligation. By the end of the 1990s, it would be the language of obligation that would come to dominate this debate.

The Defense of Marriage Act of 1996

On May 7, 1996, at the same time that welfare reform was being debated and the importance of marriage as an obligation was being asserted, legislators were arguing to limit the right of gays and lesbians to marry. Georgia representative Bob Barr (R) introduced the Defense of Marriage bill that would amend the U.S. Code to define the terms "marriage" and "spouse": "the word 'marriage' means only the legal union of one man and one woman as husband and wife, and the word 'spouse' refers only to a person of the opposite sex who is a husband or wife."[53] This bill constituted an assertion of government authority rather than a retreat from it. The congressional debate that followed underscored the longstanding dynamic of marriage's role as a contested right, which fell in the tradition of antimiscegenation laws during Reconstruction and eugenic marriage laws during the Progressive Era. Similar to these other laws, this attempt to limit to marriage was used to assert and maintain a heterosexual social and political hierarchy and stave off broader social changes.

At the same time, the limit of marriage in this case reveals a contradiction at the heart of the conservative politics of this decade. While DOMA was an attack on 1960s rights gains, it was also an extension of state power. The debate was framed by questions of who should be allowed to marry, and the stakes of civic membership, morality, and norms involved. Congress passed the Defense of Marriage Act by a vote of 85-14 in the Senate and 342-67 in the House, and Clinton signed the bill into law. DOMA defines marriage as the union of one man and one woman, excluding same-sex unions from recognition under federal law. Under the act, states can legalize gay marriages, but other states do not have to honor those marriages. Gay couples are also ineligible for spousal benefits granted by Social Security and Medicare and any other federal benefit programs reserved for different-sex married couples.[54]

DOMA made two significant changes to the institution of marriage. First, it created for the first time federal definitions of "marriage" and "spouse." DOMA establishes that where the word "spouse" appears in a federal law or regulation, the term refers exclusively to a member of a mixed-sex marriage. Second, DOMA provided that no state had to acknowledge marriage in another state despite Article IV of the Constitution, the full faith and credit clause. This clause requires each state to recognize the public acts, records, and judicial proceedings of all other states. But DOMA provided that no state "shall be required to give effect to any public act, record, or judicial proceeding of any other state respecting a relationship between persons of the same sex that is treated as a marriage under the laws of such other State."[55] DOMA also invited the states to increase their autonomy from one another by banning same-sex marriage.

DOMA legislation was part of the conservative backlash against growing gay and lesbian activism and visibility. Societal acceptance of gays and lesbians had been increasing since the 1970s, and the 1992 presidential election was widely considered a landmark for the visibility of gays and lesbians in U.S. politics.[56] Bill Clinton came into office with campaign promises to repeal the military's ban on gay service members, to focus on HIV/AIDS, and to pursue other pro-gay initiatives. At the same time, however, antigay forces were effectively mobilizing, painting gays and lesbians as deviants who threatened the nation's moral character (and its children). In the mid-1980s, groups in Colorado, Oregon, Maine, and six other states used antigay ballot initiatives to build local organizations. By the early 1990s, there were more than sixty antigay referenda around the country. In Oregon, for example, there were sixteen local antigay initiatives in 1993 and eleven more passed in 1994. Nationwide, gay rights supporters lost about three-quarters of these anti-gay ballot initiative fights.[57] Debates over gay rights took center stage in the 1990s, with the nation polarized between extending civil rights and condemning sexual practices and behavior.

Efforts to legalize gay marriage had been making their way through the courts beginning in the 1970s, as gay rights activists made legal challenges to state bans on same-sex marriage. But marriage became a central focus of gay and lesbian politics with the 1993 Hawaii Supreme Court case *Baehr v. Lewin*, which involved three same-sex couples who sued the state of Hawaii after being denied marriage licenses. The couples alleged that the state's action violated the equal rights provision of Hawaii's constitution, which mandated that all persons, regardless of gender, should be given equal protection of the law. The state marriage law did not specify that only male-female couples could be granted marriage licenses. The Hawaii Supreme Court decided in the couples' favor, declaring that denying same-sex couples a marriage license was unconstitutional.[58]

The legal case in Hawaii fueled gay rights activism around marriage and also spurred congressional action in the form of DOMA.[59] Some lawmakers in Congress expressed deep concern about the effect that legalizing same-sex marriage in Hawaii would have on other states, federal laws, the institution of marriage, traditional notions of morality, and state sovereignty.[60] On July 9, 1996, two months before DOMA was signed into law, the House Judiciary Committee submitted a report written by Florida Republican Charles T. Canady. The report explained that the Hawaii ruling brought into question states' rights vis-à-vis marriage, raising complicated issues around federalism. Thus the question of same-sex marriage was being reframed from a rights question to a structural question. In the report, the question was posed: "Which law governs—Hawaii's, as represented by the 'marriage' license, or the law of the forum state, which does not recognize same-sex 'marriage'?"[61] The report also noted that individual states had been "moved by the uncertain interstate implications" raised by Hawaii's decision and "attempted to bolster their own public policy regarding traditional, heterosexual-only marriage laws." The report went on to explain that "as of July 1, 1996, 14 states had enacted new laws designed to protect against an impending assault on their marriage laws."[62]

This situation, said the report, "is enough to persuade the [House] Committee that federal legislation is warranted."[63]

According to the report, there were four "Government interests that were advanced by DOMA," which centered on curtailing the fundamental right to marry.[64] The first was to "defend and nurture" the institution of traditional heterosexual marriage. The second was to defend traditional notions of morality. The third was to protect state sovereignty and democratic self-governance and the right of the states to formulate their own public policy regarding the legal recognition of same-sex unions. The fourth was to preserve scarce government resources. The language of "defend," "protect," and "preserve" suggests that the gay and lesbian call to marry was an assault upon rather than an appeal to the principles of equality and nondiscrimination. Marriage was shifting from a fundamental right to a limited right that was a structural anchor of the cultural, moral, political, and economic patterns of society.

The committee's report emphasized the importance of understanding the "nature of the orchestrated legal assault being waged against traditional heterosexual marriage by gay rights groups and their lawyers." [65] Where welfare recipients were seen to be rebuffing the system, gay activists were seen to be ruthlessly invading it. DOMA was thus necessary to prevent the "radical" effort to redefine marriage by extending it to homosexual couples. In claiming marriage as a full fundamental right, same-sex unions would be "equal" to heterosexual ones and would take away the power of marriage to make distinctions; in other words, it would weaken the institution. "What is really at stake," said the report, was "whether the law of this country should treat homosexual relationships as morally equivalent to heterosexual relationships." Allowing gay couples to marry would "legitimize unnatural and immoral behavior" and represent "full acceptance" of homosexuality.[66] This framing was consistent with the assertion conservatives had been successfully making since the late 1960s that groups seeking "special rights" were undermining the will of the majority.[67] The will of the majority, from this perspective, was to maintain the primacy of heterosexuality in the state. DOMA would effectively allow states to use the political institution of marriage to draw lines excluding or including certain groups.

The argument outlined in the report in favor of DOMA pulled marriage out of the realm of private decision and individual rights and placed it firmly in the public realm. The report claimed that marriage was not a private affair "but a socially important public concern," primarily because its purpose was procreation. "To discover the 'ends of marriage,'" said the report, "we need only reflect on this central, unimpeachable lesson of human nature," taken from conservative scholar Hadley Arkes: "we are, each of us, born a man or a woman. . . . At its core it is hard to detach marriage from what may be called the natural teleology of the body . . . [to] beget a child."[68] And, "at bottom, civil society has an interest in maintaining and protecting the institution of heterosexual marriage because it has a deep and abiding interest in encouraging responsible procreation and child-rearing. Simply put, government has an interest in marriage because it has an interest in children." This line of reasoning also dovetails with the argument for marriage promotion in welfare to stop entitlements, which was legitimized in the interest of children.

Harkening back to other moments when the right to marry was limited, such as the increase in antimiscegenation laws and persecutions during Reconstruction, and eugenic marriage laws in the Progressive era, marriage was also framed as a public institution in need of defending. It is important to note, however, the transformation in who was defending marriage. During Reconstruction and the Progressive Era it was the courts and judicial elites who guarded the line. In the 1990s, by contrast, it was Congress, speaking in the name of a popular mandate, that was calling to limit the right. The DOMA debate recast marriage from a rights-based issue of the courts to a policy concern of legislators and voters. Terrance Tom, a Hawaii state legislator, testifying before the committee, claimed that "I do know this: No single individual, no matter how wise and learned in the law, should be invested with the power to overturn fundamental social policies against the will of the people." He then concluded that "changes to public policies are matters reserved to legislative bodies, and not to the judiciary."[69] And homosexuality and marriage were positioned as areas of public policy. As Arkes explained in a submitted statement, "Congress, with this move [DOMA], brings this issue [homosexuality] back into the public arena of deliberation."[70] Marriage was not a protected fundamental right but was a matter subject to democratic agency, whose confines should be open to discussion and democratic debate. Marriage was cast as a state-conferred legal partnership that could be granted or withheld as society dictated.

Republicans strongly supported DOMA, and the 1996 Republican Party platform explicitly endorsed it. Democrats were divided, but Clinton supported the legislation. As early as February, he spoke on the issue at the National Prayer Breakfast:

We know that ultimately this is an affair of the heart—an affair of the heart that has enormous economic and political and social implications for America, but, most importantly, has moral implications, because families are ordained by God as a way of giving children and their parents the chance to live up to the fullest of their God-given capacities. And when we save them and strengthen them, we overcome the notion that self-gratification is more important than our obligations to others; we overcome the notion that is so prevalent in our culture that life is just a series of responses to impulses, and instead is a whole pattern, with a fabric that should be pleasing to God.[71]

Here Clinton, like Whitehead and Quayle, reframed gay rights as "self-gratification." He suggested that rights claims are selfish, and deny the importance of the "whole pattern" of life. A few months later, as DOMA was being considered in Congress, Clinton told *The Advocate*, a gay and lesbian news magazine, that "if Congress sends me the Defense of Marriage Act in the form now being considered, I will sign it." But he suggested that his position was as strategic as it was principled in regard to the potency of marriage politics, saying, "I also strongly believe that issues relating to gays and lesbians should not be used to tear our communities apart."[72]

Along with the House Judiciary Committee report arguments in favor of DOMA, Clinton's comments starkly reveal the tension between obligations and rights that has been central to shaping the institution of marriage. Like Vice President Quayle and journalist Barbara Dafoe Whitehead in the welfare debates, Clinton announces himself squarely on the side of redefining marriage as a societal obligation. The call for equal rights should not "tear the community apart." Indeed, the report itself was a collection of various moralizing and normalizing arguments that marriage was a structural obligation rather than a right of personal fulfillment. The denial of marriage rights to same-sex couples was argued and legitimized as an issue of societal stability in the name of protecting children, just as marriage promotion and marriage as an obligation were in welfare reform. Here, there is no contradiction between the promotion of marriage to welfare recipients and the denial of marriage to same sex couples.

At the same time, the negation of marriage as a right also does broader political labor. It limits civic inclusion, placing certain groups outside the boundaries of the nation. This limitation is similar to the logic behind antimiscegenation statutes during Reconstruction. Though ex-slaves were granted the right to marry and to form families when they were emancipated, this right was limited by race. African American rights to marriage and family were limited in the name of the states' responsibility to maintain the racial order of things, and to maintain societal stability in general. Echoing Reconstruction-era arguments against interracial unions, Representative Barr expressed his support of DOMA prior to the vote, exclaiming that "the very foundations of our society are in danger of being burned. The flames of hedonism, the flames of narcissism, the flames of self-centered morality are licking at the very foundation of our society: the family unit."[73]

Congressional opponents of DOMA, on the other hand, rallied to the side of marriage as a fundamental right. "This bill is a slap in the face of the Declaration of Independence," said Georgia Representative John Lewis (D). "It denies gay men and women the right to liberty and the pursuit of happiness. Marriage is a basic human right." Emphasizing marriage as a personal choice, as opposed to an obligation, Lewis explained, "You cannot tell people they cannot fall in love. Dr. Martin Luther King, Jr., used to say when people talked about interracial marriage and I quote, 'Races do not fall in love and get married. Individuals fall in love and get married.'"[74] Similarly, in the Senate debate, John Kerry said that DOMA was "a stark reminder that all citizens who play by the rules, who pay their taxes, and who contribute to the economic, social, and political vibrancy of this great melting pot do not have equal rights."[75] The references to race and "melting pot" mark an attempt to link marriage rights to civic inclusion. But ultimately, these arguments were overshadowed by the position that states should have the authority to exclude same-sex couples from marriage.

With DOMA, marriage took on the distinctive role of an institution that controls those inside as well as outside its bounds. DOMA enhanced the political role of marriage as well as altered it by federally defining "marriage" and "spouse." As federal legislation, DOMA also reset the terms of the marriage contract, which historically had been defined solely by the states and courts. In other words, as political theorist Anna Marie Smith points out, DOMA asserts that "legislation that defends patriarchal heterosexual marriage is an entirely legitimate governmental activity."[76] The phrase "define and protect" that begins the Act is thus quite apt, although it is more accurate to say that DOMA protects a particular institutional model of marriage as heterosexual and federally secured. DOMA was the first step in reshaping marriage from an individual right protected by the courts to a form of public and social policy to be decided by the legislature. DOMA made the case, which would expand in the subsequent decade, that marriage is a public obligation that functions as an anchor of society, rather than being a right of citizens.

Marital Obligations and Conservatism

As crucial as the *Loving v. Virginia* decision was to the political development of marriage, the passage of both PRWORA and DOMA was equally so. Each piece of legislation asserted that marriage was not a private right or affair, as the *Loving* decision had asserted, but a decidedly public one that some citizens were obligated to undertake and others not. By the end of the 1990s, from the right and center of the political spectrum, the potency of the claim that marriage was a civil right diminished as the notion of marriage as a social obligation took precedence in politics.

Both PRWORA and DOMA served to protect so-called traditional norms and civility in the midst of a social critique of increasing moral breakdown, whereby rights claims of the 1960s were reframed as mere expressions of selfish and self-gratifying wants and desires. Both laws were meant to stabilize the nation's dominant sexual identity at a moment when gays and lesbians threatened to gain the status of cultural normalcy. Finally, both laws served to bolster conservative advocacy of limited federal government on the one hand, and state interest in maintaining morality and heteronormativity on the other. These changes in the laws surrounding marriage began to erode the legal and cultural notion of marriage as a fundamental right. Through these transformations, marriage played a critical role in the rightward movement of the politics and culture of the nation by limiting rights claims to equality and by legitimating notions of small government and public interest.

Once enacted, PRWORA and DOMA set the stage for the robust growth of a movement that would bring together political actors across ideological boundaries and that further sought to address social and political questions. By 2000, both marriage promotion and the prevention of same-sex marriage rights had become the focus of advocacy by an emergent Marriage Movement that portrayed poor single mothers and same-sex couples as marriage offenders. The Great Society programs of the 1960s continued to be contested and the legacy of identity struggles reshaped in a marital politics that emphasized the obligations of citizens, the need for fiscal conservatism, and the legitimacy of government regulation in shaping social values. This movement institutionalized a shift that had been emerging in conservative politics and ideology.

As the question of marriage obligations and rights moved into the next decade, debates intensified over whether marriage rights for gays and lesbians buttressed the institution or threatened it. And were such questions best resolved by voters, legislatures, or judges? At the same time, welfare programs under the next presidential administration continued to shift more funds into marriage-promotion programs, taking marriage out of the realm of welfare and into a larger context of health policy. As a result, marriage became not a practice of self-fulfillment or personal happiness but a social obligation tied to economic status, stability, and order. Marriage was not a right, to be exercised or not, but an obligation in the service of society and nation.

Chapter 5

"We're in a Battle
for the Soul of the Nation"

In the wake of the 1996 PRWORA and DOMA legislation, two major developments in the political institution of marriage challenged the settlements temporarily secured by those landmark acts. One was the emergence of a national Marriage Movement, a phenomenon expressed at the local, state, and national level, and articulated across academic, public, private, and religious spheres. A second was the emergence of same-sex marriage at the forefront of lesbian and gay activism and as a central conflict in domestic politics. The debates around marriage that began in the 1990s intensified and became much more publicized. The struggle over same-sex marriage rights on the one hand, and the conservative push to promote marriage on the other, underscore marriage's role as both an obligation to be met and a right to be confined or extended. This "battle for the soul of the nation," as the head of the Georgia Christian Coalition described it,[1] reveals the continued political investment in marriage as a pivotal institution in American politics.

Three years after George W. Bush took the oath of office and two years after the 9/11 attacks, the president argued for the centrality of marriage as an anchor in uncertain times. "We are living in a time of great change," he said in his January 2004 State of the Union address, yet "the values we try to live by never change. And they are instilled in us by fundamental institutions, such as families, and schools, and religious congregations."[2] Of these institutions, which he went on to call "unseen pillars of civilization," marriage and family were essential to defining conservative politics institutionally and ideologically. In the speech, he commended Congress for passing DOMA and for protecting and defending marriage, asserting that "a strong America must value the institution of marriage." Bush's emphasis on marriage reflected the "compassionate conservatism" on which he ran in 1999. This political philosophy held that conservative values, in order to be viable and humane, had to be supported by energetic state action. Thus the Bush administration's domestic policy included national education standards and federal funding for local school districts, and faith-based initiatives that would funnel federal money for social services through religious and secular organizations. It also included the Healthy Marriage Initiative, which used welfare TANF money for marriage promotion, education, and support. At the same time, the administration vigorously opposed same-sex marriage, an issue that was thrust back into national politics by a gay and lesbian movement galvanized by DOMA. These efforts to both promote and restrict marriage were reflected at the state level across the country as well.

In marriage promotion, we see a continuation of the Clinton-era settlement between conservatives and Democratic Leadership Council (DLC) Democrats, where feminists, left-leaning communitarians, and liberals joined with figures on the right to promote marriage as a palliative for urban poverty. Under the Bush administration, that argument in favor of marriage was extended beyond welfare and poverty to become one about social well-being more generally. The advocates of welfare reform and marriage promotion made arguments consistent with the tradition stretching from the Freedman's Bureau through the Moynihan Report and PRWORA. Marriage was treated as an interest and obligation of the state. In this period, many marriage promoters advanced it as a public health issue (harkening back to Progressive Era arguments about the benefits of marriage), claiming that marriage promotion was as beneficial to society as antismoking and antidrug campaigns.

On the opposite side, proponents of same-sex marriage crossed ideological lines as well. Some liberal and libertarian supporters argued that marriage was a fundamental right with which the state should not interfere, while some conservatives claimed that same-sex marriage would stabilize gay and lesbian families and thus support the institution of marriage more generally. The push for same-sex marriage in these respects followed the path set by the *Loving* decision. Advocates argued for the obligation to marry rather than only the right to *same-sex* marriage on the grounds of normalcy and sameness rather than the grounds of difference. But just as lesbian and gay activists were increasingly successful at convincing Democratic elites that marriage was a fundamental right that should be extended them, Republicans, bolstered by social conservative activists, used the specter of gay marriage to rally their supporters.

The overall interplay between the obligations and rights of marriage continued in this decade but the meaning and politics once again shifted. Voters and non-state actors, rather than state actors and policy elites, became aggressively involved in both campaigns, attempting either to restrict or to extend the institution of marriage. Legal scholar Katherine Franke describes this shift in gay politics, specifically, as a notable transformation in which LGBT activists moved "from trying to avoid the law, to standing in town squares and on courthouse steps desperately waving our hand in the air trying to get the law's attention."[3]

In this period there was also a reframing and even co-opting of 1960s-era language of inclusion, economic equality, and rights in the service of marriage regulation. As some conservatives moved toward supporting greater government regulation, liberals adopted a moral framework that drew on the discourse of rights. In that process, the Marriage Movement, composed of elites and non-state actors, developed with the call to create a stronger marriage culture within the United States. In this process, questions that concerned social and economic inequality were viewed through the lens of marriage. At the same time, state and federal policymakers looked for ways to increase the federal government's role and promote and encourage the practice of marriage. These were interesting political reversals from the 1960s era, as non-state actors sought to use the state to regulate rather than challenge marriage, and the government sought to expand rather than limit its reach by supporting marriage programs.

Finally, another interesting turn was that debates about the norms and practices of marriage increasingly concerned the moral realm of American collective life, rather than that of social and economic equality. Exemplary of this position was a *Time* magazine cover story on the state of marriage in 2009. In it the author quotes sociologist and family scholar Andrew Cherlin's argument that in response to the rise in infidelity among our political leaders and the rapidly declining marriage rate of heterosexuals, not only was there "a great turbulence in American family life" but also, as the article surmised, a loss of "notions of sacrifice and obligation." The article went on to explain that commitments in marriage were replaced by "the ephemera of romance and happiness and . . . subject to the eternal American hope for greater happiness, for changing the hand you dealt yourself."[4] Thus marriage was posited as one of the last places where our diminishing notions of sacrifice and commitment still survived and thrived. Policymakers wanted citizens to take on the obligation of marriage, and same-sex couples also wanted to take on the obligation of marriage.

The Marriage Movement

Four years after the passage of PRWORA, the political focus on the alleged excesses of welfare had receded. Backed by influential research centers, a movement to create a "marriage culture" developed, and the marital aspects of welfare reform expanded into a more broadly defined federal marriage policy. Wade Horn, Bush's Assistant Secretary for Children and Families, supported a diverse coalition of pro-marriage constituents who advocated, not unlike Daniel Patrick Moynihan in the 1960s, for marriage promotion as federal policy. Beginning in the late 1990s, a growing coalition of conservatives, religious leaders, politicians, educators, and progressives, both inside and outside of government, made public their concerns about the decline of marriage and came together in what they called the "Marriage Movement" to promote and strengthen marriage. Social scientists, often funded by pro-marriage institutes, launched a number of studies on premarital education and the effects of marriage on children. Community-based and non-profit groups created programs to strengthen marriage, such as the Coalition for Marriage, Family, and Couples Education (CMFCE). Organized in 1996, CMFCE functions as an umbrella organization that fosters networking and collaboration among various marriage-focused groups. The primary work of the CMFCE is to sponsor an annual Smart Marriage conference, which brings together educators and policymakers to discuss and promote marriage research and education.[5] Religious groups also sponsored organizations to promote marriage, such as Promise Keepers and Marriage Savers. All of this bolstered the focus on marriage in the TANF reauthorization debates that began in 2002.

The efforts and effects of the Marriage Movement expanded well beyond social and religious organizing. By the late 1990s and early 2000s, attempts to shape the future of marriage through specific governmental or legal means had become accepted practice.[6] An increasingly prominent branch of the Marriage Movement was represented in government, and legal efforts were

passed to promote marriage and direct social dialogue. A 1998 Florida statute, for instance, was passed to create resources for premarital preparation,
and Louisiana began the trend toward "covenant marriage" with legislation
in 1997.[7] In 1998 Governor Michael Leavitt of Utah was the first to launch a
marital commission; Oklahoma Governor Frank Keating followed in 1999
and established a multi-sectored state initiative to decrease divorce rates and
strengthen marriage.[8]

The movement achieved national prominence in 2000 with the release of
The Marriage Movement: A Statement of Principles.[9] Noteworthy signatories
included advisors to Al Gore and prominent figures on the communitarian
left, such as Michael Lerner, William Galston, Amitai Etzioni, and Robert
Bellah; social conservatives such as James Q. Wilson; Bush advisors and
members of the religious right, such as Wade Horn and Don Eberly; and economic conservatives such as Francis Fukuyama.[10] The statement bemoaned
a crisis in marriage in American society, caused by trends that began in the
1960s, such as the rise of single motherhood, out of wedlock childbearing,
cohabitation, divorce, and the breakdown of African American families: "We
come together because the divorce revolution has failed. . . . We come together because the unwed-childbearing revolution has failed. . . . We come
together because we value freedom and cherish our free society. . . . We come
together to affirm that marriage is not a special interest. . . . We come together
to enlarge and energize this emerging effort to renew the marriage vow and
marriage vision."[11]

Similar to prior historical moments when marriage became politicized,
marriage here linked notions of independence, civic inclusion, and morality.
As Freedmen's Bureau officials had asserted during Reconstruction, Marriage Movement participants saw citizenship as founded on notions of freedom and independence secured through sexual order. Marriage-promotion
policies in the contraband camps during the Civil War were central to helping ex-slaves transition to freedom and citizenship by "teaching" them the
"duties" and "privileges of freedom." The nuptial reform movement in the
Progressive Era similarly attempted to rectify what it defined as disorder. It
called for creation of solemnization laws to navigate the social changes that
attended mass immigration, urbanization, and industrialization. Spurred
on by nativist and eugenic anxieties, reformers at that time succeeded in
codifying marriage as a bulwark against the unsettling of hierarchies in a
rapidly changing society. A similar dynamic emerged in the Marriage Move-

ment a century later, as advocates proposed a national marriage policy and state action. Like the societal problems of "slavery, racism, poverty, pollution, drunk driving, domestic violence, sexism and tobacco use," read the statement, "in each case, Americans proved that when a social practice, big or small, is wrong and destructive, the correct response is not fatalistic acceptance, but action."[12]

Yet there are some key differences from past struggles over marriage. The Marriage Movement did not assert that marriage was the obligation of specific groups seeking to achieve full citizenship, as had been the case with the Freedmen's Bureau. It rather articulated a "vision" for the whole of society. Whereas in the early 1990s societal breakdown was blamed on women who received public assistance, in the ideologically diverse Marriage Movement the onus was placed on society in general to take up the obligation of marriage. The Marriage Movement deployed a progressive language of equality alongside a moral language of family duty, expanding the culture of poverty argument: "The decline of marriage weakens civil society and spreads social inequality. Americans of all social classes and ethnic groups value marriage. Yet, as society retreats from supporting marriage publicly, those who succeed in achieving this aspiration are increasingly likely to be the already highly advantaged: better educated, more affluent, and white."[13] The Marriage Movement warned against marriage becoming "the private property of the privileged." Marriage "must not become the private hoard of the upper-middle class, creating a new, disturbing marital divide between the haves and have-nots in America."[14] In the Marriage Movement statement, political and ideological divides were bridged through a politics of marriage. For conservatives, the Marriage Movement asserted a traditional moral framework upholding normalized heterosexual practices and childrearing; while for liberals, it was a way to talk about social equality and the overcoming of race and class divisions.

The ultimate claim of the statement of principles was that "marriage is not just a private relationship. It is also a social institution" and therefore "strengthening marriage is a legitimate public goal." The statement lists several reasons for this: "Marriage protects the well-being of children," read the statement. "Divorce and unwed parenting generate large taxpayer costs; marriage is a unique generator of social and human capital, as important as education in building the wealth of individuals and communities; and only marriage creates a reasonable hope of permanence."[15] Marriage, like education, was an institution central to society that fostered community and stability. And as an institution, the Marriage Movement argued, marriage should be funded by the state. Whereas conservatives such as political scientist Charles Murray saw marriage as upholding the mantel of individual rights against the state, and as a private institution outside the control of the state that maintains and sustains social and economic life, the Marriage Movement endorsed federal and public support of marriage to equalize citizens across race and class divides—the Marriage Movement understood marriage as having a "public side."

The Marriage Movement claimed that behind the many examples of state involvement in marriage was "the belief that marriage is a social good and therefore a legitimate concern of the state." As examples of state involvement, Don Browning, professor at the Divinity School at the University of Chicago and scholar of marriage, cited "the 1998 green paper on family and marriage issued by the Labor government in England, the interest in marriage education in Australia, the moves into marriage preparation in Florida, Louisiana, and Arizona." The statement of principles explained that "the mass of legal codes governing marriage and family in the 50 states is also a sign of the long-standing belief that marriage deals with profound goods that must be monitored and ordered for the public good."[16] Indeed, the Marriage Movement statement identified policy and institutional areas where marriage movements were being established and were instituting new initiatives to strengthen marriage. These wide-ranging areas included the Marriage Education Movement, which targeted schools, hospitals, and the military; the Faith-Based Marriage Movement, which focused on churches; the Scholarly Marriage Movement, which conducted research and wrote reports; and other sites such as the Governors' Marriage Movement and Federal Marriage Movement.[17] Marriage preparation in particular was an area of government support. Nine states pursued efforts to promote marriage in public school curricula statewide.[18] In Utah, Florida, Arizona, Oklahoma, and Wisconsin, other educational activities were funded including the publishing of manuals, creation of classes, and the use of marriage therapists.[19]

The argument that as a public institution marriage requires government involvement can be traced as far back as 1888 and the Supreme Court case *Maynard v. Hill.* The majority decision in that case explained that "marriage, as creating the most important relation in life, as having more to do with the morals and civilization of a people than any other institution, has always been subject to the control of the legislature."[20] Marriage here was more than a contract between private parties; it was invested with rights and obligations that were protected and encouraged by law. Similarly, the Marriage Movement, in promoting a public interest in marriage, moved decisions about marriage from the purely private realm to within the purview of the state, suggesting that marriage was not a matter of personal fulfillment but one of social obligation.

This social obligation furthermore did not adhere to just one group but to all citizens. This made the Marriage Movement different from earlier marriage promotion efforts that targeted specific groups, as during Reconstruction, when the state encouraged ex-slaves to marry to obtain full civic inclusion; or the 1960s Great Society programs that promoted marriage as an obligation of poor single mothers; or the 1996 welfare reform that predicated benefits on married status. Marriage Movement advocates claimed that all citizens and their government were obligated to support and practice marriage as necessary to the stability of the nation. Similar to earlier historical calls to marital obligation, here the obligation was predicated on calls for disciplinary inclusion. Thus the emphasis shifted from controlling poor single mothers on welfare to creating the federal Healthy Marriage Initiative, which no longer was intended to address the needs of poor single mothers, but to instill morality, define economic and dependent relationships, and bolster American values.

National Marriage Policy and Welfare Reform

The shift to a national marriage policy at first targeted a specific group, as issues surrounding marriage were central to reauthorizing welfare reform under the George W. Bush administration. But as the debates progressed, a marriage culture for the nation, supported by the federal government, and not just individual state marriage programs for welfare recipients, became the focus.

Robert Rector, a fellow at the Heritage Foundation, a chief architect of Bush's welfare plan, and a self-proclaimed marriage expert, was a leader in conceptualizing a national marriage policy. In a 2001 Heritage Foundation Report entitled "Implementing Welfare and Restoring Marriage," Rector laid out his view that marriage was the work of the government and that welfare policy was the site to orchestrate it. On the question of whether government should be promoting marriage, Rector explained that the government was already "massively" involved. "Each year," he wrote in a Heritage Foundation report, "the government spends over $150 billion in subsidies to single parents. Much of this expenditure would have been avoided if mothers were married to the father of their children." Thus, he claimed, "to insist that the government has an obligation to support single parents—and to control the damage that results from the erosion of marriage—but should do nothing to strengthen marriage itself is myopic." To ask the government to support single mothers, he said, "is like arguing that the government should pay to sustain polio victims in iron lung machines but should not pay for the vaccine to prevent polio in the first place."[21] Following Rector's logic, not marrying was a social health issue, and not promoting marriage was like paying poor single mothers and their children to live in poverty, use drugs, and drop out of school. Rector called for a government campaign to eradicate what might be called the condition of un-marriage. Thus, rather than turning to marriage to "fulfill these rights" as suggested by Johnson by the beginning of the twenty-first century, conservatives turn to marriage to cure a disease.

As welfare policy progressed, it became clear that marriage-promotion money and policies did not actually target poor populations but were designed for and mostly served middle-class, educated couples who were engaged or already married.[22] The federal government permitted states to spend their welfare block grants on marriage-promotion activities that did not directly address welfare recipients. This also became evident in the 2001 congressional hearing entitled Welfare and Marriage Issues, convened to discuss the reauthorization of PRWORA. In that hearing, there were no groups brought in to testify on marriage that actually spoke to the issue of welfare recipients, poverty, or how marriage was supposed to take the place of welfare. Nor did any welfare recipients testify. Rather, the hearing focused on the dangers of dependency. "How can we prevent people from becoming dependent on the government in the first place?" asked Arizona Representative Mark Anderson in his testimony.[23] The answer was marriage. As Jerry Regier, cabinet secretary of Oklahoma, testified, "If you want strangers from the government to tell you when to see your child, how much money you should send them each month, how and when you can communicate and how to divide assets of the marriage, then file for divorce. If you want to keep government out of your life, stay married."[24] Without addressing either poverty or motherhood, these government officials promoted marriage as a way out of government regulation of private affairs. Ironically, these and other voices deployed traditional conservative arguments about keeping government out of citizens' lives to actually promote federal intervention in the form of funding for marriage programs.

This congressional hearing illustrates a critique that was developing around welfare reform and PRWORA. Beginning in 2001, the Bush Administration began working with congressional leaders on reauthorization of the welfare reform legislation. In 2002, the Administration for Children and Families (ACF) launched a Healthy Marriage Initiative and began funding research and service programs. These demonstration grants were funded under discretionary programs administered by several bureaus in ACF.[25] Though widely praised for its workfare initiatives, PRWORA was criticized by some conservatives for failing to encourage nationwide marriage programs. Critics like Rector, while drawing on 1990s assertions put forth by Charles Murray that government programs increase dependency, did not suggest that marriage replace government, but that government should fund marriage programs. He and other conservatives argued that federal funding and resources should not go toward entitling single mothers to care for their families without husbands, but rather federal money should be used to create policies that strongly encouraged poor single mothers to marry.

Rector argued that "the growth of illegitimacy and divorce are powerful factors contributing to virtually every other social problem facing the nation. Policies to reduce out-of-wedlock childbearing and strengthen marriage should be at the center of all future welfare policies."[26] In claiming that aberrant marital behavior had created "virtually every other social problem," like Rector, Charles Murray diagnosed not marrying as a public ailment. Yet, unlike Murray, he located the remedy in federal action to coerce participation in the institution.

This criticism represented a change in conservative ideology around marriage, specifically away from faith in states' rights and toward the possibility of installing a national marriage policy and marriage culture. Rector, in his policy recommendations to the Bush administration, warned against shifting full responsibility for welfare reform to the states. While the states had successfully implemented federal work requirements and had reduced welfare caseloads, states had failed to adequately promote federal marriage recommendations. Rector thus asserted that efforts to move welfare decision making to the state level would delay the essential and difficult debate over the moral and behavioral content of welfare programs. Such displacement, in other words, could be used as "a pretext for deliberately smothering the real debate needed to transform welfare," he argued. To prove his point Rector referred to the original 1996 debates over welfare reform, during which "'devolutionists' at the National Governors' Association used the slogan of state flexibility in a deliberate effort to block the national discussion on the crisis of illegitimacy."[27] Indeed, on the issue of marriage and illegitimacy, the federal government had set goals for reducing out-of-wedlock births but had left implementation up to the states. The result, lamented Rector, had been "catastrophic." According to Rector, the substance of welfare reform, what he called the behavioral content, could not properly be debated in the midst of turf wrangling between federal and state government.

Distancing himself from the traditional conservative principles of state's rights, local autonomy and privatism, Rector argued that the only strategy for welfare reform was a fundamental metamorphosis in the nature of all existing welfare programs—federal, state, and private. Rector called for a complete "transformation" in how welfare was viewed—an ideological transformation instituted through federal policies focused on regulating behavior instead of on procedure. The excesses of welfare did not stem from the failings of federal policies but from the ideological framework that generated those policies. In making this argument, Rector reserved the right for the federal government to institute social and moral policies around marriage.[28] "The policymaker's foremost job is to be an entrepreneur of ideas," Rector advised, adding that "few politicians will show open hostility to the idea of strengthening marriage. It should not be difficult to publicly co-opt prominent members of both parties into support of the issue."[29]

In addition to Robert Rector, the presence of certain other advisors and administrators in the first administration of George W. Bush suggested the president's commitment to promoting marriage. During Bush's first term, he appointed Tommy Thompson—architect of Wisconsin's welfare reform and Bridefare programs—U.S. secretary of health and human services (HHS).[30] Wade Horn, a vocal and staunch supporter of federally funded marriage-promotion programs, became assistant secretary of health and human services. Horn spent several years traveling around the country encouraging states to use their TANF dollars to promote marriage. Funding for marriage promotion increased in 2002–3 when the Department of Health and Human Services allocated $90 million to marriage-related research and demonstration projects. Finally, marriage promotion became an important platform point in 2004 when Bush was running for reelection, appealing to conservative supporters who saw it as a commitment to family values and counter to same-sex marriage.[31]

Four years after Robert Rector published his policy recommendations in the Heritage Foundation report on welfare reform, with very little fanfare, Congress reauthorized the federal welfare reform legislation of 1996 in the Deficit Reduction Act of 2005 (DRA). The DRA included $150 million each year for five years to support programs created to strengthen marriages and promote responsible fatherhood. While it was started as a demonstration project in 2002, it received its own funding stream in 2005 with the DRA. These healthy marriage programs were funded through the Office of Family Assistance (OFA). In October 2006, the OFA awarded 125 healthy marriage grants, ranging in amount from $130,000 to $2 million.[32] Thus began the second stage of the Healthy Marriage Initiative (HMI) that allocated federal money for marriage programs in general, not only for the poor. The Marriage Movement realized its greatest advances with the reauthorization of welfare reform.

The Healthy Marriage Initiative (HMI)

As it developed through welfare policy to the creation of the HMI, marriage increasingly became a central way to talk about economic inequality without addressing jobs, wages, and federal benefits to individuals. Wade Horn, the founder and director of the nonprofit National Fatherhood Initiative, was the assistant secretary for children and families within the HHS from 2001 to 2007 and was in charge of the HMI. The program had two basic components: to allocate federal money for marriage programs, though not particularly for the poor; and to support various research and demonstration projects. The funding for the program was distributed by the Administration for Children and Family Services.

The press release from February 2006 announcing the HMI quoted Wade Horn: "A key component of welfare reform is supporting healthy marriage and responsible fatherhood."[33] On September 30, 2006, the Office of Family Assistance announced grant awards to 226 organizations to promote healthy marriage and responsible fatherhood.[34] Programs varied from state to state under the HMI, but all were designed to encourage heterosexual marriage and childbearing within marriage. In most cases the populations targeted were economically disadvantaged groups, but that was not the main focus. Much of the funding was earmarked for faith-based initiatives, such as Catholic Charities, the Hebrew Immigrant Aid Society, and the Lutheran Immigration Refugee Service.[35] Grantees also included secular groups that helped minorities, such as the Boat People SOS, which aided immigrants from Vietnam; and the First Nations Community HealthSource, which aided Native Americans. Other grants targeted students, such as those who went to Auburn University, the University of Central Florida, Morehouse College, and the University of North Carolina at Chapel Hill.[36]

On the HMI website the mission statement explained that researchers have found many benefits for children and youth who are raised by parents in a healthy marriage. It asserted the following: Children are more likely not only to attend college but to succeed academically. They are physically and mentally healthier, demonstrate fewer behavioral problems in school, are less likely to use drugs or alcohol, and less likely to engage in unhealthy relationships themselves. They have better relationships with their parents and are less likely to divorce when they grow up. They are also less likely to become pregnant as teenagers or impregnate someone, or to contract a sexually transmitted disease; and finally, they are less likely to be raised in poverty. [37] Greatly expanding on the culture of poverty argument, the agency described a culture of marriage that addresses many issues together. And while matters of poverty are embedded within this framework, the primary focus is on marriage education, through for example public advertising campaigns on the value of marriage and the skills needed to increase marital stability and health.

Marriage promotion putatively became an important way to address race and class inequality. The HMI included racially specific marriage initiatives, such as the African American Healthy Marriage Initiative and the Hispanic Healthy Marriage Initiative, programs that also had earlier roots in various agencies. Beginning in 2003, the Administration of Native Americans used discretionary dollars to fund twenty-three tribal healthy marriage programs. Also in 2003, the Administration for Children and Families and the Office of

Refugee Resettlement proposed to aid refugees in establishing healthy families and marriages. Refugees encountered obstacles in the form of low-wage jobs, which forced both adults to work outside the home; low incomes, which forced refugees to live in high-crime neighborhoods; and poor public transportation, which added to time spent away from the family. In the face of these problems, the agencies explained, "marriage education can help refugee couples strengthen and adjust relationship skills and [can] help them cope with the difficulties of their new American environment."[38] In other words, instead of other kinds of programs to address low-wage jobs, high-crime neighborhoods, and poor public transportation, the government encouraged a marriage policy. In 2006, the Office of Refugee Resettlement funded about fifty-five healthy marriage programs serving refugees from Central Europe, Africa, and South Asia.

In the political maneuvering leading up to the reauthorization of TANF in 2011, the emphasis on both marriage and heteronormativity in welfare reform did not subside.[39] As an example, the American Public Human Services Association, a bipartisan, nonprofit networking and advocacy organization that represents state health and human service agencies, suggested that PRWORA wording be changed from "encourag[ing] the formation and maintenance of two-parent families" to "encourag[ing] the formation and maintenance of healthy two-parent *married* families and *responsible fatherhood*."[40]

Support for this change was reflected by the Obama administration, which supported the HMI program, but gave more funding to promoting responsible fatherhood programs. On June 29, 2011, the Administration for Children and Families announced the availability of funding for four discretionary awards totaling $150 million for "Healthy Marriage and Responsible Fatherhood" grants. The Responsible Fatherhood program received $75 million in new funding "intended to promote or sustain responsible parenting, marriage and economic stability." The other $75 million went toward funding for premarital education, marriage enrichment programs, divorce reduction programs, and marriage mentoring programs.[41]

Federally funded marriage promotion had important implications for notions of obligation. Marital obligations became one way in which policymakers and state officials talked about economic and social inequality. Giving voice to these programs, the Marriage Movement offered a path to inclusion and equality through government-funded regulatory policies on family structure and marriage. It is interesting to note the series of moves here, from empowering poor single mothers through entitlements, to obligating poor single mothers to marry, to a focus on establishing male heads of households to replace government support, thus creating a policy of compassionate patriarchy. Through the obligations of marriage, a welfare economic policy was now founded on reasserting gender roles in marriage. As Health and Human Services Secretary Kathleen Sebelius said at the announcement of the funding for Healthy Marriages and Responsible Fatherhood in 2011, "This funding provides organizations in underserved communities the tools they need to promote responsible parenting, to encourage healthy marriage and relationships, and to remove barriers to financial security and self-sufficiency."[42]

Arguments for Same-Sex Marriage

The transformation of welfare reform debates from a focus on economic inequality to one encouraging heterosexual marriage reveals the centrality of marriage in the politics of both poverty and sexual identity. This transformation has strong implications for the same-sex marriage debate that expanded and intensified over the same period. Common threads connect the two political issues. The decision in *Loving v. Virginia* focused on marriage as an individual right for the pursuance of personal fulfillment. Judicial decisions supporting same-sex marriage have followed along these same lines. However, many of the most prominent arguments for same-sex marriage in the last decade and half have focused on the socially redeeming qualities of the institution of marriage more generally.

Many proponents have argued that marriage would rein in sexual promiscuity, which would in turn make gays and lesbians better citizens. Gay conservative writer Andrew Sullivan, for instance, has argued that allowing same-sex marriage would encourage traditional familial values among gay couples.[43] In his 1995 book, *Virtually Normal*, Sullivan explained that gay politics shifted after the AIDS crisis to a focus on belonging. The Human Rights Campaign, a leading national LGBT rights organization, made similar claims in its 2004 *Cost of Marriage Inequality to Children of Same-Sex Parents*.[44] The document opened: "The Report finds great similarities between the family life of same-sex couples and heterosexual couples with children."[45] After citing statistics showing that same-sex couples were twice as likely to stay in long-term relationships as unmarried heterosexual couples, the report continued, "Since marriage is generally considered a stabilizing factor the implication seems to be that granting marriage rights to same-sex couples would lead to an even greater degree of stability in these families."[46] The Human Rights Campaign argued for same-sex marriage as a way to stabilize families, as an obligation of gays and lesbians rather than as a right they deserve.

The argument that marriage is a public obligation exists alongside opposite claims that marriage is a fundamental private right of citizens that gays and lesbians deserve. That marriage is a fundamental right is the basis on which state courts have decided in favor of marriage rights in the legal cases on same-sex marriage. In 1998, the Alaska Superior Court judged that "marriage, i.e., the recognition of one's choice of life partner, is a fundamental right. The state must therefore have a compelling interest that supports its decision to refuse to recognize the exercise of this fundamental right by those who choose same-sex partners rather than opposite-sex partners."[47] In 1999, in *Baker v. Vermont*, the state of Vermont, the city of Burlington, and two towns were sued for violating the state constitution in refusing to issue a marriage license. The Vermont Supreme Court, reversing a lower court decision, declared that the constitution required the state to extend to same-sex couples the same benefits and protections provided to opposite-sex couples. In response, the state legislature passed the Vermont Civil Union Law, which went into effect in July 2000.

In November 2003, the Massachusetts Supreme Court *Goodridge* ruling legalized same-sex marriage in that state and opened the floodgates for demands for gay marriage in local jurisdictions across the country.[48] The court held that the state law barring same-sex marriage was unconstitutional under the Massachusetts Constitution and ordered the legislature to remedy the discrimination within six months. In February 2004, the court ruled that offering civil unions instead of civil marriage would not meet the requirements set forth in *Goodridge*. As a result, in May 2004, same-sex couples gained the right to get marriage licenses and to enter into civil marriages. Massachusetts was the first state to rule that same-sex marriage was constitutionally protected.

In *Goodridge*, the court rejected the state's claim that the primary purpose of marriage was procreation. Rather, the court asserted that the history of marriage laws in the commonwealth demonstrated that "it is the exclusive and permanent commitment of the marriage partners to one another, not the begetting of children, that is the sine qua non of civil marriage." Noting that "civil marriage has long been termed a 'civil right," the court concluded that "the right to marry means little if it does not include the right to marry the person of one's choice, subject to appropriate government restrictions in the interests of public health, safety, and welfare." Here the court supported the definition of marriage as a fundamental right and individual expression of choice. The definition of civil marriage the court offered was "the voluntary union of two persons as spouses, to the exclusion of all others."[49] However, the court also asserted that same-sex marriage would not redefine marriage itself; the court's decision would "not disturb the fundamental value of marriage in our society." Rather, that "same-sex couples are willing to embrace marriage's solemn obligations of exclusivity, mutual support, and commitment to one another is a testament to the enduring place of marriage in our laws and in the human spirit."[50] Thus same-sex marriage will not change the institution because same-sex couples will embrace the obligations of marriage as well. This is similar to the 1967 *Loving* case where the Court explained that interracial marriages will follow the "orderly pursuit of happiness."

With *Goodridge*, Massachusetts became the defender of marriage rights in the tradition of *Loving v. Virginia*, marking a developmental shift in the institution of marriage. Whereas during Reconstruction the courts had prevented marriage between whites and blacks by claiming that marriage was the foundation of society, here the court asserted that the *right* to marriage established in *Loving* was the foundational concept of equality. The "marriage ban," the Massachusetts Supreme Court held, "works a deep and scarring hardship" on same-sex families "for no rational reason." It prevents children of same-sex couples "from enjoying the immeasurable advantages that flow from the assurance of 'a stable family structure in which children will be reared, educated, and socialized.'" Further, "It cannot be rational under our laws to penalize children by depriving them of State benefits because the state disapproves of their parents' sexual orientation."[51] These arguments were similar to the ones made by the judiciary in the Progressive Era in their support of family unity policies that kept immigrant husbands and wives together.

The obligation or right of marriage as expressed in the same-sex marriage debates is centrally about the role of sex in marriage. When marriage is viewed as an obligation, sex can be controlled and tamed if it occurs in marriage. When it is viewed as a right, sexual orientation does not belong, or is not the point, in the state's support of a loving and committed relationship.

While on the one hand the cases of *Loving* and *Goodridge* represent the courts' adopting an expansive notion of marriage and family, on the other this is done in the name of supporting notions of "commitment" and obligations. A crucial difference is that the *Loving* decision clearly states that race should not matter in marriage. In *Goodridge* there is no mention that sexual orientation should not matter. *Goodridge* is not a decision that affirms the civic membership of lesbians and gay men, as *Loving* affirmed racial equality. It is rather an assertion of the importance of marriage. Both today and during the 1960s, when *Loving* was decided, the assertion of the right to marriage is also a statement about the centrality of marriage to individuals and society at a moment when marriage is thought to be in crisis.

After the *Goodridge* decision was announced, gay and lesbian couples descended on their municipal governments in other states, demanding to be granted marriage licenses. On February 12, 2004, San Francisco mayor Gavin Newsom ordered city clerks to begin granting marriage licenses to same-sex couples, and more than four thousand were subsequently issued. Other U.S. cities, from Asbury Park, New Jersey, to Portland, Oregon, followed his lead, and the entire country's attention was drawn to the debate. Mayor Newsom said at the time that he was willing to sacrifice his political career over his belief that denying gay men and lesbians the right to marry "is wrong and inconsistent with the values this country holds dear." He further explained, "I think we're on firm legal footing and legal grounds, and certainly I believe very strongly and passionately we're on the right moral ground."[52]

In the wake of the *Goodridge* decision, supporters of same-sex marriage looked to capture normative claims to rights and equality in American history rather than to go against them. They tried to frame marriage rights as an assertion of American norms and values rather than as a challenge to them— they sought to assert their view of marriage as an expression of values and responsibilities. Marty Rouse, campaign director of MassEquality, the umbrella organization that directed the response to the political backlash from *Goodridge*, said the group was prepared to battle for the rights to American ideology. Activists outside the Massachusetts State House sang "God Bless America," "America the Beautiful," "This Land Is Your Land," and civil rights songs. And they waved the American flag and held signs that said, "No discrimination in the Constitution."[53] Representative Liz Malia explained how she was affected by this. She realized that the first constituency was the children of same-sex couples, saying, "there are families here. It doesn't matter whether you approve of it or not. There are kids here, and they have a future. . . . A lot of folks I think really started to see, 'This isn't a bunch of wild-eyed, crazy people out in the street protesting. This is my next-door neighbor.'"[54] The claim to same-sex marriage rights was not, in the tradition of the 1960s, radical. Rather, same-sex marriage aligned its proponents with heteronormal people and families.[55]

Two interesting shifts occurred at this moment in these normalization arguments. Whereas during Reconstruction, the Progressive Era, the 1960s, and the 1990s, state actors encouraged marriage as a form of disciplinary inclusion, in this case non-state actors were fighting for inclusion in the institution. Change was no longer elite driven; citizens now demanded the right to marry. This notion of marriage rights was interlinked with obligations, defining disciplinary inclusion. In addition, as much as conservatives co-opted the liberal language of rights and inclusion, those supporting same-sex marriage used conservative language and tactics.

Arguments against Same-Sex Marriage

In this struggle over marriage rights, one substantial difference from prior political conflicts around marriage has been the active role citizens have played in preventing the recognition of same-sex marriage, using populist arguments for majoritarianism. It has been, in other words, "the people" and voters, at least rhetorically, rather than political elites, who have sought to limit marriage through state versions of the federal Defense of Marriage Act. In fact, according to the conservative argument against same-sex marriage, it has been elites who have pressed for the fundamental right of marriage and privacy, and for rights in general, over and against the will of the people. Robert Knight, director of Concerned Women for America's Culture and Family Institute, said in response to the *Lawrence v. Texas* decision in 2003, which rendered state anti-sodomy laws unconstitutional, that "the court is now governed by an elite group that reflects the liberal opinion of major universities and even corporate boards [and] I think they will continue to function as a wrecking ball in our culture and destroy the legal framework for having a family friendly society."[56]

Opponents of same-sex marriage continued in this vein, stating that marriage was a tradition and practice—indeed an institution—to be protected. They claimed that the issue was not one of personal rights, but of whether the state can change marriage. This was a theme in the dissenting opinions in *Goodridge*. Justice Cordy wrote that, "while 'the Massachusetts Constitution protects matters of personal liberty against government intrusion at least as zealously and often more so than does the Federal Constitution,' this case is not about government intrusions into matters of personal liberty" but is "about whether the State must endorse and support [the choices of same-sex couples] by changing the institution of civil marriage to make its benefits, obligations, and responsibilities applicable to them."[57] Justice Cordy argued that the granting or denying of marriage rights was not an issue of private rights but was about the state's responsibility to maintain certain stabilizing forms of marriage. Here we see the beginnings of the argument that marriage rights for individuals should not trump the state's responsibility to protect the community.

Opponents of same-sex marriage have long pushed for a federal constitutional amendment banning gay marriage. Such an amendment was proposed first in 2001, then in 2003, and was supported by George W. Bush. When Representative Marilyn Musgrave, a Republican from Colorado, proposed the Federal Marriage Amendment (FMA, also called the Marriage Protection Amendment) in May 2003, its aim was to go beyond the Defense of Marriage Act by preventing the courts from granting the right to marry to same-sex couples. Backed by a racially and religiously diverse coalition, the FMA declared that "marriage in the United States shall consist only of the union of a man and a woman. Neither this Constitution or the constitution of any other state, nor state or federal law, shall be construed to require that marital status or the legal incidents thereof be conferred upon unmarried couples or groups."[58] The amendment was designed to prevent legislatures from using the term "marriage" for homosexual unions and to prevent courts from ordering homosexual marriage or allocating marriage benefits to gay and lesbian couples. It also prohibited the recognition of same-sex marriages performed outside the United States.[59]

In defense of the marriage amendment, Margaret Gallagher, a leading opponent of same-sex marriage and president of the Institute for Marriage and Public Policy, asserted that marriage maintains civilization and creates the next generation by "giving children the mothers and fathers they need."

She explained in a 2003 *Washington Standard* article that "the only possible effective political response" to the threat of gay marriage is a constitutional amendment. She asserted that "federalism is a poor excuse for abandoning a core social institution." Gallagher also argued that marriage is not about personal fulfillment or private rights, rather she claimed that "the social norm that needs reinforcing in the law and in the culture is not: Soul mates should marry. It is: Children need fathers and mothers."[60] Gallagher had been an arch supporter of Bush's marriage promotion programs, for which she had a government contract with the Department of Health and Human Services for $21,500.[61]

Though the amendment was defeated on the floor of the Senate, it did frame marriage as a limited right to be protected.[62] Opponents of same-sex marriage, like proponents of marriage promotion in the welfare debate, saw marriage as a social and public institution. Yet rather than arguing to extend a marriage culture, as Bush advisor Robert Rector did in the context of welfare reform, same-sex marriage opponents argued that marriage must be protected and limited. Marriage should be decided by the voters and not by the "antidemocratic" judiciary. To cite Justice Cordy's dissenting opinion in *Goodridge* again, although the plaintiffs had made a powerful case for the extension of the benefits and burdens of civil marriage to same-sex couples, the issue was "one deeply rooted in social policy" and decisions around same-sex marriage must be made by the legislature, not the court.[63] He clearly asserted that the issue was not about personal liberty. Instead, he argued, extending the benefits, obligations, and responsibilities of marriage to gay and lesbian couples would change the institution of marriage and therefore society.

Debates over the federal marriage amendment echoed this logic, as when the Alliance for Marriage, the organization at the forefront of the effort to pass the marriage amendment, asserted "gays and lesbians have a right to live as they choose. But they don't have a right to redefine marriage for our entire society."[64] The theme that began to develop for the opponents of same-sex marriage—that equal rights for gays and lesbians should not involve marriage—is similar to court arguments in the 1880s, validating antimiscegenation laws by making a distinction between political equality and social equality. In fact, the Alliance went on to explain that a federal marriage amendment is "a reasonable response to the crisis for our democratic society."[65]

Justice Spina, in a separately filed dissenting opinion in *Goodridge*, spoke to this version of a crisis. "What is at stake in this case," he wrote, "is not the unequal treatment of individuals or whether individual rights have been impermissibly burdened, but the power of the Legislature to effectuate social change without interference from the courts." Spina emphasized that the "power to regulate marriage lies with the Legislature, not with the judiciary."[66] A few months later, in May 2004, when the House Committee on the Judiciary convened a hearing on the FMA, Representative Musgrave said in her statement that "I have introduced the FMA to stop judicial activism and preserve the right of self-determination for the American people."[67] For Justices Cordy and Spina and proponents of the FMA, what needed to be protected was not the individual right to marry, but the people's democratic right to protect marriage and, by extension, society and the community.

This kind of argument provided the engine behind the state initiatives across the country to ban same-sex marriage. As state courts decided that the right to marry was a fundamental right for homosexuals, state legislatures and popular referenda moved to define marriage as strictly heterosexual. In 2004, for example, Alaskans passed Measure 2 by a wide margin of 68 to 32 percent, declaring that "each marriage contract in this State may be entered into only by one man and one woman."[68] Another example was the California Marriage Protection Act, which was passed by voter ballot in 2009 and which amended the state constitution. The voter pamphlet described the measure thus: "Proposition 8 is about preserving marriage; *it's not an attack on the gay lifestyle.* Proposition 8 doesn't take away any rights or benefits of gay or lesbian domestic partnerships."[69] While the same-sex marriage debate had been a struggle over the political status of gay men and lesbians, during and after the Proposition 8 debate, opponents of same-sex marriage reframed the debate from a judgment of sexual orientation to a question about a democratic right to maintain marriage as a distinct institution for heterosexuals. As Proposition 8 supporters argued, "the narrow decision of the California Supreme Court isn't just about 'live and let live.' State law may require teachers to instruct children as young as kindergarteners about marriage. If the gay marriage ruling is not overturned, TEACHERS COULD BE REQUIRED to teach young children there is *no difference* between gay marriage and traditional marriage."[70] In other words, gays and lesbians can have their lifestyles, but they can't marry, or it will affect other institutions. As of August 2011, forty-two states have a statute or constitutional amendment that either defines marriage as a heterosexual union or does not recognize same-sex marriage. Twenty-three states have what are called Mini-DOMAs, declaring that a same-sex relationship may not be recognized as a marriage, and nineteen states have Super DOMAs, which ban not only the title of marriage but also civil union and domestic partnership.[71]

The argument that same-sex marriage will taint the institution of marriage is based on the assertion that some cultural practices, such as heterosexual marriage, are stabilizing for society, while others are not. In this way, debates over same-sex marriage and welfare are linked. Same-sex marriage, like poor female-headed households, gets painted as destroying society. A 2004 headline in the evangelical periodical *Christianity Today* concerning the *Goodridge* decision, read, "Societal Suicide: Legalizing gay marriage will lead to more family breakdown and crime."[72] The piece argued that marriage was "the traditional building block of human society, intended both to unite couples and bring children into the world." But, "tragically, the sexual revolution led to the decoupling of marriage and procreation; same-sex 'marriage' would pull them completely apart, leading to an explosive increase in family collapse, out-of-wedlock births—and crime."

Advocates here depicted marriage as an institution of "democratic government, created, and controlled by democratic authorities."[73] In other words, since marriage is a political institution, like other public institutions, its creation, design, and performance are rooted in the political logic of the democratic system in which it resides. What Terry Moe has explained in regard to schools can also be applied to marriage—it is "what the system makes" it.[74] Yet, in addition, marriage has been defined as a fundamental right, protected by the Supreme Court.

Arguments against same-sex marriage that developed after DOMA was passed in 1996 and *Goodridge* was decided in 2003 pointedly respond to the view of marriage as a fundamental right, asserting the public nature of marriage, and thus voters' and the government's right to control who is inside and outside of marriage. The argument that the recognition of same-sex marriage is essentially antidemocratic is captured by Margaret Gallagher: If gays are allowed to join the institution, "marriage will no longer be about producing and protecting the next generation, or about getting mothers and fathers for children. In the new regime, marriage will be about legally affirming the sexual and emotional lifestyles of adults in the governing class."[75] Here, the notion of marriage rights as fulfilling grand political goals of equality is replaced with a notion of those rights as the authorization of the lifestyle choices of those who would rule over us. Rights are pitted against social obligations. Supporters of DOMA, FMA, and state versions of the federal DOMA used the argument that the status of marriage should be decided by the voters and not by an allegedly antidemocratic judiciary. They argued that the people should protect and limit the institution of marriage as a necessary foundation of society.

"We're in a Battle for the Soul of the Nation"

The culture war framework receded after 9/11, yet marriage continued to play an important role in this next stage of conservatism. Bush made marriage a central element of his domestic policy as he launched his war against terror campaign. He framed the institution of marriage as a counter to the 9/11 attacks and the instability they wrought. While marriage became increasingly defined as an obligation in the service of stabilizing the nation, it also became the site in which to talk about commitments rather than rights.

The emergence of a national Marriage Movement and an intensified fight over same-sex marriage characterized the marriage politics of this period. One effect of these developments was the reframing of marriage from a private right, undergirding personal fulfillment based in love, to one compelling duty to society and nation. The effect of this transformation was to place marriage at the center of American life as an obligation of citizens to secure national stability. The argument that marriage was an obligation and status helped to shape several important ideological shifts in the political field. These changes included a reframing of rights claims as lifestyle concerns; the rise of a conservatism that includes federal intervention; the pursuit of regulatory policies through ballot initiatives; and the cooperation between church and state. In this sense, marriage promotion in welfare illustrates the desire of the state to govern, and same-sex marriage illustrates, in legal theorist Katherine Franke's apt phrasing, "a yearning to be governed by . . . the state."[76]

These changes in the ideologies and practices of the political realm in the United States reveal then the increased role of the state in the private lives of citizens, be they gays and lesbians or poor single mothers. Whereas during the 1960s, the government protected individuals' rights, even "special rights," by 2011, government expansion has been invoked to limit individual rights and regulate citizens. In addition, this shift has created a political and social context in which critics of marriage are demonized, and the single (low-income) parent is framed as a pathological. Thus conservative expansion of the state to engage in marriage promotion is not only authorized by the historical role of the institution to protect the boundaries of the nation from undesirable members, but it also reflects the political settlement between centrist liberals and conservatives.

It also illuminates the way the institution of marriage is the place to debate the status of collective national life in the United States. In both the Marriage Movement and the struggle over same-sex marriage rights we see a continued agreement between centrist Democrats and Republicans on marriage promotion. All sides seem to agree that marriage is at the center of their politics. This period reveals a high-stakes battle that draws into its sphere institutional questions of the meaning and practice of democracy, the framing of gay and lesbian political claims as either an effort to secure a right or to legitimate a lifestyle, and policies meant to address the needs of the economically poor. In other words, marriage is the only site in which discussion of state obligation versus individual obligation is found. These questions at some basic level have to do with the community at large. Thus at the heart of the debate on marriage is a struggle to define the most pressing problems of American society and locate the institutional site to address them. Once again, marriage has been utilized to define and express political problems and then posited as central to the solution.

Conclusion

"Is There Hope for the American Marriage?"

Marriage as a Political Institution

I set out in this project with two central aims: to understand the role of marriage in U.S. politics, and to understand the role of U.S. politics in marriage. I approached these questions historically in order to examine the development of each in relation to the other, giving particular emphasis to moments of major change in U.S. politics. What I found was a patterned tension between marital obligations and rights, a tension that defined marriage in a series of passionate conflicts across the eras I examined. I was thus led to a series of interlinked questions: Why do Americans find marriage so important as an expression of political identity? Why do conflicts over the institution recur? And, ultimately, what kind of politics does marriage produce? These questions point to marriage as deeply embedded in U.S. politics, such that the institution acts as a fulcrum between two crucial and constitutive elements of the U.S. nation state: liberal conceptions of rights and feudal notions of obligations operating through the embodied statuses of race, gender, class, sexuality, and national origin. So conceived, marriage holds together and defines both of these fundamental but disparate aspects of American political culture and thus becomes central when questions of difference, hierarchy, and inclusion are at stake.

Marriage is similar in scope and design to other political institutions—it limits and defines norms and practices as it shapes the interests of those inside and outside its reach. As a political institution, marriage and family can do the work of the state, whether that work is to fortify state-bound white supremacy as Julie Novkov has argued, to play a bureaucratic role for the state as Patricia Strach has revealed, or to provide a form of governance outside the state as Patricia Strach and Kathleen Sullivan have shown.[1] This book contributes to the growing literature of political studies that shed light on the role of marriage and family in institutional and state development.[2]

Marriage can act upon citizens, limiting and shaping their actions, desires and interests. But institutions such as marriage not only shape identities and structure hierarchies. Those identities and hierarchies define and produce the practices and imperatives of institutions. For instance, we know that marriage has historically shaped gender by assigning men and women different familial roles. We know that marriage shaped our understandings of race historically, through the prevention of interracial marriage, and by normalization practices that worked to pathologize black Americans. We know that the institution has shaped our understandings of sexuality by historically limiting its availability to heterosexuals. But as we have seen in these examples from U.S. history, the meaning and role of marriage as a political institution is not static. Political actors also act as a shaping force on marriage. So even though marriage and divorce rates fluctuate, the salient pattern is continued contestation and subsequent institutional renovation over time.[3] For example, the role of gender in marriage changed when women began working; the legalization of interracial marriages altered the role of marriage in maintaining racial and economic difference; and finally, marriage promotion policies changed the institution's relationship to the state. The efforts of state and non-state actors, policymakers, judges, and journalists to challenge, recast, or maintain the political status and role of gender, race, class, and sexual identities have served to dynamically shape the institution as well. Thus marriage constitutes politics, and politics constitutes marriage. The question is when, how and in what ways.

Just as marriage is not static, nor is it apolitical. Examining the context in which struggles occur is important to any analysis of the institution. Marriage and family are unique institutions in that they link diverse elements of social, political, economic, and private life, yet are generally not considered political or open to political debate. By understanding marriage and family as embedded in state development, and state development as embedded in marriage and family, we can see how the work of the state is achieved through supposedly non-political sites. In other words, this dual embeddedness reveals how cultural discourses and practices determine institutions. The relationship between obligations and rights in marriage politics demonstrates the way that institutional imperatives express seemingly contradictory ends. In each case I examined, the repressive tendencies of marriage were matched by movement towards forms of acceptance, and forms of inclusion were matched by regulation. This study has thus shown how the impulses by the state and citizens to regulate, integrate, emancipate, or exclude must not be seen as distinct but rather as interrelated processes.

The foregoing analysis suggests a normative conclusion as well. If marriage were to be popularly viewed as a political institution, constituents might understand it as one in which they have a political interest—a role in shaping and defining it—as they might with other political institutions such as voting or public education. In other words, marriage is a site that not only shapes freedoms and opportunities, but is open to contestation and debate through which seemingly distinct political identities and interests can find common cause, a point to which I return later in this conclusion.

The Changing Institution of Marriage

I have divided the book temporally into two parts to illustrate the historical development of marriage politics and demonstrate the way it acts a fulcrum between obligations and rights across time. In Part 1, I examined the Reconstruction and Progressive eras, two moments of national crisis and instability that were resolved in part through the expansion of the American state. In these periods, state actors, such as judges in the Reconstruction cases and nuptial reformers who pushed for solemnization laws, sought to protect marriage from taint and fraud. To that end, the right to marry was limited and the obligation of certain people to marry was enforced. In other words, state actors closely regulated citizen behavior through management of the privilege of marriage in order to stabilize a changing nation—the result of war in the former case, and immigration in the latter.

The second half of the book begins with the 1960s, which was a turning point in the political development of marriage. In this period, marked by discord and instability, political actors turned to marriage to either promote or prevent political change and to shape the meaning of equality. With the *Loving v. Virginia* decision the right to marry was defined as a fundamental right of citizens. Thus the focus shifted towards marriage as a right and as an expression of individual love. However, the obligations of marriage were still present, and these were debated and used in the political arena to address issues such as civil rights and women's rights. This tension carried forward into the next stage in marriage politics, which started with the last decade of the twentieth century. The extent of the right to marry was challenged by a growing social conservative movement that used referenda and legislative regulation to advance its aims. Yet at the same time, state courts in Massachusetts and California supported the right to same-sex marriage. In the first decade of the twenty-first century, citizens and non-state political actors worked outside the state, from below one might say, organizing either to prevent marriage between same-sex couples in the name of societal stability, or to advocate for gay and lesbian marriage in the name of obligations or individual rights. In either case, there were citizens attempting to act upon the institution in a way that had previously been the role of the state, and shifting questions of public obligations onto the institution.

The political debates over whether marriage is an obligation or a right have changed marriage. Over time marriage has shifted from a matter of common law embedded in the community to an institution requiring state marriage licenses; and from an economic imperative, based on the gendered division of labor and the necessity of biological reproduction, to an expression of the personal preference of partners, based on love and companionship. The political question of same-sex marriage would not have developed the way it did had the control of marriage not shifted from local communities to state jurisdiction, or had marriage not become increasingly defined by love and companionship.[4] And yet that shift to state-sanctioned love-based relationships has maintained a historical pattern in the institution of marriage as an economic relationship, albeit a different one from the past. For single mothers on welfare, marriage is now put forth as the preferred economic alternative, a path toward independence; and same-sex marriage advocates argue for the financial benefits marriage would offer them.

These legal and bureaucratic shifts in marriage affect the kind of role it can play politically. The political development of marriage itself is not a progressive story of a march towards greater inclusion. Rather, the institution has expanded and contracted over time. While ex-slaves gained the right to marry in 1865, intermarriage was largely prohibited, and eugenic marriage laws passed in the Progressive Era placed a pseudo-genetic constraint on the availability of marriage to citizens. Antimiscegenation laws were deemed unconstitutional in 1967; thirty years hence the Defense of Marriage Act signaled a movement towards utilizing the institution to impose restrictions on civil rights and secure hierarchies. There is thus as much precedent for using the institution of marriage to limit rights as there is for using it in efforts to expand them.

The political meaning and use of marriage has changed over time, yet certain characteristics endure that mark it, such as the way political questions around marriage return to defining notions of inclusion and belonging. During Reconstruction, marriage helped define freedom and citizenship rights for ex-slaves. During the Progressive Era, marriage came to represent a path to national belonging through immigration policy and politics. After the 1960s and continuing into the last two decades of the twentieth century, marriage has become a political institution through which citizens and state actors battle over the meaning of social and economic equality. As the book demonstrates, while in the course of our history marriage has come to be viewed as a fundamental right, marriage is still very much used and understood as a way to regulate behavior, enforce specific cultural values, meet institutional imperatives, and enforce the obligations of citizenship. This development could be understood as "intercurrence" as Stephen Skowronek and Karen Orren have defined it.[5] But while the debates that began in the 1990s around marriage suggest a fight over whether marriage is a personal choice or a public obligation, it is important to see also how they are actually intermeshed and co-constitutive, even as they are brought into conflict in the political arena. In the first decade of the twenty-first century, marriage looks very different politically than it did in the past, yet at the same time, there is a "historical construction" of marriage politics "in the simultaneous operation of older and newer instruments of governance."[6]

While this work draws on notions such as intercurrence, it also assumes a deep openness to the way politics works and the way institutions develop. Though bounded by the old and newer forms of regulation and emancipation, the outcome of any particular struggle over marriage cannot be predicted in advance. This work lays the ground for future research that continues to explore and attempts to understand the interplay between obligations and rights, and the dual embeddedness of the way that institutions create politics, but also how politics creates institutions, and the importance of cultural discourse in that framework.

The Institution of Marriage and Democratic Possibilities

I have shown how marriage can foster both egalitarian and hierarchical ends, and given an account of this interplay historically. One question this study thus raises is what other kinds of public discourse can we have today on marriage? The answer may lie in treating the institution as we might treat any other political institution, as one that should be open to contestation and transparent political debate. Changes in marriage have been linked to the political context in which they occur, demonstrating the opportunity to democratize the discourse about marriage—to think collectively about marriage and family as sites of practical politics, passionate attachments and potential for both repression and emancipation, which would then have consequences in the political arena.

In looking closely at the politics of marriage we see political undercurrents that could potentially change our political dialogue. For example, the 1967 *Loving* decision was a victory of the civil rights movement and the effort to desegregate American institutions in the name of equality. As analyzed in this book, this decision pivoted marriage toward the rights view; while the Moynihan Report, in positing the importance of marriage to "broken" black families, pivoted towards obligations. Critics of the Moynihan Report dismissed it for offering a cultural (and culturally pathologizing) remedy for a political and economic problem. Yet instead of focusing on how Moynihan dodged the structural roles that racism and material oppression have played in black poverty, critics might have used the opportunity to interrogate just how marriage and family structure both economics and race.

A similar point can be made regarding welfare reform in 1996, in its push to make poor single women marry in lieu of receiving government entitlements. What is happening to the role of marriage in this development between gender, race, and class inequality? What have we lost or gained? Who else is affected by this policy change?[7] And if marriage is a political institution, how does this law shape the citizenship and economic opportunities of those on welfare? Ironically, the argument that gays and lesbians should have the right to marry because of the economic and social benefits marriage incurs can be seen as supporting the very argument made in the 1990s for why poor single mothers must marry. Political arguments in one conflict can have unintended consequences in another, but my point is that these politics are linked under marriage.

Another example is the same-sex marriage debate. In July 2011, New York Governor Andrew Cuomo signed a bill that legalized same-sex marriage in his state. New York became the sixth state to legalize same-sex marriage. While this act was celebrated as a major victory for gay and lesbian rights, many gay and queer activists and intellectuals have also been critical and cautious regarding the focus on marriage. The question that same-sex marriage raises is not *will* the institution of marriage change or stay the same if same-sex marriage rights are granted, but rather *how* it will change. In other words, the institution will change, as it has historically, but how can we collectively and openly have debate about the stakes and possibilities?

Some debate has occurred. Scholars such as Michael Warner, Lisa Duggan, and Katherine Franke, all advocates of gay rights, have raised questions about attaching an emancipatory politics to marriage rights. In other words, they highlight the normalizing and state-centered quality of marriage. In separate ways, each has explained that a focus on marriage sacrifices the progressive impulse inherent in gay politics, suggesting how the emphasis on normalization has undermined the potential of earlier queer movements. Michael Warner has argued that the focus on marriage has accelerated and privileged the more assimilationist aspects of the gay rights struggle.[8] Lisa Duggan explained that "state regulation of households and partnerships does in fact affect the basic safety, prosperity, equality and welfare of all Americans."[9] Katherine Franke wrote in a *New York Times* op-ed that she worries that this right will essentially become an obligation to marry, or, in her words, "Winning the right to marry is one thing; being forced to marry is quite another."[10] The marriage pendulum may shift back toward obligation, as it has with welfare policy and the Healthy Marriage Initiative. Franke is worried that domestic partners will be required by both public and private employers to marry their partners in order to keep health and other benefits, and the freedom to choose a relationship will be lost. Winning this right, in other words, means that gays, lesbians, and heterosexuals potentially lose other rights and privileges in the process, and become obligated to behave and institutionalize their relationships in specific ways. Franke and others pinpoint critical democratic issues here.[11] There are federally funded policies, begun under the Bush administration and continued by the Obama administration, that provide coercive incentives for poor single mothers to marry, while authorizing private faith-based as well as secular organizations to conduct marriage promotion programs.

Same-sex couples and welfare recipients are positioned outside the norm of marriage; they have been marked as marriage offenders in the 1990s culture wars. Some same-sex marriage proponents have pushed back against this claim by arguing that they are not deviant, nor even different from, but rather are equivalent to heterosexual couples. Marriage thus shapes the political field such that gays and lesbians, rather than assembling under a political banner of alternative families alongside poor single mothers, as political scientist Cathy Cohen has advocated, locate themselves on the opposite side, at a distance from them.[12] The implication is that gays and lesbians want to marry but cannot, while poor single mothers refuse to marry and choose to remain outside traditional institutions.

The current mix—welfare policy's push for marriage and the argument that same-sex couples should choose to marry—highlights the role of marriage at the beginning of the twenty-first century as largely a form of governance and public life. Since the middle of the first decade of the twenty-first century, in the context of party polarization, prolonged fiscal crisis, high unemployment rates, severe cuts in social services and public education, and a diminished progressive movement, marriage has become an institution through which to debate and discuss the notions of obligations and social responsibility. For opponents of same-sex marriage, the contemporary arguments for the right of same-sex couples to marry undermine the notion of marriage as an obligation of citizens that helps to maintain societal order and stability. In 2011, the tendency to see and enforce marriage as an obligation could be read as a corollary of the view that collective economic responsibility is a bankrupt notion, and thus we must turn to marriage to reproduce the functions of state. The turn to marriage to resolve political problems recurs historically, as this book has shown, and this may be an accurate assessment of the situation in the early twenty-first century. Understanding the potency of marriage as a political institution, we might ask, as *Time* magazine did in a 2009 cover story, "Is there hope for the American marriage?"[13] Or we might ask a different question that is more befitting a democratic society: What do we want from marriage? When we see marriage as a product of prior political conflicts and settlements, we can better see our political interest in defining the institution of marriage.

Notes

Introduction

1. Jesse McKinley and John Schwartz, "Court Rejects Same-Sex Marriage Ban in California," *New York Times*, August 4, 2010.

2. The 1996 Personal Responsibility and Work Opportunity Reconciliation Act (PRWORA) (P.L. 104–193), also known as the 1996 Welfare Reform Act, was signed in to law on August 22, 1996, by President Bill Clinton.

3. Linda K. Kerber, *No Constitutional Right to Be Ladies: Women and the Obligations of Citizenship* (New York: Hill and Wang, 1998), preface, esp. xxii.

4. Karen Orren explores her notion of "belated feudalism" in her book of the same title. She observed this tension between feudalism and liberalism in American labor. See Karen Orren, *Belated Feudalism: Labor, the Law, and Liberal Development in the United States* (Cambridge: Cambridge University Press, 1991). I am grateful to Anne Norton for raising this connection to me.

5. Nancy F. Cott, *Public Vows: A History of Marriage and the Nation* (Cambridge, Mass.: Harvard University Press, 2000).

6. Anna Marie Smith, *Welfare Reform and Sexual Regulation* (New York: Cambridge University Press, 2007), 147.

7. John Locke, *The Second Treatise of Civil Government*, (1690) (http://www.constitution.org/jl/2ndtreat.htm), chap. 7, secs. 77 and 78.

8. Stephanie Coontz, *Marriage, a History: From Obedience to Intimacy or How Love Conquered Marriage* (New York: Viking, 2005); George Chauncey, *Why Marriage?: The History Shaping Today's Debate over Gay Equality* (New York: Basic Books, 2004).

9. Carole Pateman, *The Sexual Contract* (Stanford, Calif.: Stanford University Press, 1988), 16.

10. Alexis de Tocqueville, *Democracy in America* (New York: Vintage, 1990), vol. 2, book 3, chapter 10, 201–2. Jean-Jacques Rousseau, in *The Social Contract* (1792), explained: "Marriage . . . , being a civil contract, has civil consequences without which it would be impossible for society itself to subsist."

11. For marriage rates see Centers for Disease Control and Prevention. National Vital Statistics Reports (formerly Monthly Vital Statistics Report) (http://www.cdc.gov/nchs/products/nvsr.htm) (accessed June 10, 2010).

12. Katherine Franke, "Becoming a Citizen: Reconstruction Era Regulation of African American Marriages," *Yale Journal of Law & the Humanities* 11 (1999): 251–309.

13. On the relationship between family and practices of governance see Patricia Strach and Kathleen S. Sullivan, "The State's Relations: What the Institution of Family Tells Us About Governance," *Political Science Quarterly* 64, no. 1 (2011): 94–106.

14. I rely here on Karen Orren and Stephen Skowronek's definition of "political institution." Karen Orren and Stephen Skowronek, *The Search for American Political Development* (Cambridge: Cambridge University Press, 2004), 82–86. Although Orren and Skowronek do not extend their definition to include marriage, the institution is fruitfully viewed this way.

15. Ibid., 78.

16. Brenda Cossman, *Sexual Citizens: The Legal and Cultural Regulation of Sex and Belonging* (Stanford, Calif.: Stanford University Press, 2007), 71.

17. On the hidden role of family in the state see Patricia Strach, *All in the Family: The Private Roots of American Public Policy* (Stanford, Calif.: Stanford University Press, 2007).

18. There is a growing body of literature that looks at marriage and family in American political development, including Strach, *All in the Family*; Kathleen S. Sullivan, *Constitutional Context: Women and Rights Discourse in Nineteenth-Century America*, The Johns Hopkins Series in Constitutional Thought (Baltimore: Johns Hopkins University Press, 2007); Julie Novkov, *Racial Union: Law, Intimacy, and the White State in Alabama, 1865–1954* (Ann Arbor: University of Michigan Press, 2008).

19. Pateman, *The Sexual Contract*; Susan Moller Okin, *Women in Western Political Thought* (Princeton, N.J.: Princeton University Press, 1979); Tamara Metz, *Untying the Knot: Marriage, the State, and the Case for Their Divorce* (Princeton, N.J.: Princeton University Press, 2010).

20. Cott, *Public Vows*; Coontz, *Marriage, a History*; Hendrik Hartog, *Man and Wife in America: A History* (Cambridge, Mass.: Harvard University Press, 2000); Michael Grossberg, *Governing the Hearth: Law and the Family in Nineteenth-Century America*, Studies in Legal History (Chapel Hill: University of North Carolina Press, 1985).

21. For example, this book is influenced by works of Judith Butler, *Gender Trouble: Feminism and the Subversion of Identity* (New York: Routledge, 1999); Joan Scott, "Gender: A Useful Category of Historical Analysis," in *Gender and the Politics of History* (New York: Columbia University Press, 1988); Kimberlé Williams Crenshaw, "Mapping the Margins: Intersectionality, Identity Politics and Violence against Women of Color," *Stanford Law Review* 43, no. 6 (1991): 1244–99; Michael Warner, *The Trouble with Normal: Sex, Politics, and the Ethics of Queer Life* (New York: Free Press, 1999).

22. For examples of works that examine how institutions shapes identities see Victoria Charlotte Hattam, *In the Shadow of Race: Jews, Latinos, and Immigrant Politics in the United States* (Chicago: University of Chicago Press, 2007); Daniel J. Tichenor, *Dividing Lines: The Politics of Immigration Control in America*, Princeton Studies in American Politics (Princeton, N.J.: Princeton University Press, 2002); Eileen L. McDonagh, *The Motherless State: Women's Political Leadership and American Democracy* (Chicago: University of Chicago Press, 2009); Joseph E. Lowndes, *From the New Deal*

to the New Right: Race and the Southern Origins of Modern Conservatism (New Haven, Conn.: Yale University Press, 2008); Carol Nackenoff, *The Fictional Republic: Horatio Alger and American Political Discourse* (New York: Oxford University Press, 1994); Daniel HoSang, *Racial Propositions: Ballot Initiatives and the Making of Postwar California* (Berkeley: University of California Press, 2010); Kevin Bruyneel, *The Third Space of Sovereignty: The Postcolonial Politics of U.S.-Indigenous Relations* (Minneapolis: University of Minnesota Press, 2007); Gretchen Ritter, *The Constitution as Social Design: Gender and Civic Membership in the American Constitutional Order* (Stanford, Calif.: Stanford University Press, 2006); Richard M. Valelly, *The Two Reconstructions: The Struggle for Black Enfranchisement*, American Politics and Political Economy (Chicago: University of Chicago Press, 2004).

23. Margot Canady, *The Straight State: Sexuality and Citizenship in the Twentieth-Century America* (Princeton, N.J.: Princeton University Press, 2009).

24. On this final point, see Victoria C. Hattam and Joseph E. Lowndes, "The Ground beneath Our Feet: Language, Culture and Political Change," in *Formative Acts*, ed. Stephen Skowronek and Matthew Glassman (Philadelphia: University of Pennsylvania Press, 2007).

25. Building on Judith Butler's notion of gender performativity in Butler, *Gender Trouble*.

26. Gwendolyn Mink, "Aren't Poor Single Mothers Women? Feminists, Welfare Reform and Welfare Justice?," in *Whose Welfare?* (Ithaca, N.Y.: Cornell University Press, 1999); Smith, *Welfare Reform and Sexual Regulation*.

27. Mink, "Aren't Poor Single Mothers Women?"; Smith, *Welfare Reform and Sexual Regulation*.

28. Cott, *Public Vows*. Cott argues that monogamy and heterosexuality are political discourses imbued with power relations, see in particular chapter 1 where she analyzes this. This claim builds on the work that shows how identity based ideology such as political whiteness is a political discourse. See also Lowndes, *From the New Deal to the New Right*; Bruyneel, *The Third Space of Sovereignty*; HoSang, *Racial Propositions*.

29. In developing the comparison of marriage as a political institution to voting as a political institution, I use Alexander Keyssar, *The Right to Vote: The Contested History of Democracy in the United States* (New York: Basic Books, 2000), xxiii. Keyssar explains that voting rights did not expand as the nation grew but rather that they expanded at certain times and contracted in others. I argue the same point with marriage rights, which have expanded and constricted for different individuals and couples since the Civil War.

30. I borrow this phrase from Hartog, *Man and Wife in America*, 2.

31. Homer Harrison Clark, *The Law of Domestic Relations in the United States* (St. Paul: West Pub. Co., 1968), 35.

32. Hartog, *Man and Wife in America*, chapter 1.

33. U.S. Const., art. IV, § 1.

34. Jill Elaine Hasday, "Federalism and the Family Reconstructed," *UCLA Law Review* 45, no. 5 (1998): 1297.

35. "Meeting at Augusta, Me., in Behalf of the Freedmen—Speech of General Howard," National Freedmen, August 1865, 233–39, quoted in Amy Dru Stanley, *From Bondage to Contract: Wage Labor, Marriage and the Market in the Age of Slave Emancipation* (Cambridge: Cambridge University Press, 1988), 36.

36. The debate around Mormons and polygamy is a case in point. This book does not attempt to capture all political moments around marriage.

Chapter 1

1. These include the Civil Rights Acts of 1866, 1870, 1871, and 1875, the Expatriation Act of 1868, and the Naturalization Act of 1870. See generally Rogers M. Smith, *Civic Ideals: Conflicting Visions of Citizenship in U.S. History* (New Haven, Conn.: Yale University Press, 1997).

2. "Meeting at Augusta, Me., in Behalf of the Freedmen—Speech of Gen. Howard," National Freedmen, August 1865, 233–39, quoted in Amy Dru Stanley, *From Bondage to Contract: Wage Labor, Marriage, and the Market in the Age of Slave Emancipation* (Cambridge: Cambridge University Press, 1998), 36.

3. William Blackstone, *Commentaries in the Laws of England, 1765* (Chicago: University of Chicago Press, 1979), 430–33. See text also at http://avalon.law.yale.edu/18th_century/blackstone_bk1ch15.asp (accessed November 15, 2011). On coverture and common law marriage in the United States see Hendrik Hartog, *Man and Wife in America: A History* (Cambridge, Mass.: Harvard University Press, 2000).

4. Tocqueville, *Democracy in America* (New York, Vintage, 1990), vol. 2, book 3, chapter 12, p 212. See also Rogers M. Smith, "'One United People': Second-Class Female Citizenship and the American Quest for Community," *Yale Journal of Law & Humanities* 1 (1989): 229.

5. For this paragraph see Nancy F. Cott, "Giving Character to Our Whole Civil Polity: Marriage and the Public Order the Late Nineteenth Century," in *U.S. History as Women's History: New Feminist Essays*, ed. Linda Kerber, Alice Kessler-Harris, and Kathryn Kish Sklar (Chapel Hill: University of North Carolina Press, 1995), 112–14. See also Nancy F. Cott, *Public Vows: A History of Marriage and the Nation* (Cambridge, Mass.: Harvard University Press, 2000).

6. Katherine Franke, "Becoming a Citizen: Reconstruction Era Regulation of African American Marriages," *Yale Journal of Law & the Humanities* 11 (1999): 251–309.

7. Franke, "Becoming a Citizen," 277.

8. Laura Edwards, "'The Marriage Covenant is the Foundation of all Our Rights': The Politics of Slave Marriages in North Carolina Emancipation," *Law and History Review* 14, no. 1 (Spring 1996): 85. I thank Michele McKinley for bringing this article to my attention.

9. On the connection between contract and marriage, see Stanley, *From Bondage to Contract*. See also Cott, *Public Vows*, 85.

10. Cott explains that in July 1865 the Freedmen Bureau chief O. O. Howard announced a plan to allow freedmen to rent or buy farmland left by Confederates but it

was dropped by September that same year. Lincoln's successor, President Andrew Johnson, adamantly opposed the plan. See Cott, *Public Vows*, 85. For a discussion on free labor ideology as different from slave labor see Eric Foner, *Free Soil, Free Labor, Free Men* (New York: Oxford University Press, 1971). It is interesting to compare to later developments. Carol Nackenoff, *The Fictional Republic: Horatio Alger and American Political Discourse* (New York: Oxford University Press, 1994), chapter 1. Nackenoff explains how during the late nineteenth century, gentleman did not work for wages.

11. On slave family practices, see Laura F. Edwards, *Gendered Strife and Confusion: The Political Culture of Reconstruction*, Women in American History (Urbana: University of Illinois Press, 1997); Brenda E. Stevenson, *Life in Black and White: Family and Community in the Slave South* (New York: Oxford University Press, 1996); Ann Patton Malone, *Sweet Chariot: Slave Family and Household Structure in Nineteenth Century Louisiana* (Chapel Hill: University of North Carolina Press, 1992); Herbert George Gutman, *The Black Family in Slavery and Freedom, 1750–1925* (New York: Pantheon Books, 1976). For a good discussion of the changes in slave family historiography, see Franke, "Becoming a Citizen."

12. Quoted in Cott, *Public Vows*, 83.

13. The following three quotes are taken from "Answers to Interrogatories," April 29, 1863, Memphis, Tenn., signed by John Eaton, Jr., in Ira Berlin and Leslie S. Rowland, *Families and Freedom: A Documentary History of African-American Kinship in the Civil War Era* (New York: New Press, 1997), 157.

14. Report of John Eaton, General Superintendent of Freedom, Dept. of Tennessee, April 29, 1863, quoted in Franke, "Becoming a Citizen," 279–80.

15. "Answers to Interrogatories," April 29, 1863, Memphis, Tenn., signed by John Eaton, Jr., in Berlin and Rowland, *Families and Freedom*, 157.

16. Special Orders, No. 15, March 28, 1864, in Report of John Eaton, General Superintendent of Freedmen, Dept. of Tennessee, April 29, 1863, quoted in Franke, "Becoming a Citizen," 279.

17. Cott, *Public Vows*, 83.

18. Report by Chaplain Warren, May 18, 1864, included in Report of John Eaton, General Superintendent of Freedmen, Department of Tennessee, April 29, 1863, quoted in Franke, "Becoming a Citizen," 279.

19. Eric Foner, *Reconstruction: America's Unfinished Revolution, 1863–1877*, The New American Nation Series (New York: Harper & Row, 1988), 68.

20. Statement of Col. William A. Pile, Testimony taken in Kentucky, Tennessee, and Missouri, November and December, 1863, quoted in Franke, "Becoming a Citizen," 279.

21. Stanley, *From Bondage to Contract*, 35–36.

22. Preliminary Report Touching on the Condition and Management of Emancipated Refugees, Made to the Secretary of War by the American Freedmen's Inquiry Commission, June 30, 1863, and Final Report of the American Freedmen's Inquiry Commission to the Secretary of War, in Report of the Secretary of War, S. Exec. Doc. No. 53, 38th Cong., 1st sess. (1864), quoted in Stanley, *From Bondage to Contract*, 36.

23. Franke, "Becoming a Citizen," 280.

24. American Freedmen's Inquiry Commission, Final Report of the American Freedmen's Inquiry Commission to the Secretary of War, May 15, 1864, quoted in Franke, "Becoming a Citizen," 280.

25. Ibid.

26. Randall Miller, introduction in Paul A. Cimbala and Randall M. Miller, *The Freedmen's Bureau and Reconstruction: Reconsiderations* (New York: Fordham University Press, 1999), xv. The quote is from "An Act to Establish a Bureau for the Relief of Freedmen and Refugees," March 3, 1865, reprinted in Deirdre Mullane, *Crossing the Danger Water: Three Hundred Years of African-American Writing*, 1st Anchor Books ed. (New York: Anchor Books, 1993), 301–2.

27. Miller, introduction in Cimbala and Miller, *The Freedmen's Bureau and Reconstruction*, xvi, xxiv.

28. Foner, *Reconstruction*, 159.

29. Miller, introduction in Cimbala and Miller, *The Freedmen's Bureau and Reconstruction*, xix.

30. Ibid.

31. Cott, *Public Vows*, 85.

32. Stanley, *From Bondage to Contract*, 36.

33. Mary J. Farmer, "'Because They Are Women': Gender and the Virginia Freedmen's Bureau's 'War on Dependency,'" in Cimbala and Miller, *The Freedmen's Bureau and Reconstruction*, 161.

34. Stanley, *From Bondage to Contract*, 37. See also Records of the Assistant Commissioner for the State of South Carolina, Freedmen's Bureau, General Order No. 14, Charleston, 1866, "The Marriage Rules," Causes for Dissolving Marriage Agreements, Section 4 (http://freedmensbureau.com/southcarolina/marriagerules.htm).

35. General Orders No. 8, "Marriage Rules," HQ, Asst. Comm, Freedmen's Bureau, S.C., Ga., and Fla., August 11, 1865, quoted in Cott, *Public Vows*, 86.

36. General Order No. 8, "Marriage Rules," HQ, Asst. Comm., Freedmen's Bureau, S.C., Charleston, 1866, and General Order No. 8, S.C., Ga., and Fla., August 11, 1865, quoted in ibid., 87.

37. Records of the Assistant Commissioner for the State of South Carolina, Freedmen's Bureau, General Order No. 14, Charleston, 1866, "The Marriage Rules," Section 5, Duties of Husbands and Former Wives, http://freedmensbureau.com/southcarolina/marriagerules.htm

38. Clinton B. Fisk, report of Jan. 23, 1866, to Gen. Howard, and "Address to Freedmen," Dec. 26, 1865, quoted in Cott, *Public Vows*, 87.

39. Cott explains that even amid the atrocities assistant commissioners reported during this time, they frequently mentioned marriage problems. See ibid.

40. Circular No. 7, Office of Asst. Comm., Miss, Vicksburg, July 29, 1865, H.R. Exec. Docs., 39/1, 1866, vol. 8, 154–56 , quoted in ibid., 87.

41. There is a similar argument made about polygamy in the Utah territory. See Cott, *Public Vows*, 22.

42. For a longer discussion of Freedmen's Bureau policies that focused on freed women and how the Bureau and its conception of gender helped define the meaning of freedom, see Farmer, "'Because They Are Women.'"

43. Letter of Bureau Assistant Superintendent to Captain James A. Bates, April 30, 1866, Records of the Assistant Commissioner, Virginia, Records of the Freedmen's Bureau, in Stanley, *From Bondage to Contract*, 37.

44. Cott, *Public Vows*, 92–93.

45. Foner, *Reconstruction*, 87.

46. Cott, *Public Vows*, 93–94.

47. Michael Grossberg, *Governing the Hearth: Law and the Family in Nineteenth-Century America*, Studies in Legal History (Chapel Hill: University of North Carolina Press, 1985), 133.

48. Civil Rights Act of Nov. 25, 1865, Ch. 4, 2; 1865 Miss. Laws 82, 82. According to Katharine Franke, Georgia, North Carolina, South Carolina, and Virginia passed similar laws during this period; see Franke, "Becoming a Citizen," 277.

49. Edwards, *Gendered Strife and Confusion*, 32.

50. Cott, *Public Vows*, 89.

51. Act of Jan. 11, 1866, Ch. 1469, 1, 1865 Fla. Laws 31, quoted in Franke, "Becoming a Citizen," 278.

52. See, for example, Act of December 14, 1866, ch. 1552, 1, 1866, Fla. Laws 22, quoted in Franke, "Becoming a Citizen," 278.

53. See Act of March 10, 1866, ch. 40, 6, 1866 N.C. Laws 101, quoted in Franke, "Becoming a Citizen," 278. Franke explains that the cost of a certificate was 25 cents, which many slaves could not afford.

54. Franke makes a similar argument that marriage rights constituted state coercion but in different "institutional garb." See Franke, "Becoming a Citizen," 253.

55. "Meeting at Augusta, Me., in Behalf of the Freedmen—Speech of Gen. Howard," *National Freedmen*, August 1865, 233–39, quoted in Stanley, *From Bondage to Contract*, 36.

56. Peter W. Bardaglio, "Shamefull Matches: The Regulation of Interracial Sex and Marriage in the South before 1900," in *Sex, Love, Race: Crossing Boundaries in North American History*, ed. Martha Hodes (New York: New York University Press, 1999), 123. See generally Grossberg, *Governing the Hearth*; Nancy F. Cott, "Giving Character to Our Whole Civil Polity: Marriage and the Public Order in the Late Nineteenth Century," in *U.S. History as Women's History: New Feminist Essays*, ed. Linda Kerber, Alice Kessler-Harris, and Kathryn Kish Sklar (Chapel Hill: University of North Carolina Press, 1995); Peter Winthrop Bardaglio, *Reconstructing the Household: Families, Sex, and the Law in the Nineteenth-Century South*, Studies in Legal History (Chapel Hill: University of North Carolina Press, 1995).

57. Ernest Porterfield, *Black and White Mixed Marriages* (Chicago: Nelson-Hall, 1978), 11. There was one exception when, in 1872, the Supreme Court of Alabama struck down a law of that state prohibiting intermarriage of white and black persons as being "repugnant" to the Fourteenth Amendment. However, this decision was overturned five years later in *Green v. State of Alabama*, 58 Ala. 190, 197 (1877).

58. Julie Novkov, *Racial Union: Law, Intimacy, and the White State in Alabama, 1865–1954* (Ann Arbor: University of Michigan Press, 2008), 29.

59. *State of Indiana v. Gibson*, 36 Ind. 389 (1871), is an example of a challenge to the Fourteenth Amendment. See Novkov, *Racial Union*, 45.

60. The Civil Rights Act of 1866 declared that "all persons born in the United States . . . are citizens." All persons, "of every race and color," have the privilege to contract, hold property, and testify in court. See, for example, *Green v. State of Alabama*, 58 Ala. 190 (1878); and *Doc Lonas v. State of Tennessee*, 50 Tenn. 289 (1871). For more detail, see Novkov, *Racial Union*, 50–52.

61. Porterfield, *Black and White Mixed Marriages*, 11. Except in *Burns v. State*, 48 Ala. 195 (1872) the court struck down Alabama's law in 1872. See Novkov, *Racial Union*, 45.

62. *Scott v. State of Georgia*, 39 Ga. 326 (1869).

63. Cheryl Harris, "Whiteness as Property," *Harvard Law Review* 106, no. 8 (1993): 1738. Harris argues that whiteness functions as property both theoretically and functionally. The liberal view of property is that it includes the exclusive rights of possession, use, and disposition. Its attributes are the right to transfer or alienability, the right to use and enjoyment, and the right to exclude others. White identity and whiteness were sources of privilege and protection; their absence meant being the object of property. Slavery as a system of property facilitated the merger of white identity and property. Whiteness at various times signifies identity, status, and property singularly and in tandem. See in particular pp. 1721–31.

64. *Scott v. State of Georgia*, 39 Ga. 323 (1869) (emphasis mine).

65. Edwards, *Gendered Strife and Confusion*, 19–20 and chapter 4.

66. *Doc Lonas v. State of Tennessee*, 50 Tenn. 289 (1871).

67. See generally Peggy Pascoe, "Miscegenation Law, Court Cases and Ideologies of 'Race' in Twentieth-Century America," *Journal of American History* 83, no. 1 (1996): 44–69.

68. While historical evidence is inconclusive, contemporary observers during Reconstruction believed that racial intermixture appeared to take place less often than before the war. At the same time, given the rise in antimiscegenation statutes, clearly Southern whites feared that blacks after emancipation would rush to enter into interracial unions. Thus, the *idea* of interracial marriage posed a potential political threat. In addition, it is important to note that after the Civil War marriages between ex-slaves were made legal.

69. *Green v. State of Alabama*, 58 Ala. 190, 192 (1877).

Chapter 2

1. Charles Noble, *A Compendium of Laws on Marriage and Divorce* (New York, 1881), 28, quoted in Michael Grossberg, *Governing the Hearth: Law and the Family in Nineteenth-Century America*, Studies in Legal History (Chapel Hill: University of North Carolina Press, 1985), 92.

2. Robert H. Wiebe, *The Search for Order, 1877–1920* (New York: Hill and Wang, 1967).

3. See Andrew Joseph Polsky, *The Rise of the Therapeutic State*, The City in the Twenty-First Century (Princeton, N.J.: Princeton University Press, 1991), part 1.

4. Grossberg, *Governing the Hearth*, 83; Nancy F. Cott, *Public Vows: A History of Marriage and the Nation* (Cambridge, Mass.: Harvard University Press, 2000). Cott carefully examines the public nature of marriage in the United States. She discusses three levels of public authority that shapes marriage: local community; state legislators and judges; and federal laws and policies.

5. Stephen Skowronek, *Building a New American State: The Expansion of National Administrative Capacities, 1877–1920* (Cambridge: Cambridge University Press, 1982), 24.

6. For more on the politics of the Progressive Era see Victoria Charlotte Hattam, *In the Shadow of Race: Jews, Latinos, and Immigrant Politics in the United States* (Chicago: University of Chicago Press, 2007); Rogers M. Smith, *Civic Ideals: Conflicting Visions of Citizenship in U.S. History* (New Haven, Conn.: Yale University Press, 1997); Desmond S. King, *Making Americans: Immigration, Race, and the Origins of the Diverse Democracy* (Cambridge, Mass.: Harvard University Press, 2000); Daniel J. Tichenor, *Dividing Lines: The Politics of Immigration Control in America*, Princeton Studies in American Politics (Princeton, N.J.: Princeton University Press, 2002); Gail Bederman, *Manliness and Civilization: A Cultural History of Gender and Race in the United States, 1880–1917*, Women in Culture and Society (Chicago: University of Chicago Press, 1996); Eileen McDonagh, "Forging a New Grammer of Equality and Difference: Progressive Era Suffrage and Reform," in *Formative Acts*, ed. Stephen Skowronek and Matthew Glassman (Philadelphia: University of Pennsylvania, 2007).

7. Smith, *Civic Ideals*, 18, 411.

8. James A. Morone, *Hellfire Nation: The Politics of Sin in American History* (New Haven, Conn.: Yale University Press, 2003), 226. See also the Comstock Laws as an example of legal responses to anxieties over the perceived loose morals of immigrants.

9. Maldwyn A. Jones, *American Immigration*, The Chicago History of American Civilization (Chicago: University of Chicago Press, 1992), 216–17. On nativism, see John Higham, *Strangers in the Land Patterns of the American Nativism, 1860–1925* (New Brunswick, N.J.: Rutgers University Press, 2002), 224, 338.

10. King, *Making Americans*, 3.

11. Ibid., 50–81 in particular. Immigration policy and restriction laws were based in part on a discourse of difference and inferiority. Beginning in 1882, a series of restrictive

immigration acts were passed. In 1891, one act denied entry to "paupers, polygamists, and people with disease." In 1903, "epileptics, prostitutes, professional beggars [and] anarchists" were excluded. The 1907 act excluded "imbeciles, TB sufferers, and persons who committed a crime involving moral turpitude." In 1902, Chinese immigration was suspended for an indefinite period. Fear intensified with the Russo-Japanese War, which culminated in 1907 with the Gentleman's Agreement, whereby the Japanese government denied passports to laborers immigrating to the United States. Jones, *American Immigration*, 225–27; Edward P. Hutchinson and Balch Institute for Ethnic Studies, *Legislative History of American Immigration Policy, 1798–1965* (Philadelphia: University of Pennsylvania Press, 1981).

12. Smith, *Civic Ideals*, 467–68. Also quoted in King, *Making Americans*, 127–28.

13. Legal scholar Matthew Lindsay also makes an argument about the connection between new marriage rites, eugenic marriage laws, and reproduction, but his focus is not on marriage as a political institution through which questions of civic membership, order, and exclusion get contested. See Matthew Lindsay, "Reproducing a Fit Citizenry: Dependency, Eugenics and the Law of Marriage in the United States, 1860–1920," *Law and Social Inquiry* 23 (1998): 541.

14. Ibid., 555. For histories of marriage in the nineteenth century in the United States, see Grossberg, *Governing the Hearth*; Hendrik Hartog, *Man and Wife in America: A History* (Cambridge, Mass.: Harvard University Press, 2000); Cott, *Public Vows*.

15. Grossberg, *Governing the Hearth*, 92–93. Grossberg explained that compiling statistics, while long a practice in Europe, was avidly resisted in America and marked a deviation from traditional American practices.

16. See Kathleen S. Sullivan, *Constitutional Context: Women and Rights Discourse in Nineteenth-Century America*, The Johns Hopkins Series in Constitutional Thought (Baltimore: Johns Hopkins University Press, 2007). Sullivan examines the political and legal struggle over common law and liberalism.

17. Lindsay, "Reproducing a Fit Citizenry," 553–63; Grossberg, *Governing the Hearth*, 92–94. Lindsay argues that many policymakers believed that common-law notions of marital unity were inadequate when faced with the issue of cultural and biological difference brought on by massive immigration.

18. This and the following quotes from Cook are from Frank Gaylord Cook, "The Marriage Celebration in the United States," *Atlantic Monthly* 61 (1888): 520–32, quoted in Grossberg, *Governing the Hearth*, 84; Lindsay, "Reproducing a Fit Citizenry," 557.

19. *National Divorce Reform League: Annual Report of 1888* (Montpelier: Vermont Watchman and State Journal Press, 1889), quoted in Lindsay, "Reproducing a Fit Citizenry," 558. For more on Dike, see Grossberg, *Governing the Hearth*, 90–91.

20. *In re Mclaughlin's Estate*, 4 Wash. 570 (1892).

21. *In re McLaughlin's Estate*, 4 Wash. 570, 590 (1892). See also Lindsay, "Reproducing a Fit Citizenry," 561–63, for a discussion of this case.

22. For a fuller account of the transition from common-law marriage to registered

marriages rites, see Lindsay, "Reproducing a Fit Citizenry," 553–63; Grossberg, *Governing the Hearth*, 90–94.

23. *In re McLaughlin's Estate*, 4 Wash. 570, 591 (1892) (emphasis mine).

24. On eugenics, see Nancy Ordover, *American Eugenics: Race, Queer Anatomy and the Science of Nationalism* (Minneapolis: University of Minnesota Press, 2003); Michael Willrich, "The Two Percent Solution: Eugenic Jurisprudence and the Socialization of American Law, 1900–1930," *Law and History Review* 16 (Spring 1998): 63–111; Carl N. Degler, *In Search of Human Nature* (New York: Oxford University Press, 1991); Daniel J. Kevles, *In the Name of Eugenics: Genetics and the Uses of Human Hereditary* (New York: Alfred A. Knopf, 1985); Edward Larson, *Sex, Race and Science: Eugenics in the Deep South* (Baltimore: Johns Hopkins University Press, 1995); Dorothy Roberts, "Who May Give Birth to Citizens? Reproduction, Eugenics, and Immigration," in *Immigrants Out! The New Nativism and Anti-Immigrant Impulse in the U.S.*, ed. J. F. Perea (New York: New York University Press, 1996), 205–19.

25. Grossberg, *Governing the Hearth*, 148; Lindsay, "Reproducing a Fit Citizenry," 573.

26. Grossberg, *Governing the Hearth*, 147–50; Lindsay, "Reproducing a Fit Citizenry," 542. See also Mary Ziegler, "Eugenic Feminism: Mental Hygiene, the Women's Movement and the Campaign for Eugenic Legal Reform, 1900–1935," *Harvard Journal of Law and Gender* 31 (2008): 211–36.

27. Quoted in Grossberg, *Governing the Hearth*, 144.

28. Jones, *American Immigration*, 221.

29. Ziegler, "Eugenic Feminism." Ziegler discusses the way the rise of educated women during this period also fostered concerns about race suicide because educated women were not getting married and procreating. She cites Theodore Roosevelt, "Motherhood Is the Duty of Women," *New York Times*, March 14, 1905. Roosevelt was a critic of marriages between Americans and foreign-born immigrants and discussed the problem of race suicide. He was quoted in another *New York Times* article, "Roosevelt Censures Foreign Marriage," of May 3, 1908, as saying that the American citizen who deserved the least respect was the man "whose son is a fool and his daughter a foreign Princess." Quoted in Candice Lewis Bredbenner, *A Nationality of Her Own: Women, Marriage, and the Law of Citizenship* (Berkeley: University of California Press, 1998), 62. See also Thomas G. Dyer, *Theodore Roosevelt and the Idea of Race* (Baton Rouge: Louisiana State University Press, 1980).

30. Jones, *American Immigration*, 229.

31. Quoted in Lindsay, "Reproducing a Fit Citizenry," 568.

32. Grossberg, *Governing the Hearth*, 138.

33. See Julie Novkov, *Racial Union: Law, Intimacy, and the White State in Alabama, 1865–1954* (Ann Arbor: University of Michigan Press, 2008); Peggy Pascoe, "Miscegenation Law, Court Cases and Ideologies of 'Race' in Twentieth-Century America," *Journal of American History* 83, no. 1 (1996): 44–69; Cott, *Public Vows*.

34. Elsie Clews Parsons, *The Family* (New York: G. P. Putnam, 1906), quoted in Lindsay, "Reproducing a Fit Citizenry," 569.

35. Ibid.

36. Wash. Comp. Stat. Ann. §8439, quoted in Lindsay, "Reproducing a Fit Citizenry," 572 (emphasis mine).

37. Ind. Code Ann. §8365, quoted in Lindsay, "Reproducing a Fit Citizenry," 572.

38. *Gould v. Gould*, 78 Conn. 242 (1905).

39. *Gould v. Gould*, 78 Conn. 242, 244 (1905).

40. *Gould v. Gould*, 78 Conn. 242, 244 (1905).

41. *Peterson v. Widule*, 157 Wis. 641 (1915).

42. *Peterson v. Widule*, 157 Wis. 641, 647 (1915).

43. *Schoolcraft v. O'Neil*, 81 N.H. 240 (1923).

44. *Schoolcraft v. O'Neil*, 81 N.H. 240, 241 (1923).

45. The literature that examines women and nationality rights in the United States includes: Bredbenner, *A Nationality of Her Own*; Martha Mabie Gardner, *The Qualities of a Citizen: Women, Immigration, and Citizenship, 1870–1965* (Princeton, N.J.: Princeton University Press, 2005); Eithne Luibhéid, *Entry Denied: Controlling Sexuality at the Border* (Minneapolis: University of Minnesota Press, 2002); Nancy. F. Cott, "Marriage and Women's Citizenship in the United States, 1830–1934," *American Historical Review* 103, no. 5 (1988): 1440–74; Virginia Sapiro, "Women, Citizenship, and Nationality: Immigration and Naturalization Policies in the United States," *Politics and Society* 13, no. 1 (1984): 1–26.

46. Sapiro, "Women, Citizenship, and Nationality," 7–8.

47. Act of Feb. 10, 1855, 10 Stat. 604, sec 2.

48. While this was the case in some circumstances, it was not the norm—the fear and anxiety over the potential of immigrant women fraudulently marrying outweighed the actual situation. This was also the case for fears about the prevalence of interracial marriages during Reconstruction.

49. As Nancy Cott writes, "The intertwined meanings and obligations of marriage and citizenship and male headship of the family were all deformed and devalued by prostitutes' marriages to citizens, in the eyes of bureau officials." Cott, *Public Vows*, 148.

50. *Chy Lung v. Freeman et al.*, 92 U.S. 275 (1875). For more details on the case, see Bredbenner, *A Nationality of Her Own*, 29.

51. The Supreme Court ruling in *United States v. Wong Kim Ark*, 169 U.S. 649 (1898), declared that individuals of Chinese ancestry born in the United States would get birthright citizenship.

52. *Compilation from the Records of the Bureau of Immigration of Facts Concerning the Enforcement of the Chinese-Exclusion Laws*, H.R. Doc. 847, 59th Cong., 1st sess., at 110 (1906).

53. U.S. Bureau of Immigration, *Compilation from the Records of the Bureau of Immigration of Facts Concerning the Enforcement of the Chinese-Exclusion Laws*, H.R. Doc. No. 847, 59th Cong., 1st sess., at 110 (1906). See also Suchen Chan, "The Exclusion of

Chinese Women, 1870–1943," in *Entry Denied. Exclusion and the Chinese Community in America, 1882–1943*, ed. Suchen Chan (Philadelphia: Temple University Press, 1991).

54. U.S. Bureau of Immigration, Dillingham Commission, *Importing Women for Immoral Purposes*, S. Doc. No. 196, 61st Cong., 2d sess., Appendix IV-B, at 45 (1909). See also Bredbenner, *A Nationality of Her Own*, 30–34.

55. See, for instance, Kimberlé Williams Crenshaw, "Mapping the Margins: Intersectionality, Identity Politics and Violence against Women of Color," *Stanford Law Review* 43, no. 6 (1991): 1241–99; Evelyn Brooks Higginbotham, "African-American Women's History and the Metalanguage of Race," *Signs* 17, no. 2 (1992): 251–74.

56. U.S. Bureau of Immigration, Dillingham Commission, *Importation and Harboring of Women for Immoral Purposes*, S. Doc. No. 753, 61st Cong., 3d sess., at 57–95 (1911). For more on the immigrant women's experience see Gardner, *The Qualities of a Citizen: Women, Immigration, and Citizenship, 1870–1965*; Luibhéid, *Entry Denied: Controlling Sexuality at the Border*.

57. *Official Opinion of the Attorneys-General*, H.R. Doc. No. 1013, 61st Cong., 3d sess., vol. 27, at 508 (1909).

58. *Official Opinion of the Attorneys-General*, H.R. Doc. No. 1013, 61st Cong., 3d sess., vol. 27, at 516, 519 (1909).

59. *Official Opinion of the Attorneys-General*, H.R. Doc. No. 1013, 61st Cong., 3d sess., vol. 27, at 581 (1909).

60. For more on the Cable Act, see Bredbenner, *A Nationality of Her Own*, chapter 3.

61. Act of Mar. 2, 1907, 34, Stat. 1228, sec. 3.

62. 59th Cong., 2nd sess. (January 21, 1907), Congressional Record, p. 1465. See also Bredbenner, *A Nationality of Her Own*, chapter 2 for more on marital expatriation in the U. S. more generally.

63. Bredbenner, *A Nationality of Her Own*, 57.

64. *Mackenzie v. Hare*, 239 U.S. 299, 311 (1915).

65. *Mackenzie v. Hare*, 239 U.S. 299, 300 (1915). See also Bredbenner, *A Nationality of Her Own*, 65–70, who offers an informative account of this case; Cott, "Marriage and Women's Citizenship in the United States, 1830–1934," 144.

66. The dependent status of minor children has complicated their claims to U.S. citizenship. However, generally, anyone born in the United States is automatically granted U.S. citizenship under the Fourteenth Amendment. *United States v. Wong Kim Ark*, 169 U.S. 649 (1898).

Chapter 3

1. *Loving v. Virginia*, 388 U.S. 1, 12 (1967).

2. Stephanie Coontz, *Marriage, a History: From Obedience to Intimacy or How Love Conquered Marriage* (New York: Viking, 2005), 229.

3. Milton C. Regan, Jr., "Marriage at the Millennium," 33 *Family Law Quarterly* (1999): 652.

4. Coontz, *Marriage, a History*, 252–53. Coontz argues that the spread of no-fault divorce was a result of the rising dissatisfaction with marriage rather than a cause. Marriage was a contract that was difficult to break, requiring the establishment of fault, and collusive or deceptive practices were common in order to obtain a divorce. The divorce revolution started with California's law in 1969 and continued through the 1970s and 1980s with all states except South Dakota eventually passing no-fault divorce laws by 1985. Lenore J. Weitzman, *The Divorce Revolution: The Unexpected Social and Economic Consequences for Women and Children in America* (New York; London: Free Press, 1985), 41.

5. Kenneth S. Baer, *Reinventing Democrats: The Politics of Liberalism from Reagan to Clinton* (Lawrence: University Press of Kansas, 2000); Sidney Milkis, "The Modern Presidency, Social Movements and the Administrative State: Lyndon Johnson and the Civil Rights Movement," in *Race and American Political Development*, ed. Joseph Lowndes Julie Novkov and Dorrian T. Warren (New York: Routledge, 2008), 253–87.

6. President Lyndon B. Johnson, annual address to Congress on the State of the Union, January 8, 1964. See online President Johnson library: http://www.lbjlib.utexas.edu/johnson/archives.hom/speeches.hom/640108.asp.

7. Baer, *Reinventing Democrats*, 19.

8. Michael K. Brown, *Race, Money, and the American Welfare State* (Ithaca, N.Y.: Cornell University Press, 1999), 5.

9. Baer, *Reinventing Democrats*, 17.

10. Joseph E. Lowndes, *From the New Deal to the New Right: Race and the Southern Origins of Modern Conservatism* (New Haven, Conn.: Yale University Press, 2008), chapter 5. See also for example, Kevin Phillips, *The Emerging Republican Majority* (New Rochelle, N.Y.: Arlington House, 1969).

11. This and the following quotes are from his Howard University Commencement speech: President Lyndon B. Johnson, "To Fulfill These Rights—Remarks of the President at Howard University," June 4, 1965 in *The Moynihan Report and the Politics of Controversy; a Trans-Action Social Science and Public Policy Report*, ed. Lee Rainwater and William L. Yancey (Cambridge, Mass.: MIT Press, 1967), 125–32.

12. Tom Wicker, "U.S. Likely to Aid City Rights Plan," *New York Times*, June 6, 1965.

13. Robert E. Thompson, "Johnson Takes Lead in Negro Advancement," *Los Angeles Times*, June 20, 1965.

14. Wicker, "U.S. Likely to Aid City Rights Plan."

15. This and the following quotes from Wilkins are from Roy Wilkins, "Johnson Reveals All the 'Negro Problem,'" *Los Angeles Times*, June 14, 1965.

16. Lee Rainwater and William L. Yancey, *The Moynihan Report and the Politics of Controversy; a Trans-Action Social Science and Public Policy Report* (Cambridge, Mass.: MIT Press, 1967), 4.

17. United States Department of Labor Office of Policy Planning and Research, *The Negro Family, the Case for National Action* (Washington, D.C.: Superintendent of Documents, 1965), 5.

18. Ibid., foreword.

19. Ibid., 30.

20. Quoted in James T. Patterson, *Freedom Is Not Enough: The Moynihan Report and America's Struggle over Black Family Life: From LBJ to Obama* (New York: Basic Books, 2010), 22.

21. Daryl Michael Scott, *Contempt and Pity: Social Policy and the Image of the Damaged Black Psyche, 1880–1996* (Chapel Hill: University of North Carolina Press, 1997), 151.

22. Office of Policy Planning and Research, "The Moynihan Report," 48.

23. Ann DuCille, "Marriage, Family, and Other 'Peculiar Institutions' in African-American Literary History," *American Literary History* 21, no. 3 (2009): 608. On the development of this idea see Edward Franklin Frazier and Nathan Glazer, *The Negro Family in the United States* (Chicago: University of Chicago Press, 1966). Frazier was the first to make this claim. See also white historians such as Kenneth M. Stampp, *The Peculiar Institution: Slavery in the Ante-Bellum South* (New York: Knopf, 1956); Stanley M. Elkins, *Slavery* (Chicago: University of Chicago Press, 1959).

24. For an example of this see Oscar Lewis, *La Vida; a Puerto Rican Family in the Culture of Poverty--San Juan and New York* (New York: Random House, 1966). See also Laura Briggs, *Reproducing Empire: Race, Sex, Science, and U.S. Imperialism in Puerto Rico* (Berkeley: University of California Press, 2002). Briggs gives an analysis of Lewis and culture of poverty arguments.

25. John Herbers, "Report Focuses on Negro Family," *New York Times*, August 27, 1965, reprinted in Rainwater and Yancey, *The Moynihan Report and the Politics of Controversy*, 377.

26. Rainwater and Yancey, *The Moynihan Report and the Politics of Controversy*, 139.

27. Thomas J. Foley, "Racial Unrest Laid to Negro Family Failure," *Los Angeles Times*, August 14, 1965.

28. Jean M. White, "Family Report Sparks Debate," *Washington Post*, November 17, 1965, reprinted in Rainwater and Yancey, *The Moynihan Report and the Politics of Controversy*, 379.

29. As reported in J. W. Anderson, "Negro Homes Without Fathers May Increase," *New York Times*, September 16, 1966.

30. Kay S. Hymowitz, "The Black Family: 40 Years of Lies" (http://www.city-journal.org/html/15_3_black_family.html, *City Journal*, August 25, 2005) (accessed May 31, 2011).

31. Stokely Carmichael and Charles V. Hamilton, *Black Power: The Politics of Liberation in America* (New York: Vintage Books, 1967), 40, emphasis in original, quoted in Milkis, "The Modern Presidency, Social Movements and the Administrative State: Lyndon Johnson and the Civil Rights Movement," 266.

32. Stokely Carmichael, with M. T. Ekwueme, *Ready for Revolution: The Life and Struggles of Stokely Carmichael* (New York: Scribner, 2003), 527, emphasis in original, quoted in Milkis, "The Modern Presidency, Social Movements and the Administrative State: Lyndon Johnson and the Civil Rights Movement," 266.

33. Quoted in Patterson, *Freedom Is Not Enough,* 61.

34. James Farmer, "The Controversial Moynihan Report," *Amsterdam News,* December 18, 1965, reprinted in Rainwater and Yancey, *The Moynihan Report and the Politics of Controversy,* 410.

35. Patterson, *Freedom Is Not Enough,* 61.

36. See Martin Luther King, Jr., An address delivered at the Abbott House, Westchester County, New York, October 29, 1965 (Abbott House Address), reprinted in Rainwater and Yancey, *The Moynihan Report and the Politics of Controversy,* 402–9; Whitney Young in *To Be Equal* as explained in Patterson, *Freedom Is Not Enough,* 77.

37. Patterson, *Freedom Is Not Enough,* 78.

38. Martin Luther King, Jr., Abbott House Address, reprinted in Rainwater and Yancey, *The Moynihan Report and the Politics of Controversy,* 402–5.

39. Ibid., 404.

40. Coontz, *Marriage, a History,* 248; Ann Snitow, "A Gender Diary," in *Conflicts in Feminism,* ed. Marianne Hirsch and Evelyn Fox Keller (New York: Routledge, 1990); Ruth Rosen, *The World Split Open: How the Modern Women's Movement Changed America* (New York: Penguin Books, 2006); Rosalyn Fraad Baxandall and Linda Gordon, *Dear Sisters: Dispatches from the Women's Liberation Movement* (New York: Basic Books, 2000).

41. Margaret Sanger and other reformers began advocating for birth control early in the century, but it was in 1960, with the commercial availability of the birth control pill Enovid, that the relationship between sex and reproduction immediately changed. More than six million women were taking the pill within five years of its Federal Drug Administration approval, and birth control gave women some sexual freedom. As birth rates fell within and outside marriage, the contours of marriage changed, altering the relationship between men and women. Country singer Loretta Lynn captured the mood in her hit 1975 song, "The Pill": "I'm tearin' down this brooder house 'cause now I've got the pill." See Coontz, *Marriage, a History,* 254–55.

42. Casey Hayden and Mary King, SNCC, "A Kind of Memo," on feminism and the civil rights movement, 1965, reprinted in Baxandall and Gordon, *Dear Sisters,* 21. The Feminists, "Women: Do You Know the Facts about Marriage?" 1969, reprinted in Nancy MacLean, *The American Women's Movement, 1945–2000: A Brief History with Documents* (Boston: Bedford/St. Martin's, 2009), 87.

43. NOW Statement of Purpose, adopted at NOW's first national conference, Washington, D.C., October 29, 1966 (http://www.now.org/history/purpos66.html) (accessed June 7, 2010).

44. Ibid.

45. Gloria Steinem, "After Black Power, Women's Liberation," *New York Magazine,* April 7, 1969, 8.

46. Betty Friedan, *The Feminine Mystique* (New York: W. W. Norton, 2001), 266–67, 393.

47. For more on the influence of Friedan's work see Stephanie Coontz, *A Strange*

Stirring: The Feminine Mystique and American Women at the Dawn of the 1960s (New York: Basic Books, 2011).

48. Gayle Graham Yates, *What Women Want: The Ideas of the Movement* (Cambridge, Mass.: Harvard University Press, 1975), 6.

49. Jane F. Gerhard, *Desiring Revolution: Second-Wave Feminism and the Rewriting of American Sexual Thought, 1920 to 1982* (New York: Columbia University Press, 2001), 92.

50. Kate Millett, *Sexual Politics* (Urbana: University of Illinois Press, 2000), 33 (emphasis mine).

51. Ibid., 66–68.

52. Ibid., 126–27, also quoted in Yates, *What Women Want*, 83.

53. Shulamith Firestone, *The Dialectic of Sex: the Case for a Feminist Revolution* (New York: Bantam Books, 1972), 224.

54. Reprinted in Baxandall and Gordon, *Dear Sisters*, 90.

55. The Feminists, "Marriage," written by Sheila Cronan, reprinted in Koedt, Anne, Ellen Levine, and Anita Rapone, *Radical Feminism* (New York: Quadrangle Books, 1973), 213.

56. The Feminists, "Women: Do You Know the Facts about Marriage?," 1969, reprinted in MacLean, *The American Women's Movement, 1945–2000*, 87. The pamphlet also pointedly exclaimed that, under most states' marriage laws, a husband's rape of his wife was legal.

57. Rosen, *The World Split Open*, 196.

58. Phyllis Schlafly, "What's Wrong with 'Equal Rights' for Women?" 1972, reprinted in MacLean, *The American Women's Movement, 1945–2000*, 113. For a history of the ERA, see Jane J. Mansbridge, *Why We Lost the ERA* (Chicago: University of Chicago Press, 1986). For background on Schlafly, see Donald T. Critchlow, *Phyllis Schlafly and Grassroots Conservatism: A Woman's Crusade*, Politics and Society in Twentieth-Century America (Princeton, N.J.: Princeton University Press, 2005); and Coontz, *Marriage, a History*, 249.

59. Coontz, *Marriage, a History*, 249–50.

60. *Loving v. Virginia*, 388 U. S. 1, 12 (1967).

61. Peggy Pascoe, *What Comes Naturally: Miscegenation Law and the Making of Race in America* (Oxford: Oxford University Press, 2009), 255.

62. Renee Christine Romano, *Race Mixing: Black-White Marriage in Postwar America* (Cambridge, Mass.: Harvard University Press, 2003), 190.

63. Ibid., 186.

64. The "fundamental" right of marriage came from the 1947 decision in *Perez v. Sharp* (32 Cal. 2d 711). In that case, as Peggy Pascoe explains, lawyer Dan Marshall argued that interracial marriage was a natural right, contradicting the "unnatural" label that had been a mainstay of miscegenation law since the 1880s. Marshall based his argument on the decision in *Meyer v. Nebraska* (262 U. S. 390 (1923)), a little-known case that had nothing to do with marriage but that defined the personal "liberty" guaranteed by

the Fourteenth Amendment as the individual's right "to marry, establish a home . . . and generally to enjoy those privileges, long recognized at common law as essential to the orderly pursuit of happiness by free men." The narrow 4–3 decision in *Perez* made California's miscegenation law unconstitutional. The court's decision defined marriage not as a natural right but as a fundamental right of free men. And as a fundamental right, marriage could not, under the equal protection clause of the Fourteenth Amendment, be limited on the basis of race. Pascoe, *What Comes Naturally,* 218, 278.

65. Brief of the National Association for the Advancement of Colored People as Amicus Curiae, Robert L. Carter, 1967 WL 93611, 5.

66. Ibid.

67. Pascoe, *What Comes Naturally,* 3.

68. Peggy Pascoe, "Miscegenation Law, Court Cases and Ideologies of 'Race' in Twentieth-Century America," *Journal of American History* 83, no. 1 (1996): 44–69.

69. Julie Novkov explains that the "court established an analytical structure for rejecting racialized limits on marriage" but "did not address in any substantial way the structural and institutional sources of state repression of socially subordinated racial minorities." Julie Novkov, *Racial Union: Law, Intimacy, and the White State in Alabama, 1865–1954* (Ann Arbor: University of Michigan Press, 2008), 272. In her introduction to *What Comes Naturally,* Peggy Pascoe explains two different approaches to the subject of miscegenation. One is rooted in the politics of civil rights and the tenets of liberal individualism. The other is a newer approach that, influenced by critical race studies and cultural studies, shows how law shapes identity, produces "race" categories, and a cultural "obsession" with interracial sex and marriage. Works in this vein focus on the broader processes of white supremacy and how antimiscegenation law played a role in state making. Pascoe aligns herself with this newer approach.

70. *Loving v. Virginia,* 388 U.S. 12 (1967).

71. *Meyer v. Nebraska,* 262 U.S. 390, 396 (1923).

72. Randall Kennedy captures this as a shift from the rallying cry of "We Shall Overcome" to "Black Power," during which the rejection of interracial unions gained prestige and prominence. Randall Kennedy, *Interracial Intimacies: Sex, Marriage, Identity, and Adoption* (New York: Vintage, 2004), 111.

73. Quoted in Pascoe, *What Comes Naturally,* 302.

74. Kennedy, *Interracial Intimacies,* 110–20. The argument that intermarriage was destructive to racial solidarity was the principal basis of opposition; another criticism was that it robbed black women of black men, who should be their natural partners, thus weakening women's position in the marriage market.

75. Romano, *Race Mixing,* 218.

76. Joseph R. Washington, Jr., *Marriage in Black and White* (Boston: Beacon Press, 1971), 1–2.

77. J. P. Pitts, review essay, *Marriage in Black and White* by Joseph R. Washington, Jr., in the *Journal of Black Studies* 1, no. 4 (1971): 499–502.

Chapter 4

1. Personal Responsibility and Work Opportunity Act, Public Law 104–193 (1996), sec. 101.

2. Defense of Marriage Act, Public Law 104–199 (1996).

3. George Chauncey, *Why Marriage?: The History Shaping Today's Debate over Gay Equality* (New York: Basic Books, 2004), 59 and chapter 3; Stephanie Coontz, *Marriage, a History*, in particular chapters 16–17.

4. John D'Emilio, "The Marriage Fight Is Setting Us Back," *Gay & Lesbian Review Worldwide* 13, no. 6 (2006).

5. Chauncey, *Why Marriage?*, 66–71. Chauncey explains these fundamental changes in depth.

6. Ibid., 37.

7. In the late 1970s, the lack of direct data on cohabitation, and survey questions that asked respondents to identify nonmarital cohabitation relationships required the Census Bureau to infer marriage rates based on household composition. This resulted in what became known as POSSLQ (pronounced pah-sul-cue)—"persons of the opposite sex sharing living quarters." This concept and its acronym became culturally commonplace, as witnessed by popular book titles in the 1980s such as *There's Nothing That I Wouldn't Do If You Would Be My POSSLQ* and *Will You Be My POS-SLQ?* The category "unmarried partner" first appeared in the 1990 Census and was incorporated into the monthly Current Population Survey starting in 1995, after which POSSLQ became obsolete. U.S. Census Bureau, Population Division, Fertility & Family Statistics Branch, authors Lynne M. Casper, Philip N. Cohen, and Tavia Simmons (http://www.census.gov/population/www/documentation/twps0036/twps0036.html) (accessed November 18, 2011).

8. "American Law Institute Publishes *Principles of the Law of Family Dissolution*," May 15, 2002 (http://www.ali.org/ali_old/pr051502.htm) (accessed November 18, 2011).

9. *Turner v Safley*, 482 U.S. 78, 95 (1987).

10. *Zablocki v Redhail* 434 U. S. 374, 383–84 (1978).

11. Also important was the conceptualization of privacy in marriage through reproductive cases such as *Roe v. Wade*, 410 U.S 113 (1973).

12. Phyllis Schlafly, "What's Wrong with 'Equal Rights' for Women?" 1972 reprinted in MacLean, *The American Women's Movement, 1945–2000: A Brief History with Documents* (Boston: Bedford/St. Martin's, 2009), 113. The STOP ERA campaign was successful: "The U.S. House of Representatives fails to pass the ERA by a vote of 278 for the ERA and 147 against the ERA, only 6 votes short of the required 2/3 majority for passage. Fourteen cosponsors voted NO and three cosponsors did not vote. Only 30% of the Republicans voted YES and 85% of the Democrats voted YES" (1983) (http://www.now.org/issues/economic/cea/history.html) (accessed February 11, 2010).

13. A focal point for President Reagan was the "welfare queen," a figure first raised in a 1976 speech "'Welfare Queen' Becomes Issue in Reagan Campaign," *New York Times*,

February 15, 1976, 51. See also Sharon Hays, *Flat Broke with Children: Women in the Age of Welfare Reform* (Oxford and New York: Oxford University Press, 2003); Ange-Marie Hancock, *The Politics of Disgust: The Public Identity of the Welfare Queen* (New York: New York University Press, 2004).

14. Edward G. Carmines and James A. Stimson, *Issue Evolution: Race and the Transformation of American Politics* (Princeton, N.J.: Princeton University Press, 1989).

15. James Davison Hunter, *Culture Wars: The Struggle to Define America* (New York: Basic Books, 1991).

16. "Address to the Republican National Convention," delivered by Patrick Buchanan, August 17, 1992, Houston, Tex. (http://www.americanrhetoric.com/speeches/patrickbuchanan1992rnc.htm) (accessed May 20, 2011).

17. "Address to the Commonwealth Club of California," delivered by Dan Quayle, May 19, 1992 (http://www.vicepresidentdanquayle.com/speeches_StandingFirm_CCC_1.html) (accessed May 15, 2011). The speech was penned by conservative writer Lisa Schriffen.

18. "Dan Quayle vs. Murphy Brown," *Time*, June 1, 1992 (http://www.time.com/time/magazine/article/0,9171,975627,00.html) (accessed February 11, 2010).

19. Ibid.

20. These and the following quotes from Whitehead are from Barbara Whitehead, "Dan Quayle Was Right," *The Atlantic*, March/April 1993 (http://www.theatlantic.com/magazine/print/1993/04/dan-quayle-was-right/7015/) (accessed February 11, 2010).

21. James Q. Wilson from a *Commentary* article dated March 1996, excerpted in Andrew Sullivan, *Same-Sex Marriage, Pro and Con: A Reader* (New York: Vintage Books, 1997), 163–64.

22. Ibid., 164.

23. William Bennett, "But Not a Very Good Idea, Either," *Washington Post*, May 21, 1996, quoted in House Committee on the Judiciary, Defense of Marriage Act, H.R. Report 104–664, at 15 (July 9, 1996).

24. On the genealogy of the term "dependency," see Nancy Fraser and Linda Gordon, "A Genealogy of Dependency: Tracing a Keyword of the U.S. Welfare State," *Signs* 19, no. 2 (1994): 309–36.

25. For more on the politics of behavior see Adolph Reed, Jr., "The 'Underclass' as Myth and Symbol: The Poverty of Discourse About Poverty," in *Stirrings in the Jug* (Minneapolis: University of Minnesota Press, 1999).

26. Charles Murray, "The Coming White Underclass," *Wall Street Journal*, October 29, 1993.

27. William J. Wilson, *The Truly Disadvantaged: The Inner City, the Underclass, and Public Policy* (Chicago: University of Chicago Press, 1990), 3.

28. Ibid., 83.

29. Ibid., 7, 137–78. See also Alejandra Marchevsky and Jeanne Theoharis, "Welfare Reform, Globalizaton and the Racialization of Entitlement," *American Studies* 41, nos. 2–3 (Summer/Fall 2000): 245.

30. Gayle Pollard Terry, "William Julius Wilson: Defending the Safety Net in the Welfare-Reform Debate," *Los Angeles Times*, November 3, 1996.

31. Governor Bill Clinton, "The New Covenant: Responsibility and Rebuilding the American Community," remarks to students at Georgetown University, October 23, 1991 (http://www.dlc.org/ndol_ci.cfm?kaid=128&subid=174&contentid=2783) (accessed August 17, 2010).

32. "The New American Choice Resolution" (http://www.dlc.org/documents/cleveland_proclamation.pdf) Resolutions adopted at the Democratic Leadership Council Convention, Cleveland, Ohio, May 1, 1991, 12.

33. President Clinton "State of the Union Address," January 23, 1996 (http://clinton4.nara.gov/WH/New/other/sotu.html) (accessed June 14, 2011).

34. On this point, see Gwendolyn Mink, "Aren't Poor Single Mothers Women? Feminists, Welfare Reform and Welfare Justice?," in *Whose Welfare?* (Ithaca, N.Y.: Cornell University Press, 1999).

35. "The New American Choice Resolution," 8.

36. Quoted in Holloway Sparks, "Queens, Teens, and Model Mothers: Race, Gender and the Discourse of Welfare Reform," in *Race and the Politics of Welfare Reform*, ed. Sanford Schram, Joe Soss, and Richard C. Fording (Ann Arbor: University of Michigan Press, 2003), 182.

37. Tommy Thompson on Welfare Policy, August 12, 1995 (http://www.ontheissues.org/2008/Tommy_Thompson_Welfare_+_Poverty.htm) (accessed June 14, 2011).

38. Hearing Before the Subcommittee on Human Resources of the House Committee on Ways and Means, *Contract with America—Welfare Reform*, 104th Cong., 1st sess, February 2, 1995, 852.

39. Ibid., 868.

40. Ibid., 827.

41. Hearing before the Subcommittee on Human Resources of the House Committee on Ways and Means, *Causes of Poverty, with a Focus on out-of-Wedlock Births,* 104th Cong., 2nd sess. March 12, 1996, 4.

42. Ibid., 19–20.

43. Interview: "Welfare Reform, Ten Years Later," based on Ron Haskins's book *Work over Welfare: The Inside Story of the 1996 Welfare Reform Law*, August 24, 2006 (http://www.brookings.edu/interviews/2006/0824welfare_haskins.aspx) (accessed June 14, 2011).

44. Mink, "Aren't Poor Single Mothers Women?" For an analysis of the notion of the underclass, see Adolph Reed, Jr., "The 'Underclass' as Myth and Symbol: The Poverty of Discourse About Poverty," in *Stirrings in the Jug.*

45. PRWORA, 42 U.S.C. § 601 (1996).

46. Welfare was established in the New Deal era and redefined in Supreme Court rules in the late 1960s and early 1970s as a network of entitlements that greatly enhanced Americans' citizenship rights. In 1973, in *King v. Smith*, the Supreme Court established a statutory entitlement to poverty assistance. This case was viewed as an overwhelm-

ing gain for welfare recipients. Although statutory rights are weaker than constitutional rights, since they can be eliminated by changing the federal law in question, this decision nevertheless extended a statutory entitlement to poverty assistance to welfare recipients for the first time.

47. Department of Health and Human Services, Administration for Children and Families, Major Provisions of the Personal Responsibility and Work Opportunity Reconciliation Act of 1996, P.L. 104–193 (http://www.acf.hhs.gov/programs/ofa/law-reg/finalrule/aspesum.htm) (accessed August 15, 2011); Anna Marie Smith, "The Politicization of Marriage in Contemporary American Public Policy: The Defense of Marriage Act and the Personal Responsibility Act," *Citizenship Studies* 5, no. 3 (2004): 311.

48. Mink argues this law severely limits women's citizenship rights in Mink, "Aren't Poor Single Mothers Women?" See also Sandra Morgen, Joan Acker, and Jill Michele Weigt, *Stretched Thin: Poor Families, Welfare Work, and Welfare Reform* (Ithaca, N.Y.: Cornell University Press, 2010) for in-depth analysis of welfare in Oregon.

49. P.L. 104–193, August 22, 1996, Title 1, Part A—Block Grants to States for Temporary Assistance for Needy Families; Sec. 401 Purpose, 42 U.S.C. 601.

50. Stacey Bouchet, Theodora Ooms, and Mary Parke, *Beyond Marriage Licenses: Efforts in States to Strengthen Marriage and Two-Parent Families* (Washington, D.C.: Center for Law and Social Policy, 2004); Michael Tanner, *The Poverty of Welfare: Helping Others in Civil Society* (Washington, D.C: Cato Institute, 2003), 140. For a critique of this policy, see Stephanie Coontz and Nancy Folbre, "Marriage, Poverty and Public Policy," Paper presented at Fifth Annual Council on Contemporaty Familes Conference, April 26–28, 2002 (http://www.contemporaryfamilies.org/economic-issues/povertypolicy.html) (accessed September 20, 2006).

51. Hearing before the Subcommittee on Human Resources of the House Committee on Ways and Means, *Welfare Reform*, 104th Cong., 2d sess., May 22 and 23, 1996, 80.

52. Quoted in Sparks, "Queens, Teens, and Model Mothers," 180.

53. Hearing before the Subcommittee on Human Resources of the House Committee on Ways and Means, *Defense of Marriage Act*, 104th Cong., 2d sess., May 15, 1996, H.R. 3396, Defense of Marriage Act, as introduced on May 7, 1996, 104th Cong., 2d sess., 4–5.

54. Defense of Marriage Act P.L 104–199.

55. Defense of Marriage Act P.L 204–199, Sec. 2 Powers Reserved to the States.

56. For this history, see Chauncey, *Why Marriage?*, 37, 51–54.

57. Ibid., 44–46.

58. *Baehr v. Lewin*, 74 Haw. 645, 852 P.2d 44 (1993). The case was appealed in *Baehr v. Miike* (1996). In 1998 Hawaii amended its constitution to prohibit same-sex marriage. The Supreme Court of Hawaii, in its original *Baehr v. Lewin* ruling, defined marriage as a "state-conferred legal partnership status, the existence of which gives rise to a multiplicity of rights." In 1999 (*Baehr v. Miike*) Hawaii's high court ruled that Hawaii's constitution no longer protected lesbian and gay individuals with regard to their freedom to marry.

59. U.S. House Committee on the Judiciary, Report submitted by Charles Canady, "Defense of Marriage Act," 104th Cong., 2d sess., 104–664, July 9, 1996, 2.

60. Ibid., 1–18.

61. Ibid., 8.

62. Ibid., 9–10.

63. Ibid., 10.

64. Ibid., 12–18.

65. Ibid., 2.

66. Quoted in Chauncey, *Why Marriage?*, 162.

67. For an example of this argument, see Thomas Byrne Edsall and Mary D. Edsall, *Chain Reaction: The Impact of Race, Rights, and Taxes on American Politics* (New York: W. W. Norton, 1992).

68. This quote and the following quote are from Canady, "Defense of Marriage Act," 13–14.

69. Ibid., 17.

70. Ibid., 17 n. 57 from Arkes's prepared statement.

71. Remarks by President Bill Clinton at the National Prayer Breakfast, February 1, 1996 (http://www.presidency.ucsb.edu/ws/?pid=51934#axzz1eC6U1gl1) (accessed August 15, 2011) (emphasis added).

72. J. Jennings Moss, Bill Clinton interview, 1996, *The Advocate*, June 25, 1996, p. 50.

73. *Congressional Record*, 104th Cong., 1995–96, Defense of Marriage Act, House of Representatives, July 12, 1996, p. H17170.

74. House Debate on the Defense of Marriage Act, July 11, 1996, statement from John Lewis, reprinted in Sullivan, *Same-Sex Marriage, Pro and Con*, 230.

75. Senate Debate on the Defense of Marriage Act, September 10, 1996, statement from John Kerry, reprinted in Sullivan, *Same-Sex Marriage, Pro and Con*, 231.

76. Smith, "The Politicization of Marriage in Contemporary American Public Policy," 309.

Chapter 5

1. Sadie Fields, chairwoman of the Christian Coalition of Georgia, in Bill Rankin, "Lobbyists' Face Off," *Atlanta Journal and Constitution*, February 24, 2004: B1. Pat Buchanan made a similar statement at the 1992 Republic Convention in his "culture wars" speech.

2. George W. Bush, Fourth State of the Union Address, January 20, 2004 (http://www.gpoaccess.gov/sou/index.html) (accessed April 21, 2011).

3. Katherine Franke, "The Politics of Same-Sex Marriage Politics," *Columbia Journal of Gender and Law* 15, no. 1 (2006): 241.

4. Caitlin Flanagan, "Is There Hope for the American Marriage?" *Time*, July 2, 2009 (http://www.time.com/time/nation/article/0,8599,1908243-2,00.html) (accessed April 15, 2011).

5. Sean E. Brotherson and William C. Duncan, "Rebinding the Ties That Bind: Government Efforts to Preserve and Promote Marriage," *Family Relations* 53, no. 5 (2004): 461. See also "The Emerging Field of Marriage Education: Creating Smart Marriages for the Millennium" (http://www.smartmarriages.com/fish.htm) (accessed August 15, 2011).

6. Brotherson and Duncan, "Rebinding the Ties That Bind," 461.

7. Ibid. In covenant marriage, the parties agree that they cannot dissolve the marriage without showing one of a number of fault grounds, which include adultery, felony convictions, abandonment, abuse, and two-year separation. Since 1997 at least 23 state legislatures have introduced covenant marriage statutes, but few have passed them. The Florida statute was the Marriage Preparation and Preservation Act of 1998.

8. Brotherson and Duncan, "Rebinding the Ties That Bind," 462.

9. The statement was the result of a conference on January 24–25, 2000 held in New York City and was produced by the following groups: Coalition for Marriage, Family and Couples Education; Institute for American Values; and the Religion, Culture, and the Family Project. The report was published by the Institute for American Values.

10. For the full list of signatories, see Institute for American Values (http://www.americanvalues.org/pdfs/marriagemovement.pdf).

11. Ibid., 2–3.

12. Ibid., 7.

13. Ibid., 3–4.

14. Ibid., 4.

15. Ibid., 10.

16. Ibid., 7.

17. Ibid., 13–19 for full list of initiatives.

18. Brotherson and Duncan, "Rebinding the Ties That Bind," 463.

19. Pam Belluck, "Some States Act to Save Marriage Before the 'I Dos,'" *New York Times*, April 21, 2000 (http://www.nytimes.com/00/04/21/news/national/marriage-classes.html) (http://www.smartmarriages.com/movement.nytimes.html) (accessed November 19, 2011).

20. *Maynard v. Hill*, 125 U.S. 190 (1888).

21. Robert Rector, "Implementing Welfare Reform and Restoring Marriage," in *Priorities for the President*, ed. Stuart M. Butler and Kim Holmes (Washington, D.C.: Heritage Foundation, 2001), 71–97.

22. Theodora Ooms, "Adapting Healthy Marriage Programs for Disadvantaged and Culturally Diverse Populations: What Are the Issues?" Center for Law and Social Policy, Policy Brief, No. 10, March 2007. See also Melanie Heath, "State of Our Unions: Marriage Promotion and the Contested Power of Heterosexuality," *Gender & Society* 23, no. 1 (2009): 27–48.

23. Hearing before the Subcommittee on Human Resources of the House Committee on Ways and Means, *Welfare and Marriage Issues*, 107th Cong., 1st sess., May 22, 2001, 11.

24. Ibid., 15.

25. "Introductory Guide: Administration for Children and Families Healthy Marriage Initiative, 2002–2009," National Healthy Marriage Resource Center, January 2010, U.S. Department of HHS, ACF, OFA (http://www.healthymarriageinfo.org/docs/ACF-Guideto09.pdf), 3.

26. Robert Rector, *Implementing Welfare Reform and Restoring Marriage*, 79.

27. Ibid., 75.

28. Ibid., 74.

29. Ibid., 85.

30. Kaaryn Gustafson, "Breaking Vows: Marriage Promotion, the New Patriarchy, and the Retreat from Egalitariansim," *Stanford Journal of Civil Rights & Civil Liberties* 2, no. 5 (October 2009): 287. Bridefare was a controversial 1992 reform program that encourages first-time teen parents to marry and to limit the number of children to one while on welfare.

31. Ibid., 289.

32. National Healthy Marriage Resource Center, "Introductory Guide," 9. According to the guide, grantees were located in 33 states, the District of Columbia and American Samoa. Texas was the home of the highest number of Healthy Marriage grantees with 15.

33. Health and Human Services, "Welfare Reform Reauthorized," news release, February 8, 2006 (http://archive.hhs.gov/news/press/2006pres/20060208.html) (accessed January 29, 2010).

34. "OFA Healthy Marriage and Promoting Responsible Fatherhood Initiatives" (http://www.acf.hhs.gov/programs/ofa/hmabstracts/summary.htm) (accessed January 29, 2010).

35. "Regional Map of ACF Healthy Marriage Grantees" (http://www.acf.hhs.gov/healthymarriage/pdf/comprehensive_grantees.pdf) (accessed January 29, 2010).

36. Ibid.

37. "What Is HMI?" Background Information (http://www.acf.hhs.gov/healthymarriage/about/mission.html#ms). See also Scott Coltrane, "Marketing the Marriage 'Solution': Misplaced Simplicity in the Politics of Fatherhood: 2001 Presidential Address to the Pacific Sociological Association," *Sociological Perspectives* 44, no. 4 (2001): 387–418; Nancy D. Polikoff, *Beyond Straight and Gay Marriage: Valuing All Families under the Law* (Boston: Beacon Press, 2008).

38. *Federal Register*, vol. 68, no. 139, Monday, July 21, 2003, Notices, Department of Health and Human Services, Administration of Children and Families, Refugee Resettlement Program: Proposed Notice of Allocation to State of FY 2003 Funds for Refugee Social Services, 43142–3.

39. The Temporary Assistance for Needy Families block grant program was scheduled for reauthorization in 2010. However, Congress did not work on legislation to reauthorize the program and instead they extended the TANF block grant through September 20, 2011 as part of the Claims Resolution Act (P.L. 111–291). During this period

Congress once again did not reauthorize the program but passed a three-month extension (H.R. 2943) through December 31, 2011 (http://www.clasp.org/federal_poliyc/pages?id=0021) (accessed November 20, 2011).

40. American Public Human Services Association, TANF Reauthorization Legislation, Comparison of Present Law to H.R. 240 and Senate Finance-Passed PRIDE Act, March 30, 2005 (http://aphsa.org/Policy/Doc/APHSA-side-by-side.pdf) (accessed June 25, 2001).

41. "ACF Announces $150 Million in Available Funding for Responsible Fatherhood and Healthy Marriage Grants," June 29, 2011 (http://www.acf.hhs.gov/news/press/2011/fh_hm.html) (accessed August 3, 2011).

42. Ibid.

43. Andrew Sullivan, *Virtually Normal: An Argument About Homosexuality* (New York: Alfred A. Knopf, 1995).

44. Lisa Bennett and Gary J. Gates, "The Cost of Marriage Inequality to Children and Their Same-Sex Parents," in *A Human Rights Campaign Foundation Report* (Washington, D.C.: Human Rights Campaign, 2004). See also Franke, "The Politics of Same-Sex Marriage Politics," 242.

45. Bennett and Gates, "The Cost of Marriage Inequality to Children and Their Same-Sex Parents," 2.

46. Ibid., 5.

47. *Brause v. Bureau of Vital Statistics*, No. 3AN-95-6562 CI, 1998 WL 88743, at 1 (Alaska Super. Ct 1998).

48. As said in "Marriage in Massachusetts," www.hrc.org; *Goodridge et al v. Department of Public Health*, SJC-08860 (2003) (accessed January 29, 2010).

49. *Goodridge v. Dep't of Pub. Health*, 798 NE 2d 941, 958, 1003 (2003).

50. Ibid., 965.

51. Ibid., 964, 968.

52. "Mayor Defends Same-Sex Marriage," February 22, 2004, at cnn.com (http://articles.cnn.com/2004–02–22/justic/same.sex_1_marriage-licenses-couples-political-career?_s=PM:LAW) (accessed June 23, 2010).

53. Daniel R. Pinello, *America's Struggle for Same-Sex Marriage* (Cambridge: Cambridge University Press, 2006), 48.

54. Ibid., 51.

55. As of August 2011 six states (Massachusetts, Connecticut, Iowa, Vermont, New Hampshire, and New York) plus the District of Columbia have instituted the freedom to marry for gay couples, and four more states (Maryland, Rhode Island, New Mexico, and New Jersey) have no language either prohibiting or allowing same-sex marriage. Various states now offer broad protections short of marriage, including civil unions or broad domestic partnership: Delaware, District of Columbia, California, Hawaii, Illinois, Maine, Nevada, New Jersey, Oregon, Rhode Island, Washington, and Wisconsin. (Research conducted by Erin Fine.)

56. Robert B. Bluey, "Court Uses Flimsy Principle to Strike Down Texas Sodomy

Law," July 7, 2008, at CNSNews.com (http://www.cnsnews.com/node/5644) (accessed January 29, 2010).

57. *Goodridge v. Dep't of Pub. Health*, 798 NE 2d 1000–4 (2003).

58. Committee on the Judiciary, *The Federal Marriage Amendment (Musgrave Amendment)*, H.J. Res. 56, 108th Cong., 1st sess., May 13, 2004, 1, 6.

59. Sheryl Henderson Blunt, "Defining Marriage," *Christianity Today*, posted October 1, 2001 (http://www.christianitytoday.com/ct/2001/october1/8.15.html) (accessed January 29 2010).

60. Maggie Gallagher, "Marriage Defeatists," *Weekly Standard* 9, no. 14 (December 15, 2003).

61. Her work under the contract, which ran from January through October 2002, included drafting a magazine article for the HHS official overseeing the initiative, writing brochures for the program and conducting a briefing for department officials. Howard Kurtz, "Writer Backing Bush Plan Had Gotten Federal Contract," *Washington Post*, January 26, 2005.

62. Sheryl Gay Stolberg, "Amendment's Backers Try Again on Same-Sex Marriage," *New York Times*, June 23, 2004.

63. *Goodridge v. Dep't of Pub. Health*, 798 NE 2d 1005 (2003).

64. Alliance for Marriage (http://www.realnews247.com/alliance_for_marriage.htm) (accessed January 9, 2009).

65. Ibid.

66. *Goodridge v. Dep't of Pub. Health*, 798 NE 2d 974 (2003).

67. *The Federal Marriage Amendment (Musgrave Amendment)*, H.J. Res. 56, 6–7.

68. Ibid., 25–26; Alaska Constitution, articles 1 and 25 (2004).

69. California, Official Voter Information Guide, for November 4, 2008 general election, Proposition 8, eliminates right of same-sex couples to marry; initiative constitutional amendment (emphasis in original) (http://www.voterguide.sos.ca.gov/past/2008/general/title-sum/prop8–title-sum.htm) (accessed September 10, 2010).

70. Ibid. (emphasis in original).

71. State-by-state research conducted by Erin Fine. For more on Mini-DOMAs see Dan Pinello's Web site, "The Difference Between Super-DOMAs and Mini-DOMAs" (http://www.danpinello.com/SuperDOMAs.htm) (accessed July 15, 2011). However, where Pinello limits the definition of Mini-DOMA to include only states with *constitutional* amendments that limit marriage to a heterosexual union between one man and one woman, Fine also includes states with *statutory* language limiting marriage thus. See also Daniel R. Pinello, "The Impact of State Constitutions: The Implementation and Effects of Super-DOMAs (2010)," paper presented at the annual meeting of the American Political Science Association, 2010, available at SSRN: http://ssrn.com/abstract=1643652.

72. Charles Colson with Anne Morse, "Societal Suicide," posted June 1, 2004, Christianity Today (http://www.christianitytoday.com/ct/june/8.72.html) (accessed January 20 2010).

73. Terry Moe, "The Two Democratic Purposes of Public Education," in *Rediscovering the Democratic Purposes of Education*, ed. Lorraine McDonnell, P. Michael Timpane, and Roger W. Benjamin (Lawrence: University Press of Kansas, 2000), 127.

74. Ibid.

75. Gallagher, "Marriage Defeatists."

76. Franke, "The Politics of Same-Sex Marriage Politics," 246.

Conclusion

1. Julie Novkov, *Racial Union: Law, Intimacy, and the White State in Alabama, 1865–1954* (Ann Arbor: University of Michigan Press, 2008); Patricia Strach, *All in the Family: The Private Roots of American Public Policy* (Stanford, Calif.: Stanford University Press, 2007); Patricia Strach and Kathleen S. Sullivan, "The State's Relations: What the Institution of Family Tells Us About Governance," *Political Science Quarterly* 64, no. 1 (2011): 94–106.

2. In addition to the works cited in n. 1 above, see the following as examples of work on U.S. politics that include marriage and family in political science: Jacqueline Stevens, *Reproducing the State* (Princeton, N.J.: Princeton University Press, 1999); Gwendolyn Mink, *Welfare's End* (Ithaca, N.Y.: Cornell University Press, 1998); Anna Marie Smith, *Welfare Reform and Sexual Regulation* (New York: Cambridge University Press, 2007); Kimberly J. Morgan, *Working Mothers and the Welfare State: Religion and the Politics of Work-Family Policies in Western Europe and the United States* (Stanford, Calif.: Stanford University Press, 2006). The scholarship on same-sex marriage is also growing; for example, see Daniel R. Pinello, *America's Struggle for Same-Sex Marriage* (Cambridge: Cambridge University Press, 2006). Political science journals have also run articles. See, for example, Jyl Josephson, "Citizenship, Same-Sex Marriage and the Feminist Critique of Marriage," *Perspectives on Politics* 3, no. 2 (2005): 269–84; Gary M. Segura, "A Symposium on the Politics of Same-Sex Marriage—an Introduction and Commentary," *PS: Political Science and Politics* 38, no. 2 (April 2005): 190.

3. For marriage and divorce rates see Centers for Disease Control and Prevention, *National Vital Statistics Reports* (formerly *Monthly Vital Statistics Report*) (http://www.cdc.gov/nchs/products/nvsr.htm) (accessed June 10, 2010).

4. For a discussion of how gay identity emerged with capitalism, see John D'Emilio, "Capitalism and Gay Identity," in *The Lesbian and Gay Studies Reader*, ed. Michele Aina Barale, Henry Abelove, and David M. Halperin (New York: Routledge, 1993).

5. Karen Orren and Stephen Skowronek, *The Search for American Political Development* (Cambridge: Cambridge University Press, 2004), 113.

6. Ibid.

7. For an example of an group that is asking these question, see Women's Committee of 100 at http://www.wc100.org/index.html (accessed September 30, 2009).

8. Michael Warner, *The Trouble with Normal: Sex, Politics, and the Ethics of Queer Life* (New York: Free Press, 1999).

9. Lisa Duggan, "Holy Matrimony!," *The Nation*, March 15, 2004.

10. Katherine M. Franke, "Marriage Is a Mixed Blessing," *New York Times*, June 23, 2011 (http://www.nytimes.com/2011/06/24/opinion/24franke.html) (accessed June 23, 2011).

11. See also John D'Emilio, "The Marriage Fight Is Setting Us Back," *Gay & Lesbian Review Worldwide* 13, no. 6 (2006).

12. Cathy J. Cohen, "Punks, Bulldaggers, and Welfare Queens: The Radical Potential of Queer Politics?," *Gay and Lesbian Quarterly* 3, no. 4 (1997): 437–65.

13. Caitlan Flanagan, "Is There Hope for the American Marriage?," *Time*, July 2, 2009 (http://www.time.com/time/nation/article/0,8599,1908243–2,00.html) (accessed June 23, 2011).

Bibliography

Abramovitz, Mimi. *Regulating the Lives of Women: Social Welfare Policy from Colonial Times to the Present*. Boston: South End Press, 1996.

Baer, Kenneth S. *Reinventing Democrats: The Politics of Liberalism from Reagan to Clinton*. Lawrence: University Press of Kansas, 2000.

Baehr v. Lewin, 852 P. 2d 44 (1993).

Baehr v. Miike, 910 P. 2d 112 (1996).

Bardaglio, Peter Winthrop. *Reconstructing the Household: Families, Sex, and the Law in the Nineteenth-Century South*. Studies in Legal History. Chapel Hill: University of North Carolina Press, 1995.

———. "Shamefull Matches": The Regulation of Interracial Sex and Marriage in the South before 1900." In *Sex, Love, Race: Crossing Boundaries in North American History*, edited by Martha Hodes, 112–38. New York: New York University Press, 1999.

Baxandall, Rosalyn Fraad, and Linda Gordon, eds. *Dear Sisters: Dispatches from the Women's Liberation Movement*. New York: Basic Books, 2000.

Bederman, Gail. *Manliness and Civilization: A Cultural History of Gender and Race in the United States, 1880–1917*. Women in Culture and Society. Chicago: University of Chicago Press, 1996.

Bennett, Lisa and Gary J. Gates. "The Cost of Marriage Inequality to Children and Their Same-Sex Parents." In *A Human Rights Campaign Foundation Report*. Washington, D.C.: Human Rights Campaign, 2004.

Berlin, Ira, and Leslie S. Rowland. *Families and Freedom: A Documentary History of African-American Kinship in the Civil War Era*. New York: New Press, 1997.

Blackstone, William. *Commentaries in the Laws of England, 1765*. Chicago: University of Chicago Press, 1979.

Blank, Rebecca M., and Ron Haskins. *The New World of Welfare*. Washington, D.C.: Brookings Institution Press, 2001.

Bouchet, Stacey, Theodora Ooms, and Mary Parke. *Beyond Marriage Licenses: Efforts in States to Strengthen Marriage and Two-Parent Families*. Washington, D.C.: Center for Law and Social Policy, 2004.

Brause v. Bureau of Vital Statistics, 1998 WL 88743 (1998).

Bredbenner, Candice Lewis. *A Nationality of Her Own: Women, Marriage, and the Law of Citizenship*. Berkeley: University of California Press, 1998.

Briggs, Laura. *Reproducing Empire: Race, Sex, Science, and U.S. Imperialism in Puerto Rico.* Berkeley: University of California Press, 2002.

Brotherson, Sean E. and William C. Duncan. "Rebinding the Ties That Bind: Government Efforts to Preserve and Promote Marriage." *Family Relations* 53, no. 5 (2004): 459–68.

Brown, Michael K. *Race, Money, and the American Welfare State.* Ithaca, N.Y.: Cornell University Press, 1999.

Bruyneel, Kevin. *The Third Space of Sovereignty: The Postcolonial Politics of U.S.-Indigenous Relations.* Minneapolis: University of Minnesota Press, 2007.

Burns v. State, 48 Ala. 195 (1872).

Butler, Judith. *Gender Trouble: Feminism and the Subversion of Identity.* New York: Routledge, 1999.

Cahill, Sean. "Welfare Moms and the Two Grooms: The Concurrent Promotion and Restriction of Marriage in US Public Policy." *Sexualities* 8, no. 2 (May 2005): 169–87.

Calhoun, Cheshire. *Feminism, the Family, and the Politics of the Closet: Lesbian and Gay Displacement.* Oxford: Oxford University Press, 2000.

Canaday, Margot. *The Straight State: Sexuality and Citizenship in Twentieth-Century America.* Princeton, N.J.: Princeton University Press, 2009.

Carmines, Edward G., and James A. Stimson. *Issue Evolution: Race and the Transformation of American Politics.* Princeton, N.J.: Princeton University Press, 1989.

Chan, Suchen. "The Exclusion of Chinese Women, 1870–1943." In *Entry Denied: Exclusion and the Chinese Community in America, 1882–1943,* edited by Suchen Chan, 94–146. Philadelphia: Temple University Press, 1991.

Chauncey, George. *Why Marriage?: The History Shaping Today's Debate over Gay Equality.* New York: Basic Books, 2004.

Chy Lung v. Freeman et al., 92 U.S. 275 (1875).

Cimbala, Paul A., and Randall M. Miller. *The Freedmen's Bureau and Reconstruction: Reconsiderations.* New York: Fordham University Press, 1999.

Clark, Homer Harrison. *The Law of Domestic Relations in the United States.* Hornbook Series. St. Paul, Minn.: West, 1968.

Cohen, Cathy J. "Punks, Bulldaggers, and Welfare Queens: The Radical Potential of Queer Politics?" *Gay and Lesbian Quarterly* 3, no. 4 (1997): 437–65.

Collins, Patricia Hill. "Like One Family: Race, Ethnicity, and the Paradox of US National Identity." *Ethnic and Racial Studies* 24, no. 1 (January 2001): 3–28.

Coltrane, Scott. "Marketing the Marriage 'Solution': Misplaced Simplicity in the Politics of Fatherhood: 2001 Presidential Address to the Pacific Sociological Association." *Sociological Perspectives* 44, no. 4 (Winter 2001): 387–418.

Coontz, Stephanie. *Marriage, a History: From Obedience to Intimacy, or How Love Conquered Marriage.* New York: Viking, 2005.

———. *A Strange Stirring: The Feminine Mystique and American Women at the Dawn of the 1960s.* New York: Basic Books, 2011.

Coontz, Stephanie, and Nancy Folbre. "Marriage, Poverty and Public Policy." Paper presented at Fifth Annual Council on Contemporary Families Conference, April 26–28, 2002, http://www.contemporaryfamilies.org/economic-issues/povertypolicy.html.

Cossman, Brenda. *Sexual Citizens: The Legal and Cultural Regulation of Sex and Belonging*. Stanford, Calif.: Stanford University Press, 2007.

Cott, Nancy F. "Marriage and Women's Citizenship in the United States, 1830–1934." *American Historical Review* 103, no. 5 (1988): 1440–74.

———. "Giving Character to Our Whole Civil Polity: Marriage and the Public Order in the Late Nineteenth Century." In *U.S. History as Women's History: New Feminist Essays*, edited by Linda Kerber, Alice Kessler-Harris, and Kathryn Kish Sklar, 107–21. Chapel Hill: University of North Carolina Press, 1995.

———. *Public Vows: A History of Marriage and the Nation*. Cambridge, Mass.: Harvard University Press, 2000.

Crenshaw, Kimberlé Williams. "Mapping the Margins: Intersectionality, Identity Politics and Violence against Women of Color." *Stanford Law Review* 43, no. 6 (1991): 1241–99.

Critchlow, Donald T. *Phyllis Schlafly and Grassroots Conservatism: A Woman's Crusade*. Politics and Society in Twentieth-Century America. Princeton, N.J.: Princeton University Press, 2005.

Degler, Carl N. *At Odds: Women and the Family in America from the Revolution to the Present*. New York: Oxford University Press, 1980.

———. *In Search of Human Nature: The Decline and Revival of Darwinism in American Social Thought*. New York: Oxford University Press, 1991.

D'Emilio, John. "Capitalism and Gay Identity." In *The Lesbian and Gay Studies Reader*, edited by Henry Abelove, Michele Aina Barale, and David M. Halperin, 467–76. New York: Routledge, 1993.

———. "The Marriage Fight Is Setting Us Back." *Gay & Lesbian Review Worldwide* 13, no. 6 (2006): 10–11.

DuCille, Ann. "Marriage, Family, and Other 'Peculiar Institutions' in African-American Literary History." *American Literary History* 21, no. 3 (2009): 604–17.

Duggan, Lisa. *The Twlight of Equality?* Boston, Mass.: Beacon Press, 2003.

DuPlessis, Rachel Blau, and Ann Barr Snitow, eds. *The Feminist Memoir Project: Voices from Women's Liberation*. New York: Three Rivers Press, 1998.

Dyer, Thomas G. *Theodore Roosevelt and the Idea of Race*. Baton Rouge: Louisiana State University Press, 1980.

Edsall, Thomas Byrne, and Mary D. Edsall. *Chain Reaction: The Impact of Race, Rights, and Taxes on American Politics*. New York: Norton, 1992.

Edwards, Laura. "'The Marriage Covenant Is the Foundation of All Our Rights': The Politics of Slave Marriages in North Carolina Emancipation." *Law and History Review* 14, no. 1 (Spring 1996): 81–124.

———. *Gendered Strife and Confusion: The Political Culture of Reconstruction*. Women in American History. Urbana: University of Illinois Press, 1997.

Elkins, Stanley M. *Slavery*. Chicago: University of Chicago Press, 1959.

Engels, Frederick. *The Origin of the Family, Private Property, and the State*. Translated by Ernest Untermann. Chicago: C. H. Kerr, 1902.

Eskridge, William N. *The Case for Same-Sex Marriage: From Sexual Liberty to Civilized Commitment*. New York: Free Press, 1996.

Farmer, Mary J. "'Because They Are Women': Gender and the Virginia Freedmen's Bureau's 'War on Dependency.'" In *The Freedmen's Bureau and Reconstruction: Reconsiderations*, edited by Paul A. Cimbala and Randall Miller, 161–92. New York: Fordham University Press, 1999.

Ferguson, Roderick. "The Nightmares of the Heteronormative." *Cultural Values* 4, no. 4 (2000): 419–44.

Fineman, Martha. *The Illusion of Equality: The Rhetoric and Reality of Divorce Reform*. Chicago: University of Chicago Press, 1991.

Firestone, Shulamith. *The Dialectic of Sex: the Case for a Feminist Revolution*. New York: Bantam Books, 1972.

Friedan, Betty. *The Feminine Mystique*. New York: W. W. Norton, 2001.

Foner, Eric. *Free Soil, Free Labor, Free Men*. New York: Oxford University Press, 1971.

———. *Reconstruction: America's Unfinished Revolution, 1863–1877*. The New American Nation Series. New York: Harper & Row, 1988.

Foucault, Michel. *The History of Sexuality*. Vol. 1: *An Introduction*. New York: Random House, 1990.

Franke, Katherine. "Becoming a Citizen: Reconstruction Era Regulation of African American Marriages." *Yale Journal of Law & the Humanities* 11 (1999): 251–309.

———. "The Politics of Same-Sex Marriage Politics." *Columbia Journal of Gender and Law* 15, no. 1 (2006): 235–48.

Fraser, Nancy, and Linda Gordon. "A Genealogy of Dependency: Tracing a Keyword of the U.S. Welfare State." *Signs* 19, no. 2 (1994): 309–36.

Frazier, Edward Franklin, and Nathan Glazer. *The Negro Family in the United States*. Chicago: University of Chicago Press, 1966.

Freeman, Elizabeth. *The Wedding Complex: Forms of Belonging in Modern American Culture*. Durham, N.C.: Duke University Press, 2002.

Gardner, Martha Mabie. *The Qualities of a Citizen: Women, Immigration, and Citizenship, 1870–1965*. Princeton, N.J.: Princeton University Press, 2005.

Geller, Jaclyn. *Here Comes the Bride: Women, Weddings, and the Marriage Mystique*. New York: Four Walls Eight Windows, 2001.

Gerhard, Jane F. *Desiring Revolution: Second-Wave Feminism and the Rewriting of American Sexual Thought, 1920 to 1982*. New York: Columbia University Press, 2001.

Goodridge v. Dep't of Pub. Health, 798 NE 2d 941 (2003).

Gould v. Gould, 78 Conn. 242 (1905).

Green v. State, 58 Ala. 190 (1877).

Grossberg, Michael. *Governing the Hearth: Law and the Family in Nineteenth-Century America*. Studies in Legal History. Chapel Hill: University of North Carolina Press, 1985.

Gustafson, Kaaryn. "Breaking Vows: Marriage Promotion, the New Patriarchy, and the Retreat from Egalitarianism." *Stanford Journal of Civil Rights & Civil Liberties* 2, no. 5 (October 2009): 269–308.

Gutman, Herbert George. *The Black Family in Slavery and Freedom, 1750–1925*. New York: Pantheon Books, 1976.

Hancock, Ange-Marie. *The Politics of Disgust: The Public Identity of the Welfare Queen*. New York: New York University Press, 2004.

Harris, Cheryl. "Whiteness as Property." *Harvard Law Review* 106, no. 8 (1993): 1710–91.

Hartog, Hendrik. *Man and Wife in America: A History*. Cambridge, Mass.: Harvard University Press, 2000.

Hasday, Jill Elaine. "Federalism and the Family Reconstructed." *UCLA Law Review* 45, no. 5 (1998): 1279–386.

Hattam, Victoria Charlotte. *In the Shadow of Race: Jews, Latinos, and Immigrant Politics in the United States*. Chicago: University of Chicago Press, 2007.

Hattam, Victoria C. and Joseph E. Lowndes. "The Ground beneath Our Feet: Language, Culture and Political Change." In *Formative Acts*, edited by Stephen Skowronek and Matthew Glassman, 199–222. Philadelphia: University of Pennsylvania Press, 2007.

Hays, Sharon. *Flat Broke with Children: Women in the Age of Welfare Reform*. Oxford and New York: Oxford University Press, 2003.

Heath, Melanie. "State of Our Unions: Marriage Promotion and the Contested Power of Heterosexuality." *Gender & Society* 23, no. 1 (2009): 27–48.

Higginbotham, Evelyn Brooks. "African-American Women's History and the Metalanguage of Race." *Signs* 17, no. 2 (1992): 251–74.

Higham, John. *Strangers in the Land: Patterns of the American Nativism, 1860–1925*. New Brunswick, N.J.: Rutgers University Press, 2000.

Hodes, Martha Elizabeth. *White Women, Black Men: Illicit Sex in the Nineteenth-Century South*. New Haven, Conn.: Yale University Press, 1997.

HoSang, Daniel. *Racial Propositions: Ballot Initiatives and the Making of Postwar California*. Berkeley: University of California Press, 2010.

Hull, Kathleen E. *Same-Sex Marriage: The Cultural Politics of Love and Law*. Cambridge: Cambridge University Press, 2006.

Hunter, James Davison. *Culture Wars: The Struggle to Define America*. New York: Basic Books, 1991.

Hutchinson, Edward P., and Balch Institute for Ethnic Studies. *Legislative History of American Immigration Policy, 1798–1965*. Philadelphia: University of Pennsylvania Press, 1981.

In Re Marriage Cases, 43 Cal. 4th 757 (2008).

In Re Mclaughlin's Estate, 4 Wash. 570 (1892).

Johnson, Cathy Marie, Georgia Duerst-Lahti, and Noelle H. Norton. *Creating Gender: The Sexual Politics of Welfare Policy*. Boulder, Colo.: Lynne Rienner Publishers, 2007.

Jones, Maldwyn A. *American Immigration*. The Chicago History of American Civilization. Chicago: University of Chicago Press, 1992.

Josephson, Jyl. "Citizenship, Same-Sex Marriage and the Feminist Critique of Marriage." *Perspectives on Politics* 3, no. 2 (June 2005): 269–84.

Kandaswarmy, Priya. "'You Trade in *a* man for *the* man': Domestic Violence and the U.S. Welfare State." *American Quarterly: Journal of the American Studies Association* 62, no. 2 (2010): 253–77

Kaplan, Sidney. "The Miscegenation Issue in the Election of 1864." *Journal of Negro History* 34, no. 3 (July 1949): 274–343.

Kennedy, Randall. *Interracial Intimacies: Sex, Marriage, Identity, and Adoption*. New York: Vintage, 2004.

Kerber, Linda K. *No Constitutional Right to Be Ladies: Women and the Obligations of Citizenship*. New York: Hill and Wang, 1998.

Kevles, Daniel J. *In the Name of Eugenics: Genetics and the Uses of Human Heredity*. New York: Knopf, 1985.

Keyssar, Alexander. *The Right to Vote: The Contested History of Democracy in the United States*. New York: Basic Books, 2000.

King, Desmond S. *Making Americans: Immigration, Race, and the Origins of the Diverse Democracy*. Cambridge, Mass.: Harvard University Press, 2000.

Koedt, Anne, Ellen Levine, and Anita Rapone. *Radical Feminism*. New York: Quadrangle Books, 1973.

Larson, Edward. *Sex, Race and Science: Eugenics in the Deep South*. Baltimore: Johns Hopkins University Press, 1995.

Lewis, Oscar. *La Vida: a Puerto Rican Family in the Culture of Poverty—San Juan and New York*. New York: Random House, 1966.

Lindsay, Matthew. "Reproducing a Fit Citizenry: Dependency, Eugenics and the Law of Marriage in the United States, 1860–1920." *University of Chicago Law and Social Inquiry* 23, no. 3 (1998): 541–85.

Locke, John. *Second Treatise of Government*. Edited by C. B. Macpherson. Indianapolis: Hackett, 1980.

Lonas v. State, 50 Tenn. 289 (1871).

Loving v. Virginia, 388 US 1 (1967).

Lowndes, Joseph E. *From the New Deal to the New Right: Race and the Southern Origins of Modern Conservatism*. New Haven, Conn.: Yale University Press, 2008.

Lowndes, Joseph E., Julie Novkov, and Dorian Warren. *Race and American Political Development*. New York: Routledge, 2008.

Luibhéid, Eithne. *Entry Denied: Controlling Sexuality at the Border*. Minneapolis: University of Minnesota Press, 2002.

Mackenzie v. Hare, 239 US 299 (1915).

MacLean, Nancy. *The American Women's Movement, 1945–2000: A Brief History with Documents*. Boston: Bedford/St. Martin's, 2009.

Malone, Ann Patton. *Sweet Chariot: Slave Family and Household Structure in Nineteenth Century Louisiana*. Chapel Hill: University of North Carolina Press, 1992.

Mansbridge, Jane J. *Why We Lost the ERA*. Chicago: University of Chicago Press, 1986.

Marchevsky, A., and J. Theoharis. "Welfare Reform, Globalization, and the Racialization of Entitlement." *American Studies* 41, no. 2 (2000): 235–65.

Maynard v. Hill, 125 US 190 (1888).

McDonagh, Eileen L. "Forging a New Grammar of Equality and Difference: Progressive Era Suffrage and Reform." In *Formative Acts*, edited by Stephen Skowronek and Matthew Glassman, 171–98. Philadelphia: University of Pennsylvania, 2007.

———. *The Motherless State: Women's Political Leadership and American Democracy*. Chicago: University of Chicago Press, 2009.

Metz, Tamara. *Untying the Knot: Marriage, the State, and the Case for Their Divorce*. Princeton, N.J.: Princeton University Press, 2010.

Mettler, Suzanne. *Dividing Citizens: Gender and Federalism in New Deal Public Policy*. Ithaca, N.Y.: Cornell University Press, 1998.

———. *The Submerged State*. Chicago: University of Chicago, 2011.

Meyer v. Nebraska, 262 U. S. 390 (1923).

Milkis, Sidney. "The Modern Presidency, Social Movements and the Administrative State: Lyndon Johnson and the Civil Rights Movement." In *Race and American Political Development*, edited by Joseph Lowndes, Julie Novkov, and Dorian T. Warren, 253–87. New York: Routledge, 2008.

Millett, Kate. *Sexual Politics*. Urbana: University of Illinois Press, 2000.

Mink, Gwendolyn. "Aren't Poor Single Mothers Women? Feminists, Welfare Reform and Welfare Justice?" In *Whose Welfare?* edited by Gwendolyn Mink, 171–89. Ithaca, N.Y.: Cornell University Press, 1999.

———. *Welfare's End*. Ithaca, N.Y.: Cornell University Press, 1998.

Moe, Terry. "The Two Democratic Purposes of Public Education." In *Rediscovering the Democratic Purposes of Education*, ed. Lorraine McDonnell, P. Michael Timpane, and Roger W. Benjamin, 127–47. Lawrence: University Press of Kansas, 2000.

Morgan, Kimberly J. *Working Mothers and the Welfare State: Religion and the Politics of Work-Family Policies in Western Europe and the United States*. Stanford, Calif.: Stanford University Press, 2006.

Morgen, Sandra, Joan Acker, and Jill Michele Weigt. *Stretched Thin: Poor Families, Welfare Work, and Welfare Reform*. Ithaca, N.Y.: Cornell University Press, 2010.

Morone, James A. *Hellfire Nation: The Politics of Sin in American History*. New Haven, Conn.: Yale University Press, 2003.

Nackenoff, Carol. *The Fictional Republic: Horatio Alger and American Political Discourse*. New York: Oxford University Press, 1994.

Novkov, Julie. *Racial Union: Law, Intimacy, and the White State in Alabama, 1865–1954*. Ann Arbor: University of Michigan Press, 2008.

Office of Policy Planning and Research, United States Department of Labor. *The Negro Family, the Case for National Action*. Washington, D.C.: Superintendent of Documents, 1965.

Okin, Susan Moller. *Women in Western Political Thought*. Princeton, N.J.: Princeton University Press, 1979.

Ooms, Theodora. "Adapting Healthy Marriage Programs for Disadvantaged and Culturally Diverse Populations: What Are the Issues?" Center for Law and Social Policy,
Policy Brief, No. 10, March 2007.

Ordover, Nancy. *American Eugenics: Race, Queer Anatomy and the Science of Nationalism.* Minneapolis: University of Minnesota Press, 2003.

Orren, Karen. *Belated Feudalism: Labor, the Law, and Liberal Development in the United
States.* Cambridge: Cambridge University Press, 1991.

Orren, Karen, and Stephen Skowronek. *The Search for American Political Development.*
Cambridge: Cambridge University Press, 2004.

Pascoe, Peggy. "Miscegenation Law, Court Cases and Ideologies of 'Race' in Twentieth-
Century America." *Journal of American History* 83, no. 1 (1996): 44–69.

———. *What Comes Naturally: Miscegenation Law and the Making of Race in America.*
Oxford: Oxford University Press, 2009.

Pateman, Carole. *The Sexual Contract.* Stanford, Calif.: Stanford University Press, 1988.

Patterson, James T. *Freedom Is Not Enough: The Moynihan Report and America's Struggle
over Black Family Life from LBJ to Obama.* New York: Basic Books, 2010.

Perez v. Sharp, 32 Cal. 2d 711 (1948).

Peterson v. Widule, 147 NW 966 (1914).

Phillips, Kevin. *The Emerging Republican Majority.* New Rochelle, N.Y.: Arlington
House, 1969.

Pinello, Daniel R. *America's Struggle for Same-Sex Marriage.* Cambridge: Cambridge
University Press, 2006.

Polikoff, Nancy D. *Beyond Straight and Gay Marriage: Valuing All Families under the
Law.* Boston: Beacon Press, 2008.

Polsky, Andrew Joseph. *The Rise of the Therapeutic State.* The City in the Twenty-First
Century. Princeton, N.J.: Princeton University Press, 1991.

Porterfield, Ernest. *Black and White Mixed Marriages.* Chicago: Nelson-Hall, 1978.

Rainwater, Lee and William L. Yancey, eds. *The Moynihan Report and the Politics of Controversy; a Trans-Action Social Science and Public Policy Report.* Cambridge, Mass.:
MIT Press, 1965.

Rector, Robert. "Implementing Welfare Reform and Restoring Marriage." In *Priorities
for the President,* ed. Stuart M. Butler and Kim Holmes, 71–97. Washington, D.C.:
Heritage Foundation, 2001.

Reed, Adolph, Jr. "The 'Underclass' as Myth and Symbol: The Poverty of Discourse
About Poverty." In *Stirrings in the Jug: Black Politics in the Post-Segregation Era,*
179–96. Minneapolis: University of Minnesota Press, 1999.

Regan, Milton C., Jr. "Establishing the Family and Family-Like Relationships: Marriage
at the Millennium." *Family Law Quarterly* 33 (1999): 647–62.

Ritter, Gretchen. *The Constitution as Social Design: Gender and Civic Membership in the
American Constitutional Order.* Stanford, Calif.: Stanford University Press, 2006.

Roberts, Dorothy. "Who May Give Birth to Citizens? Reproduction, Eugenics, and Immigration." In *Immigrants Out! The New Nativism and Anti-Immigrant Impulse*

in the U.S, edited by J. F. Perea, 205–19. New York: New York University Press, 1996.

———. *Killing the Black Body*. New York: Vintage Books, 1997.

Roe v. Wade, 410 US 113 (1973).

Romano, Renee Christine. *Race Mixing: Black-White Marriage in Postwar America*. Cambridge, Mass.: Harvard University Press, 2003.

Rosen, Ruth. *The World Split Open: How the Modern Women's Movement Changed America*. New York: Penguin Books, 2006.

Rubin, Gayle. "Thinking Sex." In *Culture, Society and Sexuality: A Reader*, edited by Richard G. Parker and Peter Aggleton, 150–87. London: UCL Press, 1999.

Sapiro, Virginia. "Women, Citizenship, and Nationality: Immigration and Naturalization Policies in the United States." *Politics and Society* 13, no. 1 (1984): 1–26.

Schlafly, Phyllis. *The Power of the Positive Woman*. New Rochelle, N.Y.: Arlington House, 1977.

Schoolcraft v. O'Neil, 81 NH 240 (1924).

Schram, Sanford, Joe Soss, and Richard C. Fording. *Race and the Politics of Welfare Reform*. Ann Arbor: University of Michigan Press, 2003.

Scott, Daryl Michael. *Contempt and Pity: Social Policy and the Image of the Damaged Black Psyche, 1880–1996*. Chapel Hill: University of North Carolina Press, 1997.

Scott, Joan. "Experience." In *Feminists Theorize the Political*, edited by Judith Butler and Joan Scott, 22–40. New York: Routledge, 1992.

———. "Gender: A Useful Category of Historical Analysis." In *Gender and the Politics of History*, 28–50. New York: Columbia University Press, 1988.

Scott v. State, 39 Ga. 321 (1869).

Silag, Phoebe G. "To Have, to Hold, to Receive Public Assistance: TANF and Marriage-Promotion Policies." *Journal of Race, Gender and Justice* 7 (2003).

Simmons, Christina. *Making Marriage Modern: Women's Sexuality from the Progressive Era to World War II*. Oxford: Oxford University Press, 2009.

Skowronek, Stephen. *Building a New American State: The Expansion of National Administrative Capacities, 1877–1920*. Cambridge: Cambridge University Press, 1982.

Skowronek, Stephen, and Matthew Glassman. *Formative Acts: American Politics in the Making*. Philadelphia: University of Pennsylvania Press, 2007.

Smith, Anna Marie. "The Politicization of Marriage in Contemporary American Public Policy: The Defense of Marriage Act and the Personal Responsibility Act." *Citizenship Studies* 5, no. 3 (2004): 303–20.

———. *Welfare Reform and Sexual Regulation*. New York: Cambridge University Press, 2007.

Smith, Rogers M. "'One United People': Second-Class Female Citizenship and the American Quest for Community." *Yale Journal of Law & Humanities* 1 (1989): 229–94.

———. *Civic Ideals: Conflicting Visions of Citizenship in U.S. History*. The Yale ISPS Series. New Haven, Conn.: Yale University Press, 1997.

Snitow, Ann. "A Gender Diary." In *Conflicts in Feminism*, edited by Marianne Hirsch and Evelyn Fox Keller, 9–43. New York: Routledge, 1990.

Sparks, Holloway. "Queens, Teens, and Model Mothers: Race, Gender and the Discourse of Welfare Reform." In *Race and the Politics of Welfare Reform*, ed., Sanford Schram, Joe Soss, and Richard C. Fording, 171–95. Ann Arbor: University of Michigan Press, 2003.

Stanley, Amy Dru. *From Bondage to Contract: Wage Labor, Marriage, and the Market in the Age of Slave Emancipation*. Cambridge: Cambridge University Press, 1998.

State v. Gibson, 36 Ind. 389 (1871).

Stevens, Jacqueline. "On the Marriage Question." In *Women Transforming Politics*, edited by Cathy Cohen, Kathleen Jones, and Joan Tronto, 62–83. New York: New York University Press, 1997.

———. *Reproducing the State*. Princeton, N.J.: Princeton University Press, 1999.

Stevenson, Brenda E. *Life in Black and White: Family and Community in the Slave South*. New York: Oxford University Press, 1996.

Strach, Patricia. *All in the Family: The Private Roots of American Public Policy*. Stanford, Calif.: Stanford University Press, 2007.

Strach, Patricia and Kathleen Sullivan. "The State's Relations: What the Institution of Family Tells Us About Governance." *Political Science Quarterly* 64, no. 1 (March 2011): 94–106.

Stamp, Kenneth M. *The Peculiar Institution: Slavery in the Ante-Bellum South*. New York: Knopf, 1956.

Strasser, Mark Philip. *Legally Wed: Same-Sex Marriage and the Constitution*. Ithaca, N.Y.: Cornell University Press, 1997.

Stychin, Carl F., and Didi Herman, eds. *Law and Sexuality the Global Arena*. Minneapolis: University of Minnesota Press, 2001.

Sullivan, Andrew. *Same-Sex Marriage, Pro and Con: A Reader*. New York: Vintage Books, 1997.

———. *Virtually Normal: An Argument About Homosexuality*. New York: Alfred A. Knopf, 1995.

Sullivan, Kathleen S. *Constitutional Context: Women and Rights Discourse in Nineteenth-Century America*. The Johns Hopkins Series in Constitutional Thought. Baltimore: Johns Hopkins University Press, 2007.

Swidler, Ann. *Talk of Love: How Culture Matters*. Chicago: University of Chicago Press, 2001.

Tanner, Michael. *The Poverty of Welfare: Helping Others in Civil Society*. Washington, D.C: Cato Institute, 2003.

Thomas, Gwynn Thomas. *Contesting Legitimacy in Chile: Familial Ideas, Citizenship and Political Struggle, 1970–1990*. University Park: Pennsylvania State University Press, 2011.

Tichenor, Daniel J. *Dividing Lines: The Politics of Immigration Control in America*. Princeton Studies in American Politics. Princeton, N.J.: Princeton University Press, 2002.

Tocqueville, Alexis de. *Democracy in America*. Vol. 2. Translated by Henry Reeve. Vintage Classics. New York: Vintage Books, 1990.

Turner v. Safley, 482 US 78 (1987).

U.S. Congress. House. Hearing before the Subcommittee on Human Resources of the Committee on Ways and Means. *Causes of Poverty, with a Focus on out-of-Wedlock Births*. 104th Cong, 2nd sess., March 12 1996.

U.S Congress. House. Hearing before the Subcommittee on Human Resources of the House Committee on Ways and Means. *Contract with America—Welfare Reform*. 104th Cong., 1st sess., February 2, 1995.

U.S. Congress. House. Hearing before the Subcommittee on Human Resources of the House Committee on Ways and Means. *Defense of Marriage Act*. 104th Cong., 2d sess., May 15, 1996.

U.S. Congress. House. Hearing before the Subcommittee on Human Resources of the Committee on Ways and Means. *Welfare and Marriage Issues*. 107th Cong., 1st sess., May 22, 2001.

U.S. Congress. House. Hearing before the Subcommittee on Human Resources of the Committee on Ways and Means. *Welfare Reform*. 104th Cong., 2d sess., May 22 and 23, 1996.

U.S. Congress. House. *Official Opinion of the Attorneys-General*. 61st Cong., 3d sess., 1909.

U.S. Congress. House. Committee on the Judiciary. *Defense of Marriage Act*. Report submitted by Charles Canady. Rpt 664, 104th Cong., 2d sess., July 9, 1996.

U.S. Congress. House. Committee on the Judiciary. *The Federal Marriage Amendment (Musgrave Amendment)*. H.J. Res. 56, 108th Cong., 1st sess., May 13, 2004.

U.S. Congress. House. United States Bureau of Immigration. *Compilation from the Records of the Bureau of Immigration of Facts Concerning the Enforcement of the Chinese-Exclusion Laws*. 59th Cong., 1st. sess., 1906.

U.S. Congress. Senate. United States Immigration Commission. *Importation and Harboring of Women for Immoral Purposed*, S. Doc. No. 753. 61st Cong., 3d sess., 1911.

U.S. Congress. United States Immigration Commission. *Importing Women for Immoral Purposes: A Partial Report from the Immigration Commission on the Importation and Harboring of Women for Immoral Purposes*, S. Doc. No 196. 61st Cong., 2d sess., 1910.

United States v. Wong Kim Ark, 169 U.S. 649 (1898).

Valelly, Richard M. *The Two Reconstructions: The Struggle for Black Enfranchisement*. American Politics and Political Economy. Chicago: University of Chicago Press, 2004.

Warner, Michael. *The Trouble with Normal: Sex, Politics, and the Ethics of Queer Life*. New York: Free Press, 1999.

Washington, Joseph R. *Marriage in Black and White*. Boston: Beacon Press, 1971.

Weitzman, Lenore J. *The Divorce Revolution: The Unexpected Social and Economic Consequences for Women and Children in America*. New York; London: Free Press, 1985.

Wiebe, Robert H. *The Search for Order, 1877–1920.* New York: Hill and Wang, 1967.

Willrich, Michael. "The Two Percent Solution: Eugenic Jurisprudence and the Socialization of American Law, 1900–1930." *Law and History Review* 16 (Spring 1998): 63–111.

Wilson, William J. *The Truly Disadvantaged: The Inner City, the Underclass, and Public Policy.* Chicago: University of Chicago Press, 1990.

Yates, Gayle Graham. *What Women Want: The Ideas of the Movement.* Cambridge, Mass.: Harvard University Press, 1975.

Ziegler, Mary. "Eugenic Feminism: Mental Hygiene, the Women's Movement and the Campaign for Eugenic Legal Reform, 1900–1935." *Harvard Journal of Law and Gender* 31 (2008): 211–35.

Zablocki v. Redhail 434 *U. S.* 374, 383–84 (1978).

Index

marriage debates of early twenty-first
century, (cont'd)
welfare policy/welfare reform, 123, 129–
36, 144. See also marriage promotion;
same-sex marriage debate (twenty-first
century)
Marriage Movement, 5, 18, 104, 120–22, 125–
29, 135–36, 145; Bush administration
support, 125; community-based and
non-profit groups, 104, 125; compared
to prior marriage promotion efforts,
126–27, 129; and Healthy Marriage
Initiative (HMI), 123, 129, 133–36;
marriage preparation programs and
curricula, 128; non-state actors, 18, 124;
social science studies, 125; state and
federal initiatives, 128; state government
and legal efforts to strengthen marriage,
125–26; the statement of principles
(2000), 126–28, 178n9; and TANF
reauthorization debates, 125, 135,
179n39
marriage politics from the mid-1960s to
1970s, 17–18, 68–69, 73–98; birth
control, 85, 170n41; "black power"
movement, 76, 82–83, 95; and
citizenship, 80–81, 94; civil rights
struggles, 76–78, 80, 82–83, 91–96;
"culture of poverty" arguments, 80,
82, 104; the divorce revolution, 74,
85, 168n4; the feminist challenge
to patriarchal marriage and gender
inequality, 74, 85–91; Johnson's
commencement speech at Howard
University, 78–81; Johnson's Great
Society and welfare initiatives, 73, 75,
76–78; love-based marriage model, 16,
74, 85, 149; Loving v. Virginia ruling
and interracial marriage, 4, 13, 73,
90–96, 97, 102, 120, 149, 152; marriage
ruled a fundamental civil right, 16, 92,
102–3, 171–72n64; Moynihan Report
and the obligation to marry, 78–85,

91–93, 97, 109, 152; obligations/rights,
74–75, 83–98, 102–3; patriarchal family
structure, 78–79, 80, 88–90; and racial
equality, 78–85, 91–97, 152; urban
rioting and racialized violence, 76,
81; and women's new roles in public
sphere, 85
marriage promotion, 5, 18, 100–101, 106–13,
120–36, 145–46; Bush administration's
domestic policies, 122–25, 129–33, 145;
Clinton administration, 100, 108–13;
community-based and non-profit groups,
104, 125; conferences, religious groups,
104, 125; controlling sexual behavior,
107–8; culture of poverty arguments, 127,
134; faith-based initiatives, 123, 128, 134,
153; Freedmen's Bureau policies, 5–6, 23,
25–26, 31–35, 44–45; Healthy Marriage
Initiative (HMI) and federal funding, 123,
129, 133–36; Johnson's Great Society and
welfare initiatives, 73, 75, 76–78; language
of equality/economic inequality, 12–13,
108, 127, 133–35; linking independence,
civic inclusion, and morality, 126–27;
Marriage Movement ("marriage culture"
and social obligation to marry), 5, 18, 104,
120–22, 125–29, 135–36, 145; Murray,
107–8, 131; Obama administration,
135; Progressive Era nuptial reform
movement, 51–56, 126; and PRWORA
legislation, 100–101, 106–13, 120, 131; and
PRWORA reauthorization, 113, 129–33;
as public health issue, 123; racially specific
initiatives, 134–35; Reconstruction-era,
5–6, 23, 25–35, 44–45; and Rector, 104,
112–13, 129–33, 142; social science
studies, 125; state and federal initiatives,
128; and welfare reform, 100–101, 106–13,
120, 129–33, 131, 142, 152
Marriage Protection Amendment. See
Federal Marriage Amendment (FMA)
Marriage Savers, 104, 125
Married Women's Property Acts, 15

Acknowledgments

This book is long overdue and I am glad to have the chance to recognize here the many people who helped me get to this point. I thank Rick Vallely for recommending this book for the series and for his continued support of the project. I have been fortunate to work with Peter Agree at the University of Pennsylvania Press and have benefited from his intellectual acuity and long experience as an editor. The editorial staff at the Press, including Julia Rose Roberts and Erica Ginsburg, made the process go smoothly. I also thank the anonymous reviewers for their comments and suggestions.

I am privileged to have received support from colleagues at the University of Oregon's Department of Political Science. In particular, Gerry Berk, Dan HoSang, Joe Lowndes, and Dan Tichenor not only offered great insights into American institutions and culture but also read drafts and offered encouragement. Dan HoSang especially was a steadfast writing partner. Across campus, Scott Coltrane, Ellen Herman, Sandi Morgen, and Lizzie Reis were generous with their responses to the project at different stages, particularly in relation to gender, class, and history. I thank the university's Center for the Study of Women in Society for a very useful and timely writing grant.

I benefited greatly by presenting this work in a number of venues. Dan Tichenor at the University of Oregon political science department and Margaret Hallock at the Wayne Morse Center of Law and Policy sponsored a workshop on the manuscript. I am appreciative of the thorough reflections on the manuscript provided to me by workshop participants Carol Nackenoff, Stephanie Coontz, Eileen McDonagh, and Anne Norton. Cas Mudde, Maryann Gallagher, and the Prindle Institute for Ethics invited me to present this work to their reading group, and I presented a portion of it at the Gender, Race, and Sexuality in Law and American Political Development workshop at Ohio University. Michelle McKinley and Hendrik Hartog gave me feedback on the Introduction and Chapter 1 at a workshop sponsored by the Culture, Law and Humanities Initiative at the University of Oregon Knight Law School.

This project developed through the comments and support I received over time from Lisa Duggan, Leonard Feldman, Jen Gaboury, Julie Novkov, Peggy Pascoe, Andy Polsky, Gretchen Ritter, and Gwynn Thomas. I thank Patricia Strach and Kathleen Sullivan for their continued willingness to read drafts and to reflect with me on the role of family in political development. I am indebted to Kevin Bruyneel, who read and reread many pieces of this work and who has helped shape this book.

At the New School for Social Research I thank Vicky Hattam, Ann Snitow, and Adolph Reed, whose guidance was crucial. I am privileged to have worked with each of them. Thanks also to my New York writing group: Kevin Bruyneel, Cat Celebreeze, Edmund Fong, Joe Lowndes, Ron Krabill, Jessica Blatt, Susan Hibbard, and Bill Winstead. Of this group, I especially thank Cat, Edmund, Kevin, and Joe.

Thanks to Julie Van Pelt for her edits, and to Katy Lenn at the University of Oregon Library for helping me get my bibliography in order. Erin Fine, Josh Plencner, and Brent Commoner provided excellent research assistance, and I received bibliographic support from Sam Bernofsky.

A close version of Chapter 2 first appeared in the journal *Polity* in 2009 as "The Search for Marital Order" and is reproduced here with the permission of Palgrave Macmillan.

The Lowndes family was encouraging throughout, never failing to ask, "How's the book?" The Yamin/Steinberg/Manocchia family provided great sustenance from the beginning. Pat and Deb Manocchia have been incredibly encouraging over the years, especially my sister Deb, whose love and generosity know no bounds. I also thank my parents, Joan Steinberg and Tom Yamin, and their partners, David Steinberg and Patti Yamin, who did not let their divorces and traditional notions of family get in the way of our developing into an extended inclusive family. This book was inspired in part by my grandmother Edith Levin, who at almost a century old has had a long life of navigating the institution of marriage and working within its limits.

While writing this book I had my own children, which helped my thoughts on the topic deepen. My two sons, Ben and Adam, and my partner, Joe, have given me love, encouragement, and unending patience to complete this book, and for that I am perhaps most grateful. This book is dedicated to them.

CPSIA information can be obtained at www.ICGtesting.com
Printed in the USA
BVOW03s1816060415

394680BV00001B/2/P

9 780812 223330